The Witchcraft of Dame Darrel of York

The Witchcraft of Dame Darrel of York

CHARLES GODFREY LELAND

Introduction by Professor Robert Mathiesen

The Witches' Almanac Ltd.
Publishers Providence, Rhode Island
www.TheWitchesAlmanac.com

Address all inquiries and information to
THE WITCHES' ALMANAC, LTD.
P.O. Box 1292
Newport, RI 02840-9998

ISBN: 978-0-9824323-3-4
Hardbound

ISBN: 978-0-9824323-2-7
Hardbound with slipcase

ISBN: 978-0-9824323-1-0
Leather bound with slipcase

First Printing, February 2011

Printed in China

This manuscript is published
with the permission of the
Historical Society of Pennsylvania,
Philadelphia, Penn.

The original manuscript of
The Witchcraft of Dame Darrel of York
is in Box 15 of the
Charles Godfrey Leland Papers,
which constitute manuscript collection 363
in the Library of that Society.

Cover design by Kathryn Sky-Peck
Book design by Karen Marks

Other books from
The Witches' Almanac, Ltd.

Aradia: Gospel of the Witches
Charles Leland
Introduction by Professor Robert Mathiesen

The ABC of Magical Charms
Elizabeth Pepper

The Little Book of Magical Creatures
Elizabeth Pepper and Barbara Stacy

The Horned Shepherd
Edgar Jepson

Greek Gods in Love
Barbara Stacy

Witches All
Elizabeth Pepper

For additional titles, visit: www.TheWitchesAlmanac.com

Table of Contents

Introduction

Leland's Magic

Charles Godfrey Leland (1824–1903) was fascinated by magic and Witchcraft all his life. The work that you now hold in your hands is the most beautiful fruit that fell from the tree of his fascination. That tree bore other fruit in Leland's many published works. It still casts long shadows, even today, on modern Witchcraft and Paganism.

The roots of the tree of Leland's fascination with magic reach deep down into the soil of his earliest infancy. Here is how he tells the story in his *Memoirs:*

> I should mention that my first nurse in life was an old Dutch woman named Van der Poel. I had not been born many days before I and my cradle were missing. There was a prompt outcry and search, and both were soon found in the garret or loft of the house. There I lay sleeping, on my breast an open Bible, with, I believe, a key and knife, at my head lighted candles, money, and a plate of salt. Nurse Van der Poel explained that it was done to secure my rising in life – by taking me up to the garret. I have since learned from a witch that the same is still done in exactly the same manner in Italy, and in Asia. She who does it must be, however, a *strega* or sorceress (my nurse was reputed to be one), and the child thus initiated will become deep in darksome lore, an adept in *occulta,* and a scholar.[1]

So, indeed, it came to pass with Leland. He was "reading *Paracelsus* at an age when most boys, if they read at all, are deep in

1 Leland, *Memoirs* (1894): 4.

penny dreadfuls."[2] Before he even entered college, he had read all of Agrippa's *De Occulta Philosophia* – in the original Latin! (Languages came very easily to him, and eventually he could read or speak more than a dozen of them.) During his college years at Princeton, he spent more time on his own romantic and esoteric interests than on the prescribed curriculum. He studied the *Corpus Hermeticum*, Plato, various Neo-Platonic philosophers, Jacob Boehme and other mystics, and also recent German idealistic philosophy. He even looked into theurgy as described in Iamblichus' treatise, *On the Mysteries of the Egyptians, Chaldaeans and Assyrians*. For his lighter reading there were always the works of Rabelais, Villon and Shakespeare, the old English and Scottish ballads published by Bishop Percy and by Sir Walter Scott, and other such entertaining trifles. By the time he left Princeton, he knew far more of occult, esoteric and weird things than any of his professors.

By the time Leland was about 45 years old, he had secured his financial independence, and he was free to spend the rest of his life however he saw fit. Since he was (as Elizabeth Robins Pennell, his favorite niece, wrote) a man "whose every thought, whose every emotion steered straight for the marvellous," he naturally sought out the dark and hidden corners of life, however far they might lie off the beaten track of polite society.[3] Around 1870, while living in England, Leland first encountered the Romany, or Gypsies, and was immediately fascinated by them. He soon learned to speak their unwritten language, and he took deep soundings in their magical lore. He also learned from them the art of *dukkerin'* (telling fortunes) for the *gorgio* (people who are not Romany). In England, too, he found wandering tinkers who used a secret language of their own, Shelta, which he studied. In the early 1880s, after returning to the United States, he sought out the Passamaquoddy,

2 Pennell (1905): 155.

3 Pennell (1906), II: 50.

a Native American nation in Maine and New Brunswick, and persuaded them to tell him some of their ancient legends and a little of their closely guarded lore.

Then, in 1888, Leland and his wife settled in Florence, Italy, where they were to spend the rest of their lives. In that city he met and befriended a professional fortune-teller and Witch *(strega)*, the young woman whom he called Maddalena in all his books.[4] From her and a few of her like-minded women friends he gathered vast quantities of archaic lore on magic and Witchcraft, and also on what Maddalena called *la vecchia religione* – the Old Religion of the Gods and Goddesses before Christianity came into the land of Italy.

At the same time, quite out of the blue, another woman, Mary Alicia Owen, an amateur folklorist living in Missouri, opened a correspondence with Leland on the subject of African-American folk magic. They proved to be kindred spirits, and for the rest of Leland's life they wrote regularly to one another, trading spells and charms, and reinforcing one another's interest in magic.

All these women seem to have inspired Leland to turn his attention ever more toward the problems that the study of magic will pose to any inquiring mind. The result was a long series of books on that subject. The first to appear was *Gypsy Sorcery and Fortune-Telling* (1891). It was closely followed by five volumes of the magical lore and legends of Italy: *Etruscan-Roman Remains in Popular Tradition* (1892), *Legends of Florence Collected from the People* (in two volumes, 1895 and 1896), *Aradia, or the Gospel of the Witches of Italy* (1899), and finally *The Unpublished Legends of Virgil* (1899). The series was concluded by two books on magic in general: *Have You a Strong Will?* (1899, later titled *The Mystic*

---

4 Her actual given name was Margherita, according to Roma Lister (1926: 123-124). Her surname was Taluti (Ordish 1892: 454). Raven Grimassi was the first to notice this reference, the only known place where Leland himself mentioned her surname in print. In my earlier article on Leland, I had misread her surname as Talenti (Mathiesen 1998: 32).

Will) and *The Alternate Sex; or, The Female Intellect in Man, and the Masculine in Woman* (1904, published posthumously). Related to the last two books, but a work of fiction, was Leland's *Flaxius: Leaves from the Life of an Immortal* (1902).

Despite all these books that he published on magic, Leland was never content just to sit in his study and write. Every inch a man of action, he had to be out and about almost every day of his life, ever on the move, conducting his research not just in the books of other men, but in the alleys and the woods and along the wild back roads of the great wide world. And whatever he learned there, he was keen to try out for himself, over and over, before he ever put pen to paper. And so it was with magic. He practiced it avidly and repeatedly, to see whether he could make it work for himself and others, and how well; and also to figure out, if he could, how it *really* worked. He could no more have held back from trying out the magic he learned, and trying to understand it, than a cat can resist fresh catnip.

Nor did any religious scruples hold him back. He had spent his youth in very progressive circles, among Unitarians, Transcendentalists and Free Thinkers. Later he went his own way in religion, as in everything else. His niece writes:

> I have said nothing whatever of his religion hitherto, for the simple reason that according to the usual standard of church-going as a test of religion, he had none. Since the days when he went to hear Dr. Furness preach in the Unitarian church at Philadelphia, and, to escape the prevailing Presbyterianism, attended the Episcopal church at Princeton, no church of any kind had often seen him. But he had the religious temperament. He could not dispense with some sort of religion, and he felt the need, – the more as he grew older. Through science and mysticism, he had gradually evolved a creed for himself.[5]

5 Pennell (1906), II: 46-47.

This creed of his was a sort of nature religion, a mysticism of the material world. As his niece elsewhere put it:

> ...in his religion, which was a sort of mystical materialism, love of nature played a large part.[6]

As such, it grew naturally and equally from two roots. One of them was his wide reading in occultism, esotericism and mysticism. The other was the strictly materialistic science of the late nineteenth century. These two things seem incompatible to many people, but Leland made them work together in his service.

Leland was constantly practicing small magics. His pockets were always stuffed with charms and amulets. Every stone with a hole in it, every discarded piece of red string, caught his eye; he would pick it up and save it for its magical uses. As his niece wrote, he "not only studied witchcraft with the impersonal curiosity of the scholar, but practiced it with the zest of the initiated."[7] Here, for an example, is an extract from a letter of his to Mary Alicia Owen on the power of a Black Stone, once owned by an African-American magician named King Alexander, which she had sent to him:

> ...I must tell you that King Alexander's fetich has been working the most delightful miracles. Firstly, to go from Stockholm to Copenhagen, we had 400 Orientalists, a night's railway journey, and only about 30 places in the sleeping cars. And I had hardly ever spoken to the Secretary, who was a hard, grim, *dour* man. However, I invoked the little spirit and put him in my pocket. Mrs. Leland went with me and asked for our tickets – only expecting, of course, common seats, as the sleeping cars were reserved for the magnates. What was our *fainting amazement* when Count Landberg

6 Pennell (1905): 156.

7 Pennell (1906), I: 6-7.

volunteered us a compartment in a sleeping car. *The Spirit had spoken!*

From Christiania to Gottenburg – the same thing, but more marvellous. I again invoked the spirit, and this time Count Landsberg said he had only *one* ticket, but calling a stately Oriental in turban, etc., made him disgorge *his* ticket! We were absolutely awed at such good fortune!

Und noch weiter, on the steamboat to England Mrs. Leland found that a diamond worth perhaps $40 or $50 had fallen from her ring, probably while asleep in her berth. The whole stateroom was overhauled in vain. I invoked the spirit and I predicted its recovery. A few days after, here in Brighton, she found it loose at the bottom of her travelling bag. And I had another invocation to find a friend who I was confidentially assured had left Brighton. One day I invoked the spirit and he bade me follow two girls on the other side of the way. I did so for some distance, when I met my friend, who had just returned to Brighton; I might have been here a year without doing so...

As for my little spirit, I can only say, Blessings on him and on her who sent him to me.

With regards to King Alexander – and love to all around...[8]

Two years later, in 1891, Leland attended the International Congress of Folk-Lorists at London, where there was an exhibition of artifacts in support of the papers given. To his niece he wrote:

We all contributed folk-lore articles to the Exhibition. I had only to pick out of one tray in one trunk to get 31 articles, which filled two glass cases. As Belle [Mrs. Leland] says, she can't turn over a shirt without

8 Pennell (1906), II: 321-322.

> having a fetish roll out. And I couldn't distinguish between those of my own make and those of others. For I am so used to picking up stones with holes in them, and driftwood, and tying red rags around chicken-bones for luck, etc., that I consider my own just as powerful as anybody's.[9]

All this magical practice is best summed up by Leland himself in yet another letter to his niece, in 1895:

> There is a great difference between collecting folk-lore as a curiosity and living in it in truth. I do not believe that in all the Folk-Lore Societies there is one person who lives in it in reality as I do. I cannot describe it – what it *once* was is lost to the world. You cannot understand it at second hand... the more I know such people [as Maddalena and her friend Marietta], the more bewildered I am, and the more lost in a kind of elfin-land of mystery...[10]

An active mind such as Leland's could not be content with the mere practice of magic, however successful he might become at it. Such a mind had to understand *how* it worked – or rather, *how* it could be made to work. Experience had shown him that magic did not work by itself like some sort of mechanical device, but needed a skilled and knowledgeable operator to set and keep it in motion. But just what skills, what knowledge, must this operator have to make magic work?

By the time he wrote his first book on magic, *Gypsy Sorcery and Fortune-Telling* (1891), he had come up with a rough sort of theory to answer this question.

Leland began with the easy observation that there lies hidden in every person a second self, an *alter ego*, that can do things

---

9 Pennell (1906), II: 352. Ordish (1892: 453-454) lists Leland's contributions to that exhibition.

10 Pennell (1906), II: 379.

which the ordinary, waking self cannot. It can recall things that the latter has wholly forgotten, and it displays a different sort of fanciful creativity, and more of it, than the latter ever does. It will work against the waking self and even thwart the latter's purposes. It delights in all kinds of mystification, mystery, befuddlement and deceit.

Also, this *alter ego* comes into its full power when the waking self is asleep, and it is the author of our dreams. The two selves need not be in sympathy with one another, but may exhibit a fundamental difference in character. If ever one has just woken up from a dream that was utterly disgusting and revolting, one has experienced at that moment just how great this difference in character can be between the *alter ego* and the waking self.

As a rule, too, the *alter ego* is more perceptive than the waking self, and its leaps of intuition hit the mark far more often, and with less effort, than the waking self ever does by reason alone. Also, the *alter ego* has access to memories of everything – absolutely everything! – that a person ever experienced in his life, whether he paid attention to it at the time or not.

Whoever, therefore, can manage, by any means, to persuade or compel his *alter ego* to do the bidding of his waking self, will have power and knowledge beyond the capacity of ordinary people. In short, such a person will *seem* to most people to be possessed of supernatural abilities – though there is nothing supernatural about them at all. He (or she) will appear to be a magician, a sorcerer, a Witch, a wizard, a prophet, or whatever name one gives to people who are able to do and know things that most people cannot, and who also do and know them by means that lie beyond the ken of most people.

So how can a person actually persuade or compel his *alter ego* to do the bidding of his waking self? This is the problem with which Leland wrestled for several more years. By the end of 1897 he had arrived at an answer that satisfied him, which he expounded in a small book under the misleading title, *Have You a Strong Will?*

(1899).[11] In the United States, the third edition soon caught the eye of William Walker Atkinson, who published it in 1907 under a new title, *The Mystic Will*.[12] In this form, it has remained in print for over a century.

At the very end of his life, Leland made a last few adjustments to this theory of his, and he included them in his last book, *The Alternate Sex* (1904). The book was not quite ready for publication at the time of his death, but his niece saw it through the press. His earlier book, *Have You a Strong Will?* was *not* revised by him to incorporate these final insights, but continued to appear without further change after his death.

In *Gypsy Sorcery and Fortune-Telling* (1891), the best advice that Leland could offer for bringing one's *alter ego* under control was to become very skilled at what is now called "cold-reading" by mentalists and other stage magicians. This is an art of *apparent* mind-reading which relies on a deep knowledge of human nature and human life, on an ability to weave plausible narratives of the inquirer's own life and present concerns, and on the keenest possible observation of every small shift in the inquirer's posture, muscle tension, coloration, breathing, and so forth, that can show how the inquirer is reacting to each word in such a narrative. Beginning with banal generalities, the reader steadily refines his narrative of the inquirer's life by slow degrees, making it reflect more and more closely what the inquirer's true concerns are. Then the reader knows enough to offer plausible or palatable advice to relieve the inquirer's anxiety and guide his future actions.

Cold-reading may be characterized as humbug or deceit. If that's what you want to call it, then the only means that Leland knows in 1891 to bring the *alter ego* under control is to develop

---

11 See Pennell (1906), II: 388-391. The second edition (1902) has an added chapter on Kant, the third edition (1903) a second added chapter on Paracelsus. Later editions with this title reproduce the third edition.

12 In this edition, the chapter on Kant is omitted, though the one on Paracelsus is retained.

great skill in this sort of humbug or deceit, and to practice it often. In *Gypsy Sorcery and Fortune-Telling* his theory goes no farther.

Soon, however, he found another, more powerful and subtle means to the same end, which he expounded in *Have You a Strong Will?* alias, *The Mystic Will*. The process is a slow one, but it does give results. It is also complicated, so that a very brief summary – all that I have room to give here – will not be enough to let anyone master the process. Essentially, it moves through several stages. First you cultivate what Leland calls **Forethought,** and you use it to strengthen your power of **Suggestion**. (By Suggestion, Leland means what is now called auto-suggestion or self-suggestion. By Forethought he means a focused meditation, before you fall asleep, on whatever auto-suggestion that you plan to carry out the next day.) Suggestion, strengthened by Forethought, is first employed to increase **Perseverence** in yourself. Once you have learned to persevere at any task, the next step is to persevere at keeping your **Attention** closely fixed on whatever task lies at hand, not allowing it to wander. Attention will *naturally* produce **Interest** in whatever object you fix your attention on, if you persevere in fixing it there. Once you have learned how to create for yourself a deep Interest in any task or object you choose, you can then apply your fixed and cultivated Attention, which can create Interest, to the task of strengthening your **Memory** and to the similar task of strengthening your **Will**. When you have mastered these seven abilities in their proper order, you will be able to perceive and accomplish things beyond the abilities of most other people. According to Leland:

> All that Man has ever attributed to an Invisible World without, lies, in fact, within him, and the magic key which will confer the faculty of sight and the power to conquer is the *Will*.[13]

Having mastered these seven abilities, you can then shape and train your *alter ego* to serve you, in effect, as a kind of immaterial

---

13 Leland, *Strong Will* (1899): xxvii; *Mystic Will* (1907): 16.

being, "gifted with greater powers than those possessed by Conscious Intellect."[14] This brings "a power by means of which we can learn mysteries," Leland says somewhat rhetorically.[15]

This very short summary leaves out a variety of practical techniques that one may, if one wishes, use to help each step of the process along. If you wish to try it out, get the book and read it through. It is not very long, and you will have a fuller grasp of the details of Leland's theory of magic than my summary can give you.

Yet even this is not quite all. For quite some time Leland had been struck by the ways in which, in a man, this *alter ego* often seems to have womanly qualities, and in a woman, manly qualities. In his final book, *The Alternate Sex*, he pushes this observation to a logical conclusion, and claims, as a general rule (allowing many exceptions), that the *alter ego* is of the opposite sex from the waking self, and also from the body that houses both selves. In a man, the *alter ego* is feminine; in a woman, masculine. It can best be approached by the waking self, and its latent powers most fully developed, only if this difference is kept in view.

Readers may be struck, as I was, by the way in which Leland anticipates some features of Jung's psychology, and some of Freud's. As it happens, all three authors have their roots in the same soil: each of them was very well read in the psychological literature of the nineteenth century, which was much less scientific than it now is, and also much more interested in things that scientific psychology later shunned as "the black tide of mud of occultism."[16]

One such nineteenth-century psychologist was C. Lloyd Tuckey, M.D. (1855–1925). His most influential book was titled *Psycho-Therapeutics, or Treatment by Sleep and Suggestion* (1889).

---

14 Leland, *Strong Will* (1899): 180; *Mystic Will* (1907): 90.

15 Leland, *Strong Will* (1899): 181-182; *Mystic Will* (1907): 91.

16 Jung (1963: 149-155), writing decades after the event, attributed this phrase to Freud.

Leland cites the work in his *Gypsy Sorcery and Fortune-Telling* and commends it "to all persons interested in ethnology as casting light on some of the most interesting and perplexing problems of humanity, and especially of 'magic.'"[17] He also mentions Dr. Tuckey twice in *Have You a Strong Will?* What Leland may not have known, was that Dr. Tuckey became a member of the Hermetic Order of the Golden Dawn in 1894, thereby entering the charmed circle of practicing occultists and magicians.[18] Tuckey also kept up his membership in the Society for Psychical Research, and he published a brief review of Leland's *Have You a Strong Will?* in the *Proceedings* of that Society.[19] Though I have not taken the trouble to check, it would not surprise me if evidence could be found, as well, that both Sigmund Freud and Carl Gustav Jung had read Tuckey's book.

The Witchcraft of Dame Darrel of York

Leland also loved practicing what he called "the minor arts" – such arts and crafts as drawing, wood carving, leather working, bookbinding and calligraphy. It was only natural for him to combine this love with his love of magic, and make small handwritten, illuminated books of magic lore for himself and others. We know of three such books. Two of them he certainly made for his niece; the third is likely to have been meant for her also, if he did not make it for himself alone. It seems possible to me that Leland also made a few other such books for some of his best friends and closest confidants who shared his interest in magic, for instance, the folklorists Mary Alicia Owen and Roma Lister. If so, they have been lost.

Two of these three handwritten, illuminated books were titled *Dukkerin Lil* (the title is in the Romany language). Here is how Leland described such a book:

---

17 Leland, *Gypsy Sorcery* (1891): 5.

18 Howe (1972): 51; Gilbert (1986): 153.

19 Tuckey (1903).

> The reader must understand that, among the women Gypsies, there is no treasure so coveted as a so-called *dukkerin-lil*, or fortune-telling book. By this is not meant a dime dream-book or a cheap fortune-teller, such as are generally to be found associated with cent-broadside ballads, but some quaint and ancient little work on chiromancy or magic, garnished with pictures of hands and strange cabalistic devices, such as abound in Agrippa and Trithemius. Such a book is to a fortune-teller what a wand was to a sorcerer or a broom to a witch. The possession of a really remarkable specimen of such literature confers a species of renown. One hears that a certain family owns it as one hears of another's owning a famous horse or a superior wagon.[20]

In the early 1880s, Leland and his niece had a chance to visit an encampment of the Rom in Philadelphia, where they went to meet an ancient woman, Rosanna Lovel, who was perhaps a hundred years old, and was reputed to know more of bygone Romany customs and lore than anyone else. While there, his niece had reason to show the old woman her own *dukkerin-lil*, "a small book bound in old red morocco," which Leland further described in the following words:

> That which my niece had was a curiosity in its way, being filled with marvelous illuminated hands, dragons, and other monsters, in vermillion, gold, or silver, and looked as well able to raise Mephistopheles as any specimen of occult philosophy which eyes ever beheld.[21]

The old woman visibly coveted the volume and offered to buy it from Leland's niece, who instead offered it to her as a present.[22]

---

20 Leland, "Visiting the Gypsies" (1883): 906-907.

21 Leland, "Visiting the Gypsies" (1883): 907.

22 Leland, "Visiting the Gypsies" (1883): 907, 909.

If it has survived the intervening 130 years, it is probably still cherished as a great treasure by one of her descendants.

Leland, however, seems to have made good his niece's loss, for photographs of three pages from a second *dukkerin-lil* of the same description can be seen in her *Biography* of Leland.[23] It, too, is in Leland's handwriting, just 30 pages long, wholly in the Romany language. It is now in the British Library, where it has been bound up with many other papers to make volume V of the C. G. Leland Collection.[24]

The last of these three books is *The Witchcraft of Dame Darrel of York*. It is now part of the large archive of Leland's papers that was given to the Historical Society of Pennsylvania by his niece.

I still remember that day in the summer of 1992 when I first saw the book. I had gone to the Society's library to look through Leland's archive there. I was hoping to find letters and other papers that had been sent to him by Maddalena, on the basis of which he had written another book of his, *Aradia, or the Gospel of the Witches of Italy*. At the time, Leland's archive consisted of fourteen banker's boxes filled with loose papers, many of them jumbled together almost at random. (They have been put in order since my visit.) Though I looked at every sheet of paper in those fourteen boxes, I did not find anything of Maddalena's among them. However, I soon found something else almost as useful. I recognized a loose page of *Aradia* in Leland's handwriting. Soon I found another, and then many others; in the end I had found almost every page of the book and put them in their proper order. What I had on the table before me, when I had finished, was the original printer's copy for *Aradia*, which Leland had written out by hand and sent to the publisher, David Nutt. It had evidently been returned to him once the book was printed, and he had never discarded it. Though none

---

23 Pennell (1906), II: facing pp. 184, 186.

24 British Museum (1907): 367-368: Additional Ms. 37172, ff. 132-146: "'Dukkerin Lil,' a fortune-telling book, in *Romany*, with fantastic diagrams, by C. G. Leland."

of it was in Maddalena's hand, it still offered clear evidence that Leland had been working from texts in Italian written by someone else, and had not just made the whole thing up himself.[25]

When I had finished my work and was preparing to leave the library for the last time, one of the librarians asked with some diffidence – as if expecting a negative answer – whether I might also be interested in seeing a bound book, written in Leland's hand,which was kept on the same shelf as the fourteen banker's boxes. Of course I would, I replied; I had not known that such a book existed.

And the librarian put into my hands what at first appeared to be a centuries-old volume bound in plain, cream-colored vellum, not quite nine inches tall by seven inches wide, containing about 200 pages (in fact, there are 182 pages). There was nothing on the spine or cover to indicate its contents. Then I opened the cover and saw the title page, and I leafed quickly through the whole book – and I stood there thunderstruck at what I was seeing, at the beauty of Leland's art and at the quaint and curious text that he had written.

My remaining time in Philadelphia was very limited indeed. I could only skim the book and place my order for a microfilm of it. But I could not forget what I had seen, or the strong impression it made on me that day. Now, almost twenty years later, I – or anyone – can peruse it at leisure in this facsimile edition. But the thrill that came with seeing for the first time an unknown treasure, and recognizing its great value – *that* I cannot bring back through the mists of twenty intervening years.[26]

If you, too, go to Philadelphia, hold the actual volume in your hands, and then open its front cover, you will immediately see the

---

25 See Mathiesen (1998) for the argument and the evidence that supports it.

26 I briefly mentioned *The Witchcraft of Dame Darrel of York* in my article on Leland (Mathiesen 1998: 56-57). Since 1992, other scholars with similar interests have gone to Philadelphia and examined the manuscript (e.g. Chas S. Clifton, Raven Grimassi), and one of them, Marion Gibson, has even briefly mentioned it in print (2007: 142-143, 147).

first title page (p. 1). Inside a medieval-style arch, supported by a human figure on each side, you can read:

> The Witchcraft of Dame Darrel of York.

The next page is blank, but the page after that gives a much fuller form of the title (p. 3):

> Here followeth ye Book of *ye Witchcraft of Dame Darrel of York* with account of all kinde of Fairys, *Elves*, Goblines, Bargests, *Ghostes*, Gasters, Bendys, Pixys, Pillicockes, Hobthrushes, Friar Rushes, Pictrees, Dules, Night Hagges, Giantes, Yeth-Hounds, Devilkins, Spoornes, *Robin Goodfelows* and all *theyr Kinde*.

This is followed by three more blank pages, and then you come to the start of the book itself, which tells who the writer is and why the book was written. It begins with these words (pp. 7-8):

> *Dame Darrell* was called *the Wise Woman of York*. What I here write I heard her tell from time to time. *Veritas non semper valet*, he who tells great truths will pass for a Liar, but those who are wise know Truth from Lyes *and if ye can tell a Fly in a Milk-pan ye may know whether what is written here be meant for you or for your betters*. Now a *Wise Woman* is a *White Witch*, much as a Broom is a Besom, and so she was called of her best Friends but to my Mind what she did not know of *Witchcraft* be it white or black was little worth knowing and might be put in a Flea's Eye not to speak of Anything smaller. And as I was her own Sister's Child and dwelt with her Ten Years I knew her like my pocket from the time when I came from the Ile of Jersey to dwel with her.

The book claims, therefore, to give a first-hand account of the Witchcraft of a very knowledgeable Wise Woman of the previous generation. She was called Dame Darrel, and she lived in York, which is the foremost city of Yorkshire, in the North of England. The writer, Dame Darrel's "own sister's child," however, had been born and raised on the Isle of Jersey (where they spoke French though it belonged to the English Crown), and knew something of the Witchcraft of that island. Elsewhere in the book the writer recounts a tale told "among us Wise Women" (p. 31), thereby implying that she is a Wise Woman herself, that is, Dame Darrel's *niece*, not her nephew. Toward the end of the book she mentions her own given name, Peronell or Pernel (p. 177) – which reminds one of Leland's niece, Elizabeth Robins Pennell, whom he fondly called "Pen."

Yet the writer is a man, Charles G. Leland himself. The whole book is written in his distinctive literary style, and it reflects his uncommonly wide knowledge of magic and folklore. The text is entirely in his own well-known handwriting, and all the artwork in it is by him also, as can be seen by comparing it with all the illustrations in his later published works. In short, Leland the man has put on the mask – or adopted the literary *persona* – of a Wise Woman.

For Leland, this may have been something more than merely a literary device. Toward the end of his life he developed a strong interest in what he called "the female intellect in man," and the very last book that he ever wrote, which was released just after his death, had the title: *The Alternate Sex; or, The Female Intellect in Man, and the Masculine in Woman* (1904). Moreover, Leland thought that Witchcraft was the birthright of all women, but a rare oddity in men. In his books on magic, he expressed surprise when, in his own research, he encountered some mention of a man who was regarded as a Witch. In several of his books he quoted a verse from an unidentified poem:

> For every woman is at heart a witch.[27]

As you continue to leaf through *The Witchcraft of Dame Darrel of York*, you will soon see that it is an odd cross between a memoir, a grimoire and a dictionary of magical creatures.

---

27 Leland, *Gypsy Sorcery* (1891): 208; *Aradia* (1899): 111; *Alternate Sex* (1904): 75. I suspect that the line may come from an unpublished poem by Leland himself.

It begins with several handy spells for women to have good luck in love. The last of them ends by saying that "the fairies have no mind unto some" (p. 13), and no spell can help such a person.

This leads naturally enough into a long account of fairies in general, and their several races, including various kinds of *Elves*, *Goblins*, *Brownies*, *Durgans*, *Hamans* (or *Hemans*), *Thurses*, and *Ouphs*. Here the writer gives several connected legends to account for the origin and character of some of the races of fairies, as well as a number of spells for securing their favor and assistance, and a few tales of fairy magic and the role it once played in the affairs of some men and women. This amounts to somewhat more than a fourth part of the entire volume (pp. 14-58).

Having come to this point in the book, the writer is at a momentary loss how to present the lore about the many other magical creatures that remain to be treated. In what is clearly a jerry-rigged solution to the problem, the Elves are now renamed *Alfs* with the letter A, and as such are given first place in an alphabetical dictionary of these creatures:

> *Now I will here as well as I can, not being over Learned as ye can well see, give all the names of the Faireys* and *Goblins according to the Letters of the Christcross* and with them such Words as pertain to their kind. And first are the Alfs or Elves of whom I have written all that I know or what we call Awvish or Elvish things (p. 59).

The rest of the volume (pp. 59-172) is a series of about ninety entries, more or less in alphabetical order, treating close to one hundred magical creatures from the *Annet* and the *Bo* to the *Woodwose* and the *Yeth-Hound*. They are treated in much the same manner as the kinds of Elves. That is, the accounts of them include legends of their origin, tales of their interaction with men and women, and spells for securing their favor or aid.

The writer ends – that is, had originally planned to end – with the following summary (pp. 173-175):

This is al that I call to mind to this daye and Hour of Dame Darrell, *though God wote If I had wil to write all I ever heard I should nat* have moneye no credit enow to buy me ye paper and *Ink and pennes to do soe*. Now here I have to saye that I being ignorant with no skill to write have natheless sett downe what I wene are strange and unkent things and whatt are cald here *Uncoths* or News to many Scollars, tho I have done it many a time clumpish and awkert. Lett it all goe in one Stewe as the Good wyfe saide whan she put meate and fysshe, cole and coines and apples all to stew in one pott and make a Cockagrice, whiche is a ***[long blank space]*** dish that never cometh twise alike. Now tis a strange Thing yet true that there bee many unlered Folke who are full of quainte and rare Wisdom who would be all of a dither iff made to write down what they can tell and talke, as crousely and cannily as Hearte coulde wish. and *per contra* I ever find that those who learne to write with Skil, *as Scollars, whenn they get there, have nothing left to saye or sett downe*. like Rob of the Greene who did goe from York to London to sell a wagonload of Stuffe, but whann hee got there the wagone was bare, for hee had traded away all hee hadd on the way for Bait for him and his horses. So that he had learned muche yet loste more. *Or I may liken too too many scollers to the man who* to jumpe over a dike did firste tak a Runn ere hee lepped, but run so long that ere he gott to ye Ditch was fain to sit down and reste. And so itt is with Folke who put all theyr Witt into learning how to write well, soe that whan 'tis learnt they have no thing left to say. so there they sitt like so many Dobbeys by the brook which they don't jump over to ye other side where is the House of Fame where all are famoused who dwel therein

Wherein I tell you verily
We all of Us would like to bee.
And wherein to fess it plain
If we Could we'd ay remain.

Yet this is not quite the end of the book as it stands now. The volume contains seven more pages, all of them originally blank. Now four of these pages are no longer blank, but hold entries for three more magical creatures, which had been omitted by mistake from their proper places in the alphabet. The first of the three was for *Dobby*. It was clearly provoked by the reference to "so many Dobbeys" in the paragraph just quoted, for Leland begins it with the sentence, "Nowe this word Dobby minds me that I forgat to tell whatt a Dobby is..." (p. 175-177). Next follow entries for *Boll* and *Black Bugg* (pp. 177-179). The last three pages (pp. 180-182) of the volume are still blank.

How and When Did Leland Make This Book?

Let us now take a look at *The Witchcraft of Dame Darrel of York* as a material object, an artifact that Leland made at his desk or in his workshop.

As noted above, the volume is made up of 91 leaves of paper (that is, 182 pages), not counting the single leaves pasted down on the inside of the front and the back covers. When you look more closely at the manuscript, you can see that almost all of these leaves were made by folding larger sheets of paper in half, and each leaf is, for the most part, still attached to its other half. A certain number of these large folded leaves have been placed together, one inside the next, and have been sewn together at the fold. The result is called a **gathering**. A gathering will naturally have an even number of leaves, twice as many as the number of large folded sheets of paper that make it up. (If we count by pages instead of leaves, a gathering will have four times as many pages as the number of large folded sheets of paper that make it up.) Thus, for example, a gathering of 6 large sheets of paper, folded and sewn together, will necessarily have 12 leaves, which is the same thing as having 24 pages.

In the facsimile, you can see the threads that hold many of the gatherings together. They can be seen, for example, between pages 2 and 3, pages 10 and 11, pages 28 and 29, and so forth.[28] These mark the mid-points of the gatherings.

When someone creates such a book, and has filled all of his gatherings with text and decorations, the next step is to sew all the gatherings together, thereby making a solid block of gatherings that can be put into a cover. He will sew them together at the spine, that is, at the back of their folds. Then he will fit a cover to the book and attach it to the block of gatherings that he has just made. The spine of that cover will hide the threads that hold the gatherings together at the spine. However, if the sewing is not tight enough, you may occasionally catch a glimpse of these threads where two gatherings come together. In the facsimile, you can glimpse these threads between pages 6 and 7.

One of the problems you face, when you sew the gatherings together, is to keep them in their correct order. You can solve this problem by numbering (or lettering) each gathering as soon as you finish it, usually in some inconspicuous or temporary way. In the fascimile, you can see some of the numbers that Leland used to keep the gatherings in their correct order. The number "2," in pencil, is easily seen in the upper left corner of page 15, the first page in what is now the *third* gathering in the volume. The number "1," somewhat fainter, can be seen in the same place on page 7, the first page in what is now the *second* gathering.

By paying attention to such details, we can see how Leland made and put together this particular volume. He began with what is now page 7, and he wrote out his text, page by page and gathering by gathering, until he came to page 175, not quite all the way to the foot of that page. And that was the end of his book, at least for the moment.

---

28 They can also be seen between pages 56 and 57, 80 and 81, 96 and 97, 110 and 111, 136 and 137, 148 and 149, 162 and 163, and 176 and 177.

However, Leland had not quite come to the middle of his last gathering, which fell between pages 176 and 177.[29] Rather, that gathering contained nine more pages (four and a half more leaves), which he left blank. When, at the end of all his labor, he put the book inside its vellum cover, he would paste the last of these blank leaves down onto the inside of the back cover. After doing this, he would still have seven blank pages left (pp. 176-182).[30]

But he had not given his work a title page yet. So he made one more gathering, which contained just four leaves. He put the short title (in its decorative arch) on the front side of the second leaf (p. 1), the longer title on the front side of the third leaf (p. 3), and left everything else blank. Then he put this gathering in the front of his book. (This is why the gatherings that *now* stand second and third in the volume bear the numbers "1" and "2." The gathering that is *now* the first was an afterthought. Next he sewed all the gatherings together in their proper order to make a solid block.

Finally Leland cut cardboard and vellum to size, and made his cover. The first and the last leaf of his book were wholly blank, so to finish the job properly and strengthen the whole book, he pasted the first leaf and the last leaf down onto the insides of the front and the back cover. And then his book was finished.

One last question remains. When did Leland write out *The Witchcraft of Dame Darrel of York?* It bears no date that might give us an answer. The work clearly belongs to the last years of his life, from about 1890 onward, when his interest in magic and Witchcraft was at its peak.

Moreover, the work, as we have it, clearly stood at the end of a long process of note-taking and creativity. In one place, by

---

29 The last gathering seems to be the tenth that he had completed so far, but it is hard to be completely certain from the facsimile just where each gathering begins and ends.

30 Later he would write more text, beginning at the foot of p. 175 (where a few lines had been left blank) and continuing through the first four of the seven blank pages (pp. 176-179). The last three pages (pp. 180-182) remain blank.

chance, we can even watch Leland copying from an earlier note of his that he could no longer quite read. Having ended one tale with the words, "So the Gaster served as a horrorr and a Scar to the Crows," he then continues: "(Illegible)... Jankin who made a *Scar for Crowes* so terrible... he was wel-nye scart to death of Itt him selfe" (p. 108). The ellipses and the word "(Illegible)" are there in Leland's own handwriting, showing where his own note of another short tale, about Jankin and a scarecrow he had made, had become illegible with the passage of time, even to Leland himself.

In 1890, he wrote to his niece that he had

> begun a book on strange Beings, such as Nightmares, Stone Men, Headless Men, Tree Men, Smoke Men, etc., but a book with a purpose, to show the world how little difference there is between all religion of our time and old sorcery, etc. I am taking great pains to combine in it a serious philosophy of Folk-Lore with nice stories, new to all readers and all kinds of quaint and merry plays of my most peculiar style."[31]

In the end, Leland did not write or publish that book. Nor is *The Witchcraft of Dame Darrel of York* that book, although it draws on the material that Leland was collecting for it.

Ten years later, in the autmun of 1900, Leland wrote to his niece, mentioning various books he wanted to write, including "a book to be called 'The Gothic Mother Goose,' the old nursery rhymes illustrated by Gothic grotesques."[32] This work, too, or rather, the notes he had taken for it, have left their clear traces in *The Witchcraft of Dame Darrell of York.* However, all his plans were derailed when his wife suffered a severe paralytic stroke on December 29, 1900. She remained an invalid until her death not quite two years later.

---

31 Pennell (1906), II: 339-340.

32 Pennell (1906), II: 413-414.

I suspect, therefore, that *The Witchcraft of Dame Darrell of York* was one of the very last books that Leland ever wrote, sometime after 1900, and probably after his wife's death on July 9, 1902. The shock of her death was almost more than he could bear, after more than forty years of marriage. On September 22, 1902, two and a half months later, he wrote in a letter to his niece, "When Belle died, I took to drawing all day and often in the evening."[33] These two and a half months may well be the period when he worked on *The Witchcraft of Dame Darrell of York*. If he did not finish the work then, he must have finished it not too long thereafter, for Leland joined his wife in death about six months later, on March 20, 1903.

The Witchcraft of Dame Darrel and the Book of Shadows

As many of my readers will already have noticed, Leland's manuscript of *The Witchcraft of Dame Darrel of York* bears a striking outward resemblance to other handwritten books of the rituals, legends and lore of Witchcraft that were copied and circulated during the second half of the twentieth century. These other books are generally called *Books of Shadows* by the Witches who make and use them.

The oldest known *Books of Shadows* were made – that is, written out by hand and decorated – by Gerald B. Gardner. (The very earliest of them has a different title, *Ye Bok of ye Art Magical*, though it has much the same content as the others.) To judge from the available photographs of pages from Gardner's *Books of Shadows*, and also from my own examination of the *Ye Bok of ye Art Magical*, he wanted all these books of his to look very old, like illuminated manuscripts from the Middle Ages. However, Gardner had much less skill as an artist than Leland, and very little knowledge of authentic historical book design.

---

33 Pennell (1906), II: 418.

Despite their outward and superficial similarity, there are no points of contact at all between the text of *The Witchcraft of Dame Darrel of York* and the texts found in any of Gardner's *Books of Shadows*. There is no reason whatever to think that Gardner himself had ever seen this particular manuscript of Leland's.

And yet, the question remains: could this outward and superficial similarity point to some kind of a thin link between the two? After all, only about half a century separates Leland's workshop from Gardner's in time.

Let us speculate just a little, perhaps too wildly...

We know of three handwritten books of magic that Leland wrote and decorated, two of which still exist. At least two of them, and probably all three, were made for his niece and close confidant, Elizabeth Robins Pennell. Yet these three need not have been the only such books that Leland ever made. He obviously enjoyed the work of making such a book. Also he had other, younger friends who shared his interest in magic and Witchcraft.

One such friend was Mary Alicia Owen. Another was Roma Lister, also a folklorist.[34] Yet another was Rev. J. Wood Brown, author of a book about the Medieval philosopher, Michael Scot, who in later legends had also been a great wizard.[35] One more may have been Ethel Mary "Tessa" Arbuthnot.[36]

Leland *might* have given any of them, or any other friend, one of his handwritten books of magic as a present. That person *might* have carried it to England later, and *might* have shown it to like-minded friends there as late as the 1930s, or even later. (Tessa Arbuthnot died in 1965, 101 years old.) Moving forward in time from Leland, this line of speculation narrows the gap between his workshop and Gardner's, or eliminates it altogether.

---

34 Pennell (1906), II: 338, 369-371.

35 Pennell (1906), II: 338-339, 413-414, 423-426.

36 Pennell (1906), II: 338, 424; Leland, *Flaxius* (1902): vii.

We can also move backward in time from Gardner, and narrow the gap in the other direction.

There are good reasons to think that Gardner's own surviving manuscripts of *A Book of Shadows* (especially the oldest of them all, *Ye Bok of ye Art Magical*) were copied – at least in part – from some earlier Witch's book, now lost. Philip Heselton has summarized some of the textual arguments favoring that conclusion, and I think it would be possible to make other arguments along the same lines using just the texts published by Aidan Kelly and others.[37] However, textual arguments of this sort turn precisely on very fine details in the specific wording of this or that text. They are very tedious for a casual reader to follow, so this is not the place to present them.

One argument, however, can be made here that will not be too hard to follow.

Some of the most important texts in *Ye Bok of ye Art Magical*, including the rituals of initiation into the three degrees, are written in an extremely elaborate calligraphy, which has a Medieval look to it. In a printed book or newspaper, letter-forms of this kind would be called an "Old English" or "black-letter" type-font. Black-letter fonts are most commonly used, these days, to print the title of a newspaper in large letters at the top of the front page, for example, **The New York Times**. Gardner used this sort of elaborate calligraphy elsewhere as well, for example, in a charter written out by him, and signed by Aleister Crowley, authorizing him to establish "a camp of the Ordo Templi Orientis, in the degree Minerval."[38]

There are, however, subtle differences between the letter-forms of his elaborate calligraphy in this charter (and elsewhere), and the letter-forms that are found in the rituals of initiation and a few other texts in *Ye Bok of ye Art Magical*, and replicated in

---

37 Heselton (2003): 304-310. See Kelly (1991, 2007).

38 Heselton (2003): 197.

his other early *Books of Shadows*. The most striking, and also the most revealing, of these differences is the form of the capital letter M. In the charter it has the form commonly used by English calligraphers, namely, 𝔐. In the elaborate calligraphy of *Ye Bok of ye Art Magical*, however, the capital M has a very odd shape, which was hardly ever used by any English calligrapher anywhere. This bizarre letter-form looks rather like a zero run together with an immediately following closing parenthesis, or a numeral 7. That is, it looks roughly like 0) or 07, but with the two parts connected at the top to make a single letter-form.[39] [*see figure 1*]

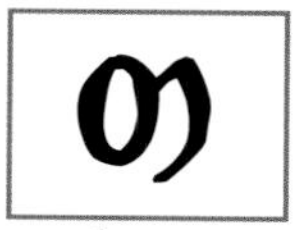

figure 1

Now this bizarre form of the capital letter M does have a history in England, in a very small and strictly limited way. During the early 1900s, a small group of artistically sophisticated men set out to reform typography and calligraphy in England, and one of their sources of inspiration was the black-letter type-fonts that had been used in Germany during the late 1400s.[40] At the center of this group stood the distinguished type-designer Stanley Morison (1889-1967), who created the font now known as Times New Roman, as well as many other fonts still used today. From the 1920s onward, Morison was a much respected figure within the very narrow circle of professional typographers and calligraphers. Outside that circle he was hardly known at all; he influenced only a few sophisticated artists and esthetes. An artistically unsophisticated man like Gardner would hardly have been aware of these artists and their work, much less of their taste for odd type-fonts and bizarre letter-forms.

---

39 Valiente (1989: plates 10-11) publishes photographs of two pages from one of Gardner's early *Books of Shadows*, where you can see two examples of such a capital letter M in the abbreviation M. S. The form of the capital M here – more like 00) or 007 – is not quite the same as the form 0) or 07 in *Ye Bok of ye Art Magical*.

40 See, for instance, Morison (1928, 1942).

From this we may draw a pretty firm conclusion: wherever we find this odd form of the capital letter M in *Ye Bok of ye Art Magical,* there we probably have a text that Gardner had originally copied from an earlier manuscript written by some other person, also copying that person's calligraphy, odd letter-forms and all. Who this other person might have been we do not know for certain, though Gardner's close Witch friend, Dafo (Edith Woodford-Grimes), seems to have been the sort of cultured person who might fill that bill. Did she, or someone like her, have a Witch's book of her own, written by hand in her own elaborate black-letter calligraphy, containing rituals of initiation and some other texts, that she had made for herself before she ever met Gardner? If so, did Gardner copy some or all of that older book into *Ye Bok of ye Art Magical?* I think it quite likely that both of these questions should be answered with a resounding "Yes"!

For what it may be worth, the late Cecil Williamson told several people that he had often seen just such an earlier Witch's book in Gardner's possession, which the latter always guarded with the greatest care – until one unlucky day, in a moment of carelessness, he left it unguarded on a table in the lunchroom for a while, and it was stolen from him – never to be recovered. According to Williamson, it was a handwritten book, apparently old, not very big, and it had two large sheets of thin paper folded and tucked inside its binding.[41]

This evidence can take us back at least a little ways, perhaps as much as a decade and a half even, before the time when Gardner began to make *Ye Bok of ye Art Magical,* at his desk or in his workshop. Since Gardner started to make that book in the second half of the 1940s, this kind of argument can take us back even as far as the early 1930s, to the years before Gardner's own initiation into Witchcraft in 1939. It reduces the gap between Leland's workshop and Gardner's in the other direction.

---

41 Heselton (2003): 305-309; Howard (2009): 91-92.

Or *none* of these things might actually have happened. It is all just a matter of speculation, even wild speculation, however likely it may seem to the reader.

Instead, the truth may be much simpler. The notion, the image, the ideal of such an ancient book of Witchcraft or magic *may* have been popular at the time, *may* have been reflected in art and literature. Ancient books, written out by hand and decorated with fanciful artwork, can easily seem to be mysterious objects of forgotten power. As such, they meshed well with the general fascination with the Middle Ages that characterized the late Victorian Age, when Leland was old and Gardner was young. Each man could have drawn the inspiration for his books from this ideal independently. Maybe that should be enough.

And yet the question remains: could one of Leland's handwritten and decorated books of Witchcraft and magic, a lost volume along the lines of *The Witchcraft of Dame Darrel of York*, somehow have been an inspiration for the very first *Books of Shadows?* Indeed, might *The Witchcraft of Dame Darrel of York* count as the very first known book of Witch-magic from the pen of a person who actually practiced it?

You, the reader, will have to answer that question for yourself, at least until more hard evidence is discovered one way or the other.

How to Read This Book and Not Get Too Confused

The transcription you have here represents the original manuscript as Leland wrote it, warts and all. This sort of transcription makes more work for a casual reader, though less work for a meticulous and careful one. It is for the sake of careful and slow readers that the warts seemed to me worth keeping.

Leland often did not capitalize the first letter of a new sentence, or distinguish between a comma and a period with any clarity. Sometimes he did not even bother with punctuation at all. Often it was enough for him that he had come to the end of a line in his manuscript at a point where someone else would have put a mark of punctuation. As a rule, he saw no need for any punctuation at the end of a line. Nor is it certain that Leland always knew when he had arrived at the end of one sentence and begun another: run-on sentences seem to be a feature of his literary style.

On the whole, I have kept all these features, or flaws, in the transcription, though where the end of a line seems to serve in place of a punctuation mark, I have often added the mark that seems most appropriate, to help the reader along a little. The facsimile will always serve to resolve any doubt.

Leland also delighted in creative misspelling, probably to make his manuscript look like it was the work of an unlettered rustic Wise Woman. Even the name of the Wise Woman herself is not spelled consistently: she is Dame Darrel, Darrell, Darel, or Darell, with no rhyme or reason to the choice of spelling.

Leland also used a certain number of archaic or obscure abbreviations, sometimes just to save space, sometimes to make the book look old and rustic. Thus, *ye* stands for *the* and *y't* for *that; wh'h* or *w'h* stands for *which* (and once for *Witch*), *w't* or *w'th* or even *wi'* for *with*. Less common are *the'* for *then* and *wh'n* for *when*. All the others should be clear enough from their context.

Leland "loved strange words as truly as strange people," wrote his niece.[42] As he worked on *The Witchcraft of Dame Darrel of York*, he delighted in finding and using words that no reader was likely to have seen ever before, or to have had any idea what they mean. These words, too, Leland creatively misspelled, which made them much harder for the reader to find in any dictionary. "For this they shall dearly abye," he wrote in one place (p. 133), and the context suggests that *abye* means something like "pay." Is *abye* an outright mistake, not a real word at all? Is it a familiar word creatively misspelled, or misspelled by accident – perhaps Leland meant to write *pay* or *obey* or *abide?* No, it is none of these things. Rather, it is a creative misspelling of a word so very obscure that it is almost impossible to find it in any dictionary at all. James Orchard

42 Pennell (1906), II: 293.

Halliwell's *A Dictionary of Archaic and Provincial Words* (first published in 1847) gives the word as *abie* "to pay for, to expiate."

As if this weren't enough thoroughly to perplex his readers, Leland's handwriting is not always clear enough for one to be certain just how he meant to spell, or misspell, these unfamiliar words. At first I read *Cockagnce* in one place (p. 147), but I could come no closer than *Cockayne* to such a hypothetical word in any dictionary. Eventually I found *Cockagrice* in Halliwell's *Dictionary*, which fit the context perfectly.

From the same dictionary Leland drew almost all of his really obscure words for kinds of magical creatures or objects, for example, *havel, hella, jemmy-burty, laurence, laverock, ouph, pictree, sooner, spoorne, swaithe, spellicoat, thrummy-cap, tilsterre, tod loury,* and *yeth-hound*. Only a very few words of this kind, such as *coricane* and *quimby*, are not found in Halliwell, but must have been taken by Leland from some other source.

In fact, Leland seems to have ransacked Halliwell's *Dictionary* from its first page to its last for words that he might use to puzzle his readers. Thus, he wrote of "a Jack o lanthorn such as ye teen" (p. 162), where *teen* means "to light."

Because of this, readers may want to keep a copy of Halliwell's *Dictionary* close at hand while they read the transcription. Fortunately, several editions of it can be found online.

My own very few additions to the transcription are printed in ***bold italics*** in square brackets. I have noted the presence of a full-page illustration without any text on pages 105 and 158. Also, on a few pages Leland left a long blank space in the text where, probably, he meant to write a place-name or some other word once he got around to looking it up. I have marked these places by adding the words ***[long blank space]***.

In the original, the first letter of a page or a section of the text was often ornamented or worked into a drawing, usually in color. This has usually, but not always, been marked by the use of an extra-large upper-case letter. (A few of these ornamented letters seem to be somewhat out of place in the original manuscript, and have been left unmarked.)

In one place only, I have corrected such an initial letter, and printed "She" where Leland actually drew and wrote "Hhe" (p. 47). The context makes it certain that *She* is the correct reading here.

Leland frequently underlined individual words, phrases or whole sentences, even though it is sometimes hard to understand why he has done so. I have marked all these words, phrases and sentences by the use of *italic type* (not bolded). The first title page (p. 1) is an exception to this rule, as underlining seems to be part of the artwork here.

There are 182 pages in the original volume. The facsimiles reproduce them in their full size. There are also facsimiles of the outside and inside of the front cover, the inside and outside of the back cover, and the spine. In the transcription, each page corresponds to a page of the facsimile, and is numbered at its top to show this correspondence.

This transcription was originally made, with great care and labor, by my colleague Yakov Rabinovich in the 1990s. Unfortunately, he had to work from a black-and-white printout of the microfilm that I had ordered in 1992, in which certain words and sentences were barely legible, or not legible at all. Three former students of mine, Jaime Zuckerman, Isabel Kunkle and Michelle Menard, checked large parts of his transcription against the same photoprints. I am much obliged to them for their painstaking work from so difficult an original.

Once color scans of the original manuscript finally became available, I read the entire transcription against them one more time, and corrected it wherever I found any discrepancy. Most of the corrections I made were minor; my colleague's original transcription had been made as carefully as the old printouts allowed, and the mistakes that my former students had already caught were also generally minor slips.

No doubt here and there I have misread or overlooked something, but I hope that such errors are few. If you find any errors, they are my fault, not theirs.

Robert Mathiesen
Professor Emeritus
Brown University

References

British Museum. 1907. *Catalogue of Additions to the Manuscripts in the British Museum in the Years MDCCCC-MDCCCCV.* London: The British Museum. (The C. G. Leland Collection is described on pp. 367-369.)

Gibson, Marion. 2007. *Witchcraft Myths in American Culture*. New York–London: Routledge.

Gilbert, R. A. 1986. *The Golden Dawn Companion: A Guide to the History, Structure, and Workings of the Hermetic Order of the Golden Dawn*. Wellingborough (UK): Aquarian.

Halliwell, James Orchard. 1924. *A Dictionary of Archaic and Provincial Words*. London: Routledge. [First published in 1847.]

Heselton, Philip. 2003. *Gerald Gardner and the Cauldron of Inspiration*. Chievely (UK): Capall Bann.

Howard, Michael. 2009. *Modern Wicca: A History from Gardner to the Present*. Woodbury, MN: Llewellyn.

Howe, Ellic. 1972. *The Magicians of the Golden Dawn: A Documentary History of a Magical Order, 1887–1923*. London: Routledge & Kegan Paul.

Jung, C. G. 1963. *Memories, Dreams, Reflections*. Revised ed. Translated by Richard and Clara Winston. New York: Random House (Vintage).

Kelly, Aidan A. 1991. *Crafting the Art of Magic*, Book I: *A History of Modern Witchcraft, 1939–1964*. St. Paul, MN: Llewellyn.

——. 2007. *Inventing Witchcraft: A Case Study in the Creation of a New Religion*. Loughborough (UK): Thoth.

Leland, Charles Godfrey. 1883. "Visiting the Gypsies." *The Century Illustrated Monthly Magazine*, vol. 25 (Nov. 1882 – April 1883): 905-912.

——. 1891. *Gypsy Sorcery and Fortune Telling, Illustrated by Numerous Incantations, Specimens of Medical Magic, Anecdotes and Tales*. London: T. Fisher Unwin.

——. 1892. *Etruscan Roman Remains in Popular Tradition*. London: T. Fisher Unwin.

——. 1894. *Memoirs*. 2nd edition. London: William Heinemann.

——. 1895 & 1896. *Legends of Florence Collected from the People*. 2 vols. London: David Nutt.

——. 1899. *Aradia, or the Gospel of the Witches of Italy*. London: David Nutt.

——. 1899. *The Unpublished Legends of Virgil*. London: Elliot Stock.

——. 1899. *Have You a Strong Will? Or How to Develop and Strengthen Will-Power, Memory, or Any Other Faculty or Attribute of the Mind, by the Easy Process of Self-Hypnotism*. London: George Redway. (2nd ed., 1902, and 3rd ed., 1903: London; Philip Wellby.)

——. 1902. *Flaxius: Leaves from the Life of an Immortal*. London: Philip Wellby.

——. 1904. *The Alternate Sex, or The Female Intellect in Man, and the Masculine in Woman*. New York: Funk & Wagnalls.

——. 1904. *The Mystic Will: A Method of Developing and Strengthening the Faculties of the Mind, Through the Awakened Will, by a Simple, Scientific Process Possible to Any Person of Ordinary Intelligence*. Chicago: Yogi Publication Society.

Lister, Roma. 1926. *Reminiscences – Social and Political*. 2nd ed. London: Hutchinson.

Mathiesen, Robert. 1998. "Charles G. Leland and the Witches of Italy: The Origin of the Aradia." Pp. 25-57 in the critical edition: Charles G. Leland. *Aradia, or the Gospel of the Witches*. Trans. Mario and Dina Pazzaglini. Blaine, WA: Phoenix.

Morison, Stanley. 1928. *German Incunabula in the British Museum: One Hundred & Fifty-Two Facsimile Plates of Fine Book Pages from Presses of Germany, German-Switzerland and Austria-Hungary printed in the Fifteenth Century in Gothic Letter and Derived Founts*. London: V. Gollancz.

——. 1942. *"Black-Letter" Text*. Cambridge (UK): The University Press.

[Ordish, Thomas Fairman.] 1892. "Catalogue of the Exhibition of Objects Connected with Folk-Lore." *The International Folk-Lore Congress, 1891: Papers and Transactions*: 433-460. London: David Nutt.

Pennell, Elizabeth Robins. 1905. "Hans Breitmann as Romany Rye." *The Atlantic Monthly: A Magazine of Literature, Science, Art, and Politics*, vol. 95 (1905): 154-168.

——. 1906. *Charles Godfrey Leland: A Biography*. 2 vols. Boston – New York: Houghton, Mifflin.

Tuckey, Charles Lloyd. 1889. *Psycho-Therapeutics, or Treatment by Sleep and Suggestion*. London: Bailliere.

——. 1903. [Review of Leland's *Have You a Strong Will?* 2nd ed, 1902.] *Proceedings of the Society for Psychical Research*, vol. 17 (1901-3): 424.

Valiente, Doreen. 1989. *The Rebirth of Witchcraft*. Custer, WA: Phoenix.

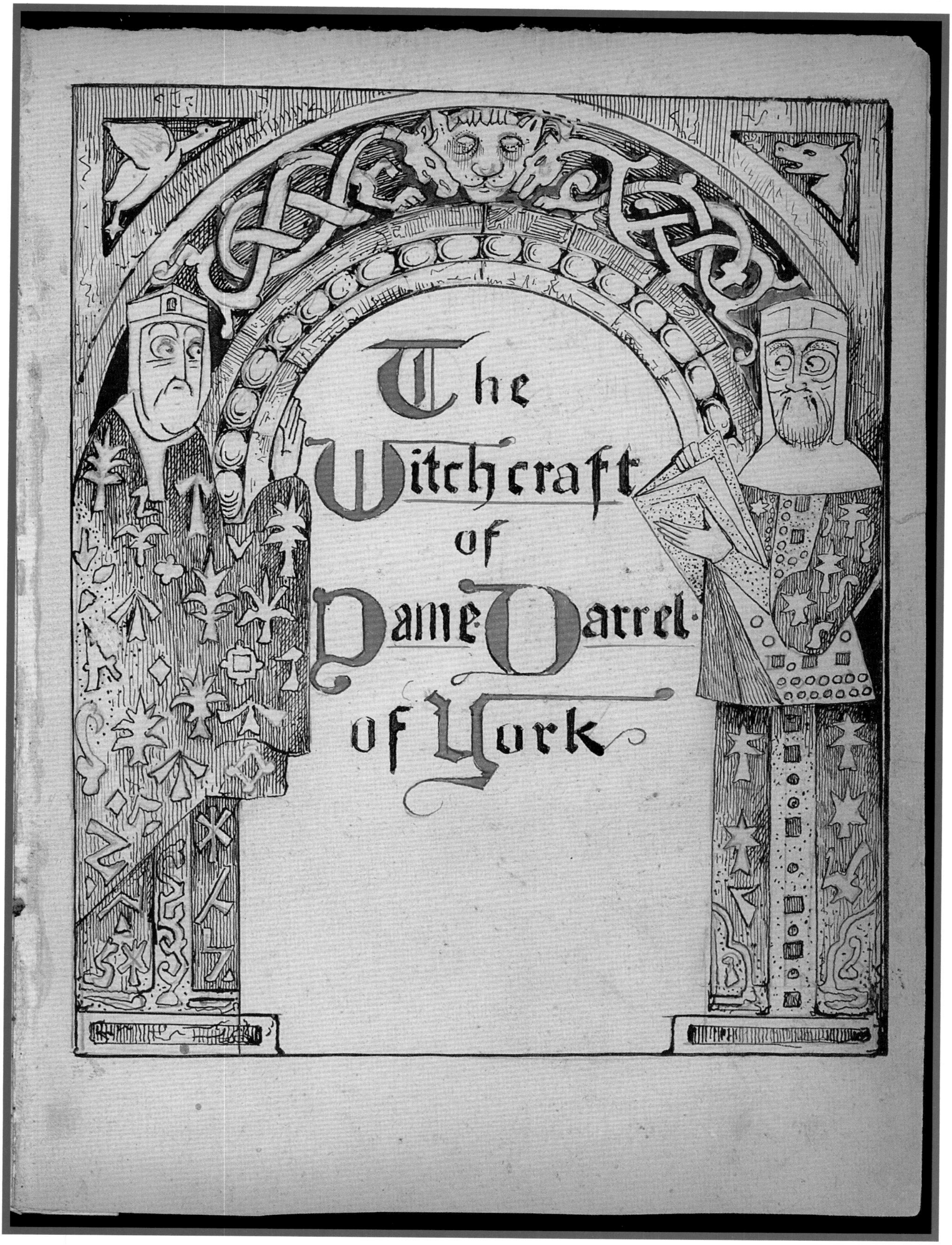
The Witchcraft
of
Dame Darrel
of York

Here followeth ye Book
of ye Witchcraft of
Dame Darrel of
York with account
of all kinde of Fairys · Elves ·
Goblines · Bargests · Ghostes
Gasters · Bendys · Pixys
Pillicockes Hobthrushes ·
Friar Rushes · Pictrees Dules
Night Hagges Giantes Yeth-
Hounds Devilkins · Spoornes
Robin Goodfelows and all ·
theyr Kinde ·

Dame Darrell was called the Wise Woman of York. What I here write I heard her tell from time to time. Veritas non semper valet, he who tells great truths will pass for a Liar, but those who are wise know Truth from Lyes, and if ye can tell a Fly in a Milk-pan ye may know whether what is written here be meant for you or for your Betters. Now a Wise Woman is a White Witch, much as a Broom is a Besom, and so she was called of her best Friends but to my Mind what she did not know of Witchcraft be it white or black was little worth knowing and might be put in a Flea's Eye not to speak of Anything smaller. And as I was her own Sister's Child and dwelt with her Ten Years I knew her like my pocket from the time when I came from the Ile of Jersey to dwel with her.

And when she would give a man or woman good Luck in Love she bade them in their Walks watch to find a red string or Ribbon or even a piece of red rag, howbeit clean red wool is best. And when any one pickt it up he should say

Red is my heart's blood
Even as this string is redd,
Therefore I pray thee
Bind her Love unto me
Until seven Doves I see,
And seven roses on a tree,
Let it no longer bee.

Then when he or she had pickt seven Roses from one tree and seen seven Doves he would have his will, howbeit there were other ways, and this was one— Take the red string and if you can not finde one then beg or buy it, however it is best if found. And then take a stone with a hole in it, but if this fails to be had take any good little pebble, and cord the string all about and round it, and knot and tie it. And while you do this say:

All other maids above
[Here the name], I do love,
As this string on this stone
I bind;
May my love round her heart
entwine
By the power of Night
And the moon's light
While ash trees grow
And roses blow
And rain falls in the sea
Shall her heart turn to me.

Now this must be carried in the pocket and when you

meet Maid or Man whom you
want, bee bold, and you may
have your will with them
Which has been full often
assayed and never failed
that I know of.

Another way and a rare one
is this. You must paint or lim
the exact Picture of the one
whom you love, quite naked,
and note that the better the
Likeness the better will be the
success. Keep this secret, let
none know thereof and often
look upon it. And keep about
it sweet scents, musk and
spices. And when the Moone is
full at Midnight, or in the
Season of the New Moon burne
these perfumerys and Spices
before it. And as you do so sing:

Sweet is this Spicerye
But sweeter is her fair Body.
Lady Moon on high
Who seest all Things from the
Sky
If my Love thou findest

Moon as thou shinest
Turn her thoughts unto me
So I will worship thee!

Fairies haunt old thorn bushes, ruins of old castles and towers, fairy rings on the downs near the sea and open places in forests. And if you find a large Snail Shell in such a place keep it for it is a fine Charm. Now this is for a Maid and she must rub it all over her Body by Night. And while so doing sing or say:

Shell if thou hast fairys seen
And has dwelt where they have been
Mind thou my conjuration
While I make this aplication

Then she shall put into the shell so many dried Peas as it will hold. And if a shell was so large that it could hold fifty Peas not one more nor less the Charm was a sure one. Then it comes to pass that in so many Days as there be Peasen she will win the love of him whom she would have. Of which Charm I can truly say Probatum est as Dame Dorel always said when I asked her if any charms was good.

Now it comes to pass and that many a time and oft and perchance oftener that a Charme fails as a Physitian be he never so wise cannot cure as men did say in Jersey where I dwelt, Medecin est bon voisin me ne reussi pas tojours. So there came once to my Aunt a grand lady who had tride three Spells for Love of which one had mist, one had failed and the third had nout availed. To her Dame Darell said "Yea and if thou hadst pissed thrice it would have done as much good. For thou hast a hard head and no Faith. The Devil take such a seeker who hath no will to find. Thou art blind because thou wilt not see, thou Bitch". So my Aunt always spoke to people of Quality who thought the more of her for it, but to the Poorer kind she was Soft as a Kitten. Then she saide, "Now I will give thee a spell which would charm the Devil out of Hell.

Thou must when the moon is full and bright and every star is in sight at mid-night walk stark-naked three times round about thy House and that without an Eye sees Thee. And while thou walkest say seven times.

"I a maiden fair forlorn,
Naked now as I was born,
As three times I pass around
This my House and Gardenes bound,
So may I thrice entwine
Round thy Heart oh Love of mine,
Ash and Beech & Oaken Tree
Grant no eye may look on me!

And if thou findest aught while so walking be it only a Peble or a Flower keep it for a Charm. And if this fail thee nothing will avail thee, for the Fairies have no mind unto time, and if thou beest of them, then is my Game at an end, even as FIN IS the end of a fish.—

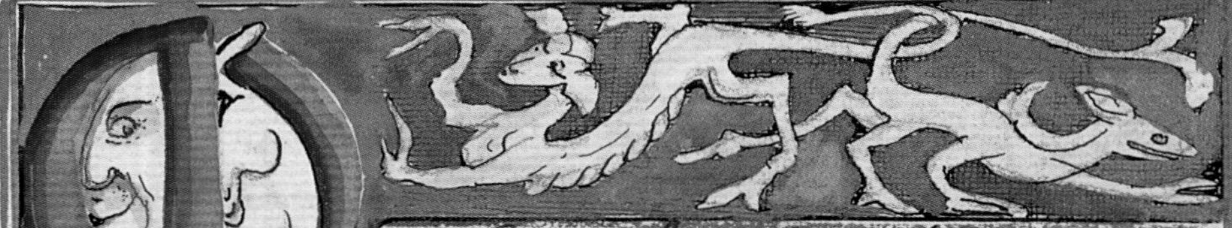

One day I asked Dame
Darrel how one could
know where Faireys
dwelt or came! And she said
"Wherever Nettles grow there
are the places where they go
a downe into the Ground dwel
one kind, and they are what
are called Swart-Elves and
of that there is a strange History. When the Father made
the World, first he created Men
and then all kinds of Fairys
Goblins, Pookas, and ye like.
Now one kind of Elfs were
made first and left to drie
in the Sun-light, but they were
left too long and were mislayd, so that the first pair
Brother and Sister were very
dark. Then all were told to
wait till Wives and Hus-
bands were made for them.
And all the other Fairies
waited as they were told to do.

But the Swart Elf and his Sister being like all dark folk warm blooded would not wait and so Coupled at once. And therefore the Father condemned them to live underground. Then Swart Elf sang.

Hard is the fate
Of me and my mate;
Left in the sun
We were over done;
Thence came the Harm
That our blood is so warm
For that we must go
To the cold Earth below
And live out of sight
Of the sun's light.

So the Father said Thou speakest truly, therefore thou shalt not want Light or Warmness. For there is Fire within the Earth and a great light. And thou shalt have rule over Gems and Gold. So Swart Elf and his Sister rule in the Earth. And because they abide in Heat they love all hot and prickly things and the Nettle and Thistle and Thorns are dear to them, so that where they come forth Nettles grow. And he who would have Luck in seeking Women, or Gold or Gems, if he know how to find them and become their friend may got all these. [redacted] Now note that if you take a cup and leave it by night, near a nettle, and let it be full of wine or mead or milk, and come the next day, and what was therein be gone, this is a beginning and note that the Cup be a new one out of which no one has ever drunk at all. Then another time do the same and so forth on, many times But if ye once begin to do this cease not so long as ye find it emptied.

And when you want the love of any one write on clean Parchment and that as well as ye can with all your Skill.

Elves whom no one sees
Under the Roots of Trees
Deep in the antient Hills
I pray of your good Wils
By the white bear's paw,
And the grey wolf's jaw,
The Serpent's back,
And Foxes track!

Give me the Stone
Whose power is known
Unto you alone!

Then you will find a Stone in the cup, be it a Pebble or a Gemm. And if ye touch a Man or Woman on the Brows with it you will get their Love. But this is not lightly come by for they give not this stone to everybody.

The Swart Elves be allways thirsty because their Nature is heat. But the Elves of the Woods and Forests do incline to dainty food, because when they were made and left to dry, as soon as ever they were done, and they were right shaply and fair, but shatter and harebrained. So insted of lying still as the Master bade them the Sister seeing an Appletre, full of fruit said I hunger, let us eat yon coddes! To which her brother said. "Climb my crabbat, and throw them down". And as she was picking and eating and throwing, came the Master who seeing the Elfe up in the tree, tho' she tried to hide her Nakedness behinde the Leaves, said, Since ye are so fond of Trees ye shall ever dwell in the Woods, and for your haste to eat ye shall ever be given to eating. So it came to pass that to this day they dwell in the Forests. And he or she, devill the difference, who will have a favour of them shall take a dish of spiced Frumenty, or a dish of figgy which is made with almones figs, raisins ginger and honey, or sugar-fruiters, or a Mince Pye, and let it be in a wood Test under an Oak if it may be, but where it can not be seen of Mankind. And if it be gone the next day, do the like again. And so at last lay with your gift a Boar's tusk, and if the next day the dainty be gone and the Boar's Tusk be there, but turned over on the other side, it will be an exceeding good charm, be it for Love or any other Luck.

of which Dame Darrel told me. There was once a girl named <u>Bessy Locken</u>, she had no kith or kin and was of good blood yet exceeding poor. And one day she came to my Aunt and said Dame I am as thou knowest a poor destitute, but I have here an <u>Egg-pye</u> and a good one, this is all I have and I will give it to thee if ye will give me a Charm to bring me Luck." Then Dame said. Take thy Pye, child, into the Wood and leave it under an Oak, and the next time thou canst leave such things with this <u>Boar's Tush</u>. And when she went one day, with the tush, and it was in her poke, she sat beneath the Oak and thinking how forlorn she was, wept. Then there came out of a Hollow in the Oak a Wood Elf, a young man he seemed, dressed all in green.

Bessy had never in all her young Life seen or dreamt of any man one hundred the part as comely as this Elfe and her foolish little Hearte bumpt for Love. Then he said Good day, Bessy, I have brought thee thy Fairing, and with this he gave her a Boars tooth, and lo it was the very same one wh. she deemed she had in her poke. And yet again "Bessy, if thou throw that Tusk into any mans Lap, he will marry thee. Now do thou mind my words. To-morrow the King's son and all his Train will pass through York. And when he is seated do thou draw near and he seeing thee will bid thee come to him. Then as thou cast the Boars Tusk into his Lap and he wil wed thee. More than that my sweet Child I can not give thee."

Bessy sat still for a little time with a beating heart and then burst into tears and said: Thou canst give me a far better Gift and that I will have. Saying this she threw the Ring into the Elf's lap. And he halsed and kissed her and said. As thou hast chosen Bessy so be it and truly it has been best for us both. And I am King of the Wood Elves in all the North. but if thou comest with me thou must leave men for evermore" Bessy answered — "Little good have men ever been to me or women either, save the Fairy-Dame Danel." And from that day Bessy was never more seen by any one save my Aunt who said that now and then she had met her of moon-lit nights at the Fairy Dancings in the Forest.

Now there is another kind of Fairys which live in rivers and Lakes and these are the strangest of their Kinde. For many times they live as Men and Women in the World among us and pass for Humane and this came to pass in such Wise. When ye Water Elf and his Sister were made and layd in the Sunshine to dry the Father bade them ly still till they were well baked, but when they found it hot, and seeing a river near by in wh a human maid and youth were swimming and wantoning, in they jumped and began to bop and play at bawdey-bo-peep, belly-bumpers and Tommy-come-tickle-me; flinking, flisking and flipping about in the water, as merry as a thousand Griggs, for they had found stolen waters were sweet. Then came the Father and said "Since ye have found water so pleasant in water ye shall dwell. So they became Water Elves, and because they began by mingling with man

and women they are ever exceed
ing fond of them. And the Water
man in old times often ravisht
maides who went in to swim,
while the Water witches sing
sweetly to intrap young.
How be it there came
a new law among them be-
cause of their exceeding Lust
fulness, there being Danger
that all Mankind would turn
to Elves or the Elves change
to men. So now they only dare
to couple with human kind
when they are asleep. Then
the Elf cometh and lyeth
with a Damsel, and when he
hath had his pleasure of
her Bodie, he layeth his
hand on her Heart; when
she straightway forgets it
all, nor knows anything
of what has been done to her.
But if a Water Elf carry this
too far and spende all his
nights with Women, or if a
Water-lady lye every night
with men, neglecting her
own Kind, they are so punisht

by being sent to dwell among them in humane Form, and while so they must be good and break no Laws else they must remain many Years longer away from their river or Lakes.

Now it came to pass that a very beautiful but withal wanton young lady drew the love of a Water Elf and he came and laid with her every night, nor was there one in which he did not couple with her nine times. Then he would press his Hand on her Head and when she awoke she had clean forgot all that had happened. Yet she plainly perceived, not being quite an Innocent, that something had happened and that the posnet, as Northern Folk call a little pot, had been on the fire. Therewith she came to Dame Darrel and askt what it might mean. Then the Dame said "Truly

I see how it is. Thou art Elf-rid
den every night, and that with
a woman for when such a
rider hath so faire a mare
if he once gets on the saddle
he spareth not ye Spur. But
if thou wilt catch and keep
this Frog, go in the garden early
and eate of four kind of Leaves,
Rue, Cummin, Mint and
Marjoram. Then the morning
ere the Sun shines he will
lay his Hand on thy Heart
but twill not availe, and
he must obey thee like a slave.
So that nighte when the Elf
came she knew it and saw
to her great joy that he was a
very comely youth tho his
Haire was green as an Emer
ald. And she had her joy with
him to her Heart's Content.
And when both were full fed
with amorous daintys, he
laid his hand on heart, but
it was of no avail for she did
but laugh and say as Dame
Daniel had taught her:

As the Rain falls on ye Hills
And to their Rivulets distils,
As the Riveret seeks the River,
Running to the Sea forever,
As the Sea doth rise to Rain,
Coming to the Hils again,
In a Ring which hath no End
And a Chain which none can rend
So I bind thee Water Elf
In my Service, to Myself.

So my lady Marian got herself a brave Leman and as the saying is they slept well sweetly samely in one bed for many a year.

Those who would have aught from these Water Elves must take a new earthen Pot or Tankard with a close Top. and put therein some such toy as a Stringe of Beads which a Girl hath worn or a Silver Ring

or chain or any such but they
prize mostly a little looking
glass or a pretty combe. And
write on a clean paper these
words and they name.

Elf of river sea or lake
As I came my thirst to slake
Here unto you I bring
With my love an offering
As the men of ancient days
Made their Offering al-
ways
So whoever ye may be
I make my Offering to
thee.

Then drinke of the lake or Riveret and cast the pot in as far as ye can and sit there awhile, and so come day by day, <u>till an Elf comes</u>. But if ye value your Virtue one straw it is a great risk, for verily one may as well entrust a Black pudding to a hungry Dog as a Maidenhead to such merry gentlemen or a pretty innocent boy to their Ladies.

And it was said that at once it became the talk of a Town that every Day three Sisters who were very fair Maides went to a wood a hidden place by a River, and none knew why. So they were trackt and were seen to go the rivers Edge, and took off all their Cloathes, and when they were star-naked one cast a peble into the river, saying some words. Then there came up a Water Elf, on whom the three maids fastened like Bees on a Clot of Honey, and so they all rutted and randied and he had his will of them on the green bank, a they theirs of him. And it is told that when this fine tale was bruited abroad the three Sisters drowned themselves for shame, but others report that they did but become Water-Elfies themselves and have been seen many a time by moonlight playing about the place where they were seen with the Water Elf.

Adam and Eve and all mankind came to the Fall by Curiosity, and the Elves because they were so wild and wanton and feaky and full of fegarys that they could not rest when they were bid. And when the Elves of the Air were created they were exceeding fair bonny and bright. And as these two pretty fantekins lay in the sunshine a drying there came a Breeze and the two without more ado flew away on it merrily over hills and dales. And when the Master missed 'em and saw where they were he said Stay where ye be. And so from that time they have been Aeriall Sprites. To them go men who are axious as to absent friends or expected events or who would fain know their fate. But women seek them who would have children. This comes of a very old story that among them there are a certain Some who would become human, and so when a woman prayed them for a child, they went into her Belly and lay there for nine months, till borned. And there is an old song which was sung by an Elf while he lay in his new Mothers womb.

Once over all in sunshine high
I flew on Windes thro' ye Sky
Now in a Prison cell I ly
Yet for that ne Whit care I,
Though I be in dungeon dark
Star-naked eke without en Sark
And no Sun or Moone I see
Here I live so merrily
All about is soft and warm
With no trouble or alarm
Little knows my Lady fair
Whom she doth in Belly bear

And there is a tale told all among us <u>Wise Women</u> that in the old time a heathen Dane who had taken a Thegn in the North Umber land put him to torture and said Ile let thee go free if thou wilt no more be a Christen man but knele to my gods. Then the Thagn laughed and said "Little dost thou kenn

thou Heathen Fool with whom
thou hast to do. For my Father
and Mother when they grew
older and had no Heir went
to a wise Woman who prom
ist them a child. And she
went to the Chief of the Sprites
of the Air and asked for Aid.
And because I was of Mind
to be a Christen Man I went
into the dark cell which we
call Mother's Womb till I was
borned a Babe. And for all
thy Torture I care never a Whit.
Thou art a Dog and all thy
gods, dogs and Bitches. —
And saying this he dyed.
And men say that the Dane
who was an Earl and all his
Following became Chrisom
men. —

These Sprites of the Air
love Musick and Flowers and
sweet Smels. But they fear to
go near Gardens for fear of ther
Enemys who guard them, or
they may steal Roses. And
if one can play the Lute a Pipe
or anything, and has a Garden
let him go therein by Night

and play as well as he may
and sing.

Ye who live in Air above
Unto you I give my Love
Now this garden shall be fe
Unto you as tis to me.
Every flower whitch is mine
From this Hour shall be thine
By the Wild Goose & the Swan
By the Eagle and the Pawn
All that flies oer Land & Sea
They shall all my Witness
be.

Then speak thy Wish and it may be that one will appear, but it ever comes to pass that they will haunt the Garden and grant thy desire. These be easy Sprites to win, and there are more in number than other of the Fairey kind. When you dream that you are flying then one of them or more has come into thy Dreaming. And to draw them into thy Dreams, put a lute or the like by thy Window so that the Aire blows over its Cords and make Musick and they will be atracted to come.

These are all the Chief Kinds of Elves, Some say that those of the Earth and Fire are of two Kinds but my Aunt reckoned em as one. Now there are lesser Tribes akin to them such as the House Fairys or Goblins, who come from the Wood Elves. And it is said that in the old days when the Saxones and Danes dwelt in England and much more so among the Britones before time, these House Elves lay about Houses like Cats and had no fear of Men and did much work all for a Bowl of Milk or a Jack of Ale and a Loafe. But when the Christen Faith came in they became less common though many of them were still lovesome to the gawds and glitter and

gimbols of the Papists. But when the Reform drove out the Prestes, it was gone Day and Iack over the Stile with them, and they cared no more to live with Folk who looked at them all as meer Witches and Impes. Howsoever there are still some old Castles and Manors, and antient Farm Houses where a Goblin or twain still dwel secretely, and come out by night to lye by the coles in the Chimney-place and pilfer some Scraps of Food. And of these Browny's tis said they much love Children being but a simple Folk themselves among the Fairey kind. And they often play with them but always touch them to make them forget. And if the Master of the House be a Man of an old Family and knows the true name of the Browney, he can call him forth. And tis told of a young Lord who was in sad case from the Warrs with ner a Penny in his purse and his Land forfet, he came back to his Castel to find it bare. and as he sat all amort and alone he remembered of a Browny that he loved much when he was a Boy and was wont to play with him: So he called his Name and loe, the Goblin came forth from the Chimney-back, and with his Wyfe danced for Joy and hugged and embracet him. The the Fairey led him into the Vaults and showed him in a secret Place a very great Treasure of Coyn, Jewels, gold-inlayd arms and Plate and said All this I give Thee. I have gathred it this nine hundred Years where Men were slain or ever an evill man or a foe came into this castle to do harm him did I despoile This I give thee and know that I was in great Fear less thou shouled die, for when thy race is at an end we two must perish for we began and shall end with thy Family. So the yg. Lad was now rich and wedded well and his Monument in the Church shows that he had fourteen Boys and two maids.

The old name for these Faireys was Durgans or Derger, by which name some folk still call a very little man, or if one be very small and heavy-set they say he is dergy. And of some kinds it is hard to say with whom they fellowship. Now there are Feck-Elves who are mightyful and strong, and such as these used of yore to dwell in Swords and Spears which were sure death to some one when taken in hand, and others wond in a silken kirtle for which no weapon could cut or stab. Others would live in a staff which pointed out where gold lay hid or secret Springs and fountains ran under ground. Or they had their homes in rings and coins which brought luck or in shoes in which a man could run like the wind or in caps which made those who wore them invisible.

Of a strange kind are those
whom my Aunt calld
in her old Northern fash
ion Logh-Elves or the
Laughing Faerys though they be
not rightly Faireys nor Elves nor
Goblins but Spirites of a sort wh
no one knows ther Family. They
appear ever as Men among Men
sometimes as Minstrels or Jesters
and like Merry Nighters in the
sky flash and go no one doth
know whither or whereuntoe. And
all ther Delight is to make mischief and jape folk. Now of one of
these there is a very old and strange
tale. There was an Earl in North
Umber Land an evil Trole Carl the
Dame calld him, in some sort a
devil or Enchanter; what he loved
above all things was Ridlings, as
country folk call Riddels. There
was a certain old Lord whom the
Earl had so trapt in his nets that
he held his life. And he sent him word

To come on a day to his Castle to be doomed but if he could make any Riddel which the Earl could not guess he should be scathless. Now ye Lord knew as little of Riddels as an old Bawd of Grace. And the Eve before the day of Tryal he sat all adrad in his home when there came a Pilgrim who craved lodging unto whom the poor lord told his trouble. "Little needs thou rack for that," quoth ye Pilgrim. Do thou lend me thy Garments and Ile go and riddel him so riddlingly that thou shall be rid of him forevermore. And in the morning when he had don'd the Lords Cloaths he saw so like him even in the Face that no man could tell Whitch. And when he came to the Earl, the Earl said wilt thou be doomed by my Council or has thou a Riddel? "I trow," said the Pilgrim that Doomed and damned is all one here. Ile een abide by my Riddels. So he put one after the other till he had given ninety eight and the Earl guessed them every one, and then said, More than an Hundred I will not answer. Quoth the Pilgrim: [redacted]

[redacted] "As I came to thy Castel I saw in the house a Creature which had eight legs and four Heads yet of all this I saw but one Head. Earl of North Umbr Land guess thou my Riddel!"

What thou didst see answered ye Earl was a woman with child but thou art uncanny and a wizard if thou speakest truly. For it is a woman with three unborn Babes in her Belly. And as he spoke there came a man who said "My Lord there is a strange Thing happened For while ye sat here the wife of thy Gardener has given birth to three children". Then the Earl lookt Askant at the Pilgrim and said. "Give me thy hundred th Riddel thou Son of the Riding Hag, and a curse on thy riddening." Then the Pilgrim laughed and said This is my Last Riddel.

Tell me oh Earl of Northumberland who it was lay with thy Mother the Night thou wast begotten."

The Earl roared in a rage Who else but my Father the Earl of this Land. The Pilgrim answered: Thou lyest between thy teeth and on thy Tongue. To the

Earl was but thy Trow-father.
For thy Mother was a leacherous
Trull and over-troxy, and coupled with all her Man-servants.
And a Witch-wife gave her Lovers
the Form and Figure of ye Earl,
and made him sleep while
these Bullys went in unto her.
And the worst of them all who
swiked the Earl was his own
Swine-heard, and his Son art
thou as all thy Manners shows.

Then the Earl in a rage
drew his Sword and hewed at
the Pilgrim, so that the blade
passed clean through his
Neck, but he heeded it not, and
laught again like a sper
or a devil, and said: Thou dids
bid me here on thy word, and
said I should be safe if I could
give thee a Riddel beyond thy
getting. Now for thy falset
thou shalt die the death of
a dog and truly a dogs death
it shall be. And saying this
he vanisht out of sight, before
their eyes. And as all men know
that Earl was torn to death by his dogs.

In the City of York there is
a Street called ye Shambles
Therein was an Ale House
And every Chrismas Eve
thereto came a Man in
strange cloaths, no one knew
whence he came but they cald
him Youel, for the first word he
always spake he cryed out three
times Yuell Yuel, Yuell! Then
he would play on a lute & sing
Songs which no man had ever
heard, and make Mirth & Game
Once there came Some one who
said that a great Wolf, exceeding
bold and dreadfull, because it
was a very cold Winter and the
Wolves were starved had come
into Town and rusht into a stal
and then the Door was shut on
to him, and no man dared to
slay him because of his great
Fiercenes. Then Youell laught
and said If ye will see good Sport
come with me. And when they
were at the Stall he said | Now
I will slay the Wolf. | And because
Yuell had no Arm some one
offred him a Sword but he said

A cat needs not a Knife to slay
a mouse, which was true of
old times and yet holdeth good
and I am born as I be|. Saying
this he went in and closed the
door, and then there was heard
a great noise, but it seemed
more like two men in rage
danging and illipping one the
other than a man and a Wolf.
But they spoke in a tongue wh-
no man understood. And all
thought it was a gabbery and
japery of Yuell who was only
playing at two Voices, for
he was very swipper with
his Tongue. Then all was stil
and Youel came forth and
fastened the door and said that
no man should go in till the
next day and then we should
have a rare and merry Jest.
But that Night he was gone
and the next Morning when
men went to see the Wolf there
lay a dead man; ster-naked
and it was plain that he had
been strangled for his neck
was writhed arynt. And by
him lay a wolf's skin. And the
dead man was one very ill

liked, cruel and evil and men were afeared of him because he was thought to be a wizard and deal with the devill. And now twas known he had been a <u>Were Wolf</u> such as we in the Ile of Jersey call in our French <u>Loup garou</u>.

Of this appearing to be as animals there are some things which I do not very well know. Once I asked Dame Darrel wherein a <u>Fay</u> was unlike a Fairy. For in ye Isle of Jersey what we call a <u>Fé</u> or Fay is a spirit like a very fair Lady as large as a natural Woman who is mostly in all ye Tales as benevolent and very friendly. And Dame Darrel said that a Fay was properly the same as a <u>Hamen</u> or <u>Hemen</u> which was a Home Spirit by a mans <u>Luck or Fate</u>. And they always appear in the Form of an Animal at first, and always <u>in Dreams</u>; And whenever ye see an <u>Animal</u> in a

Dream it is some mans or womans Hamin. It was thought in
the old Time that Everybody had one
though Some said there was one to
a Family, and some believed they
brought good fortune. So they
seem to be somewhat akin to
the House Elves which belongd
to Families. Of this Kind is
the Thrummy Cap who ap
pears like a Dergy little old
man. he liveth in the Vaults
of Castles and there are many
tales of him and his Kind.
Yet he is not Hamin for they
seem to fly in the Air. And
there are Followers who are
much like them, they fly after
men as Birds or in other Forms.
If a man see his Follower ap
pear to him as a Woman and
lye with her she looses all
her power and becomes like
any other woman. There was
a Lord of great riches, he was
forth from the land in a boat
and saw a Hawk which flew
after; one of his men said I tro
that is your Follower. That
may be he answered, I will
make her an Offering, and say

ing this he threw out a gold
Ring. The Hawk flew scoop
ing and scuting down and
took up the Ring ere it sunk
and flew away. Then arose
a great Storm, the Boat was
sunk all the men drowned.
The Earl swam long and
saw come flying over him a
very beautiful woman who
taking him by the Scruff
or behind his Neck held him
up and so drew him ashore.
Then she took him up to a
Castle among ye Rocks and
made a fire and gave him
meat and wine. And as he
sat there he saw on her arm
the gold ring which he had
thrown to the Falcon. Then
he said Art thou not my
Hammen and Follower? And
she said I am. The Earl an
swered For that I am glad
but I would thou wert as
other Women because thou
art so beautiful. But I will
not ask it of thee to love me
because then thou wouldst
lose all thy fairy power.

She answered I love thee so that if thou wouldst fain have me thou mayst and I will be a woman and no longer a virgin. So he lay with her and wedded her and from them came a famous family. Of them it was said that the daughters could all fly and they kept it a great secret; but once or twice something came to light. There was a randy, rascally young gentleman who meeting a young Lady of this Family one Evening as she walkt out alone in the Moonlight by the Edge of a very high Clift would fain have ravisht her, and thought himself Cock-sure to succeed But she ran and leaped over the Clift and he swore that she did not fall but sailed out on the Wind like a Bird afar till he could see her no more. But the next day shee was at Home and as well as ever.

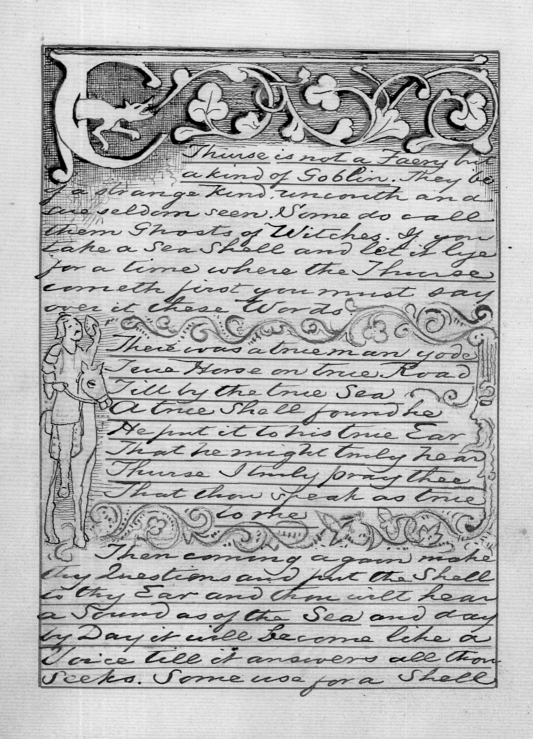

Thurse is not a Faery but a kind of Goblin. They be of a strange Kind, uncouth and are seldom seen. Some do call them Ghosts of Witches. If you take a Sea Shell and let it lye for a time where the Thurse cometh first you must say over it these Words:

There was a true man an yode
True Horse on true Road
Till by the true Sea
A true Shell found he
He put it to his true Ear
That he might truly hear
Thurse I truly pray thee
That thou speak as true
to me

Then coming again make thy Questions and put the Shell to thy Ear and thou wilt hear a Sound as of the Sea and day by Day it will become like a Voice till it answers all thou seeks. Some use for a Shell

an old Beake or Mug or Cup—
such as are fisht out of the sea
or are found in Stangs wherein
Men cast them in old times
for offerings, there is a Man in
Beverly who hath twelve, all
of them he found in a Deep
Hole in a Burn. But if ye find
a Shell and there in the Mark
ings can see the Word Thurse
or Thrs it is exceeding good
to answer. And Dame Darel
told of a Rock in a lone Place
where was an old Ruin there
dwelt a Thurs. In the Rock
was a Hole throw which the
Wind blew. Who put his Ear
to that Hole on a Thursday
could hear a Voice tell him
strange Things. And in old
Drinking Horns often dwells
a Thurse. There was a Knight
who had one of these old Horns
& Whenever he was in great Peril
the Thurse would make it
sound aloud. One day he had
gone forth to hunt and he was
waylaid by a certain Enemy
with Twelve Men. About this
time his Lady took up ye Horn
and heard it sound, and prom

it came the Words Hurry Hurry
Hurry! Then she took twenty
of her Men well armed and
rode forth and found her Lad
in a sore strait fighting all
Thirteen. Then there was a
rattling and rasing fight,
so that all the thirteen were
slain and bury'd in one hill.
Then that Lad took a Horn
for his Arms with the words
Free for a blast. tho' some say
it was Hurry Hurry. Hurry.
And when made game of him
he said he cared not how
many Horns his Lady set
him so that they were of that
kind. And because he had very
rich Lands men said that
he never wanted Corn. for
so they call with us the unseen
Horns which grow on the Heads
of some married Men, whence
the saying of a certain wife
who lay with other men that
she had sent her husband
to Cornwall in an open
Boat and that he lacked not
an Oar [or a Whore] while
she lived.

Some think that Fays be the very little merry Faireys of whom ther are so many pleas ant Tales. Others wil have them to be Ouphs. Dame Darrel said that when the Elfs were made there was left but a little Piece of Clay and from this the Father made two teeny pretty little Sprights and that these alone behaved well so that they are ever happy and dance and ride on Butter Flys and sleep in Flowers. One kind of these little Ones live by the Sea. The Land Ouphes greatly esteem fine Limpet Shells which they wear for Helmets or use for Cups and these the Sea Ouphes guard with great Jealousy. Once there was a Little Girl and Boy who had been told this and when they were taken on a Time to the Sea they made good provants of such Shells

And coming home they went to
a place where they deemed these
Ouphes dwelt and threw there
all their Shells. And who so
merry and glad as these smal
folk when they found this ex
ceeding great and valuable
Treasure, truly they danced for
joy. Now the Mother of these
Children was so poor that when
Christmas Even came there was
no bite or Sup in the House
nor any Gifts, and the Children sat a-cold and cried for
Hunger and Grief. When lo
there came a great Light in
to the Room and a great Yule
Log with Fire was in the Herth
and there came in a great
Processioun of Ouphes, every
one who had got a Limpet
Shell from them wearing it
proudly on his head like a
mighty Warrior. And their
Musicians blew on Trumpets
made of Straws a Solemn
March and as they Paraded
round the Room and passed
the Children Every Ouph
gave them a Silver Two-

Penny Piece or a Coin of the
Fairy Money as Men call
old Money some say it is of
the Romans or Saxones
Dame Darrel gave me two
for a Fairing. And so they
went forth leaving the
Children as a-joyed as they
had been sorrowfull. And
their Mother grew so rich
that she bought a Manor
and set apart a Field and in that
since it was never toucht and
no one entered it it was called
the Fairys Field and they filled
it with Fairy Rings and danced
there every Night.

There is another Tale
which is of a Youth
who heard that when
one eats an Egg, he
should break the Shel
lest Witches or Faireys
make of them Boats or Cups.
But he threw a whole Shell into
a Bush saying Take it ye
Faireys and much good may
it do you, and this he did

whenever he ate an Egg. Now it
came to pass that one day he
was in a Tavern and held an
Egg when a strange Man in a
very ancient Attire said, That
Egg thou wilt never eat. Truly
I will try he said, but when the
Egg was opened it was full of
Wool, and in the Wool was a
Mark of Gold full weight. The
Strange Man said Go in the
Morning to the Bridge and thou
wilt meet a Man with Sheep
and I counsel thee to buy them
whatever his Price may be. The
Youth promist to do so. And in
the Morning he found the Man
who had six Sheep and his
Price was a Gold Mark for all
The Youth said such a Price was
never paid in all England for
Sheep but for his Words sake he
bought them. And as he drove
them homewards at every mile
he found one more Sheep in the
Flock, and this was ever so every
Day that whenever he drove em
they encreased. Then the Youth
remembered an old Tale, how
that there was in a certain
Mountain a Drove of such Fairey

Sheep which belonged to an old King in Days of Yore. And he told his Secret to none and grew to be as rich as an Earl.

here is a round stone of many sites from that of a nut to an apple which Men find in Rocks or Gravell. These they call Fairey Faces or Colt Pixy or Elves Heads. Dame Darell told me that ere as Men were in the Land were only Giants and this kind of Faireys and they were a hard dour race and ill to knap with. So when the Master came he turned them all into Stone, of the Gyants were made the Rocks but of the Faireys only the Heads were steaned. A Wise men do so make with these Heades, they take one on which a Face appears and make a small Body of Wood, Beech is best, and set ye Head on it. And when it is made set it in an honourable place and Say:

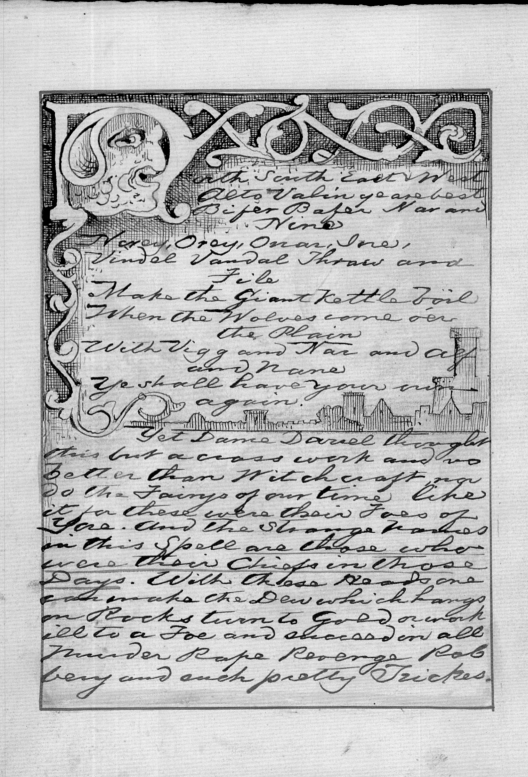

North South East & West
Alto Valin ye are best
Bifer Bafer Nar and
Nine
Nery, Orey, Onar, Ire,
Vindel Vandal Thraw and
File
Make the Giant Kettle Boil
When the Wolves come o'er
the Plain
With Vigg and Nar and Alf
and Nane
Ye shall have your own
again.

Yet Dame Darel thought this but a cross work and no better than Witchcraft nor do the Fairys of our time like it for these were their Foes of Yore. And the Strange Names in this Spell are those who were their Chiefs in those Days. With these Heads one can make the Dew which hangs on Rocks turn to Gold or work ill to a Foe and succeed in all Murder Rape Revenge Robbery and such pretty Tricks.

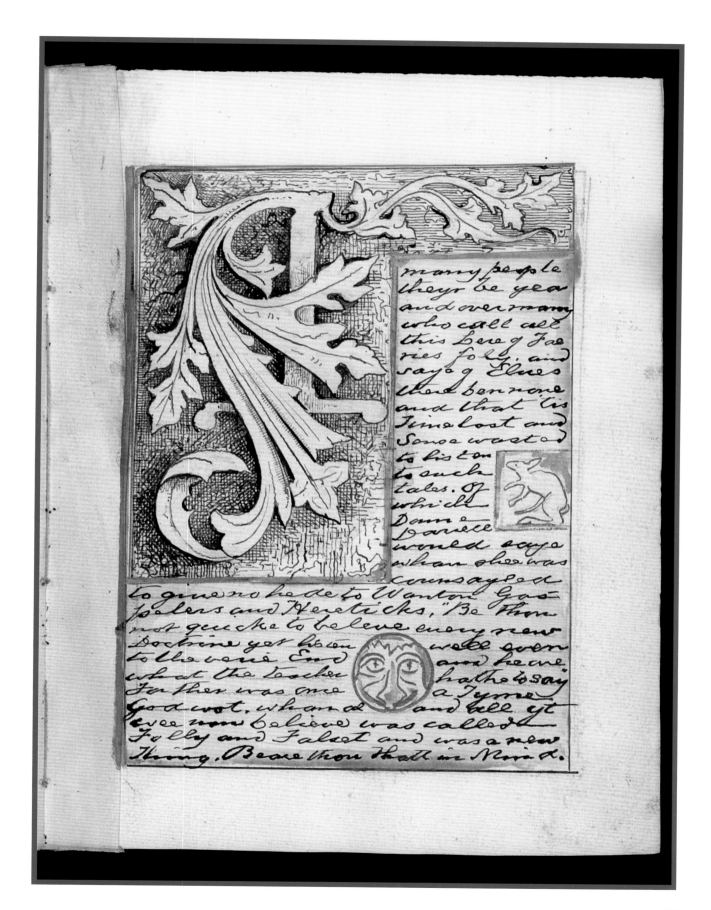

many people theyr be yea and over many who call all this Lore of Faeries foly, and say of Elves there ben none and that 'tis Time lost and Sense wasted to listen

to such tales. Of which Dame Darell would saye when shee was counsayled to give no hede to Wanton Gospelers and Hereticks, "Be thou not quicke to beleve every new Doctrine yet heare well even to the verie End and heare what the teacher hathe to say.

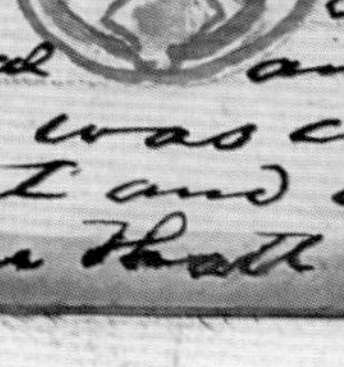

For ther was one a Tyme God wot, whom I and all yt ever now believe was called Folly and Falset and was a new thing. Beare thou that in Mind."

owe there was one thinge of which D. Danell spoke noe worde to any other and but litel to mee and that was she had but small faith in Blacke Witchcrafte or that We men solde themselves to ye Devill for she had knowen ful many who was sayd to serve the Devill and devill a one was there who could conjer up half a crown or shoore my Aunt anything new. But in White Witchcrafte the Dame had great beleefe, saying that Faithe in Spels and Charmes and great hope would cure or holpen Folke when the Devill and all his folk were afraid. Twas with them fraying tales like Rob o the Dale who when a man was scart att some Frogges, said "Beeg good Cheare I trow itt, is nothing but a Noyse."

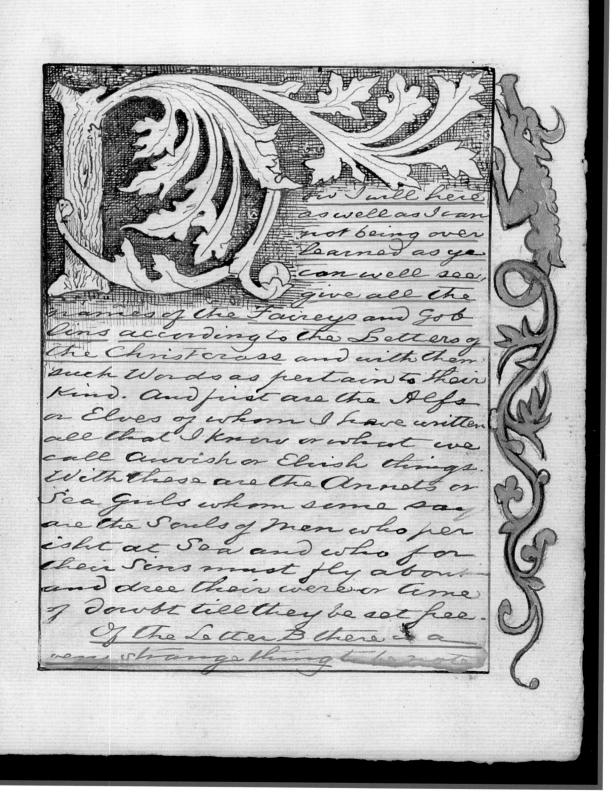

So I will here
as well as I can
not being over
learned as ye
can well see,
give all the
names of the Faireys and Gob
lins according to the Letters of
the Christcross and with them
such Words as pertain to their
Kind. And first are the Alfs
or Elves of whom I have written
all that I know or what we
call Auvish or Elvish things.
With these are the Annets or
Sea Gulls whom some say
are the Souls of Men who per
isht at Sea and who for
their Sins must fly about
and dree their were or time
of Dowbt till they be set free.

Of the Letter B there is a
very strange thing to be note

And this is that of the beings
whose names begin with it are
a kind of mysticall terrifying
sprights who seem more like
Devills and Demons with all
than Fairys. They are all
believed to be Horrific in figure
be they spinney and thin, or
dwergy and dumpy. They seem
to be all much the same, as
their names seem to be in one.
These be called firstly, the
Bo, who is a hobbgoblin also
the Bogg or Bugg which I
take to be all the same with
Boo, Bogy-bo and the Boman
who carrys childer away or
who is used to frighten them.
With them and all one and
the same is Boggert, whom
some account to be a ghost
as the North Umbrians call
him Bogle, and Boogan
who is sometimes the Devil.
And there is the Bloody Bo
or Bloody Bone, but Bone
means here a Bon or Boman
and not that which is in our
body. And with him goes the
one called Boneless, but
Dame Darrell said that this

meant only a smaller Bone or
his Wife. Now of this it is to be
said that Ghosts and Goblins
when they speak their first
word is Bow or Boo. And this
is to frighten Folk, and so the
wild Irish in their Warrs do
always rush on screaming
A-boo, which made them so
mad that as I have heard
Dame Darell say there was
a law made against the
Word. Now whether the word
came from Bo a goblin, or
the goblin's name from the
cry is more than my small
Wit can discern. Like unto
these is the Bargaste or Barguest who is horrible over
all the others to behold and
who when some bad man is
about to die goes howling and
shrieking and skirling and
skrithing a nights where
men dwell and which hath
been heard not long ago in
York through ye Streets.

All of a kind are the Brag
the Breer and the Bull Beggar
which last is a Boo-Bugess
as Dame Darel declared.

C standeth for Church in a picture book of the Alphabett which I have seen so I will be gin by the

which are the very strange images which we see in Churches on the gabels and Everywhere and which are often plainly enough the carved pictures and portraits of Imps, Goblins, Jack-devills, Bogeys and the like. The Story runs that the Masons who built these Churches were exceeding wise and of a kind Magicians. And while they worked these Imps who served the Heathen priests and Witches and Warlocks came and vext them all they could, mislaying their Tools breaking their timbers and doing all the Devillments

in their power. Then the Master
of the Masons turned the Imps
into Stone and made them
hold up arches and all kind
of heavy weights for a punish
ment, and be trod under foot
by Saints. Now there is a tale
that when there is a full moon
on Saint John's Eve then they
all come down from their
nooks and Horns where they
sit as the Saying is | In a
Horn when the Devill is
blind | and dance and talke
over the good old Time when
everybody went to Hell and
they were all so happy. And
some say that of every Hund
red, one is then set free if he will
become a Christian sprite.

There was a Carpenter
in York who being drunke
one Saint John's Eve went
into Church and fell asleep
and was not noted and so
he staid there. And it was a
full moon and when he
awoke lo all the Images
of the Cathedral came
crowding in. After that he
came no more. and then it
was marked that one of
the Goblins in the Church

had no more the same Face
or Form or Holding that hee
had afore but was all one am
the same as the Carpenter -
yea and his Cloaths there - to
But the Carpenter man saw
never mo here below. If to
the Divel he did go is more
than I or any Know. 

C standeth also for a
Cuckoo which is a
kinde of Faerie. When
ye hede it for the first
Time in Spring when
birds sing then say
alowd | Cuckoo. Cuckoo
as thou art true Let me have that
which I crave, As what I got
to the Poor I gave, So give unto
me If so good it seems to be |
Then make thy wish. and so much
as thou has given so much
wilt thou get, but if thou asks
for more thou wilt get nout.
unless it be a pair of Hans.
And note that all this cometh
best if you see Cuckoo a sitting
Therefore, unto, men say of ye Gowk.

If you see the Cucko sitting
And the Swalow a-flitting
And a filley Foal lying still
You all the Year shall have
your Will.

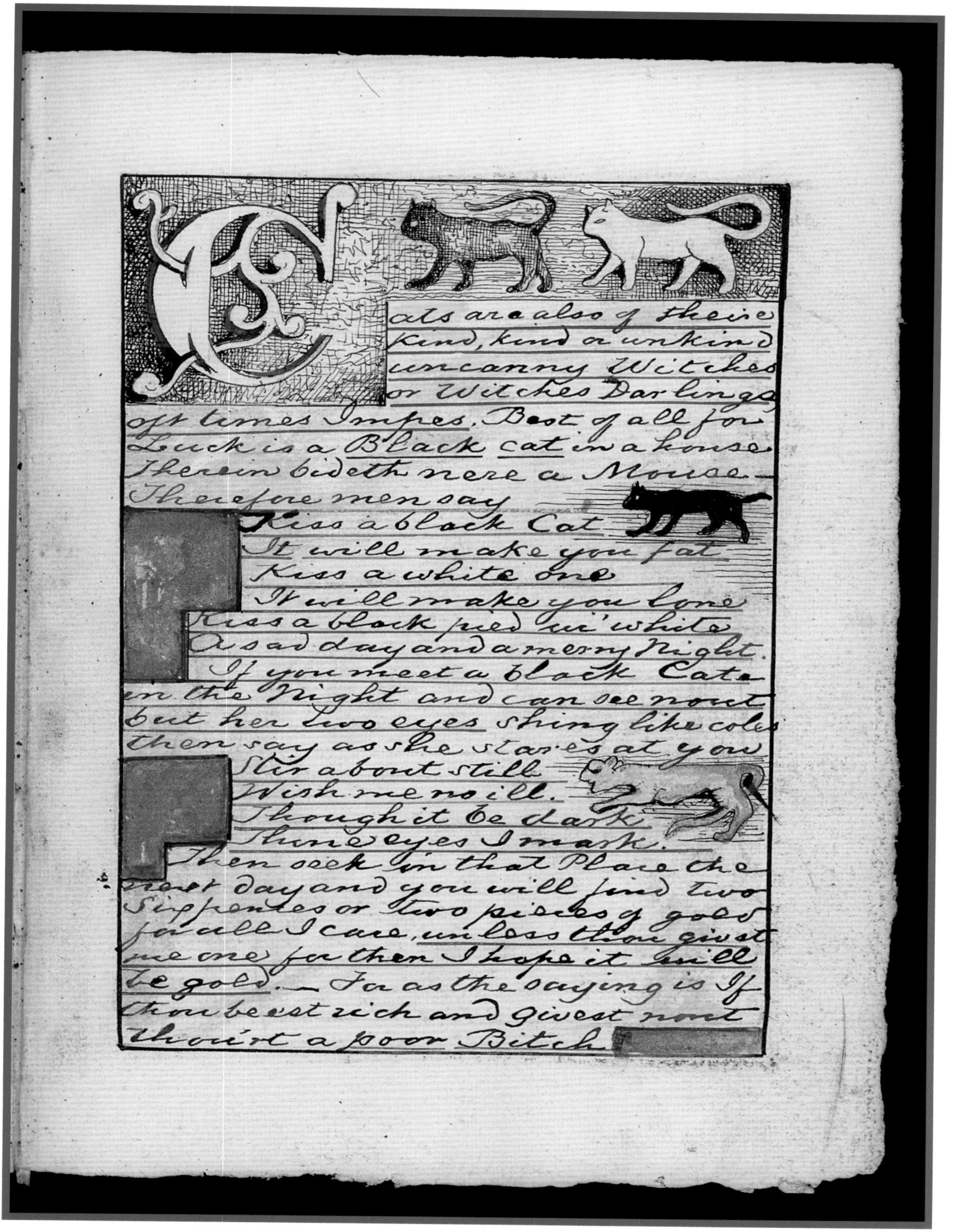

Cats are also of theire kind, kind or unkind uncanny Witches or Witches Darlings oft times Impes. Best of all for Luck is a Black cat in a house Therein bideth nere a Mouse— Therefore men say

Kiss a black Cat
It will make you fat
Kiss a white one
It will make you lone
Kiss a black pied wi' white
A sad day and a merry Night.

If you meet a black Cat in the Night and can see nout but her two eyes shing like coles then say as she stares at you

Stir about still
Wish me no ill.
Though it be dark
Thine eyes I mark.

Then seek in that Place the next day and you will find two Sippences or two pieces of gold for all I care, unless thou givst me one for then I hope it will be gold.— For as the saying is If thou beest rich and givest nout thou'rt a poor Bitch

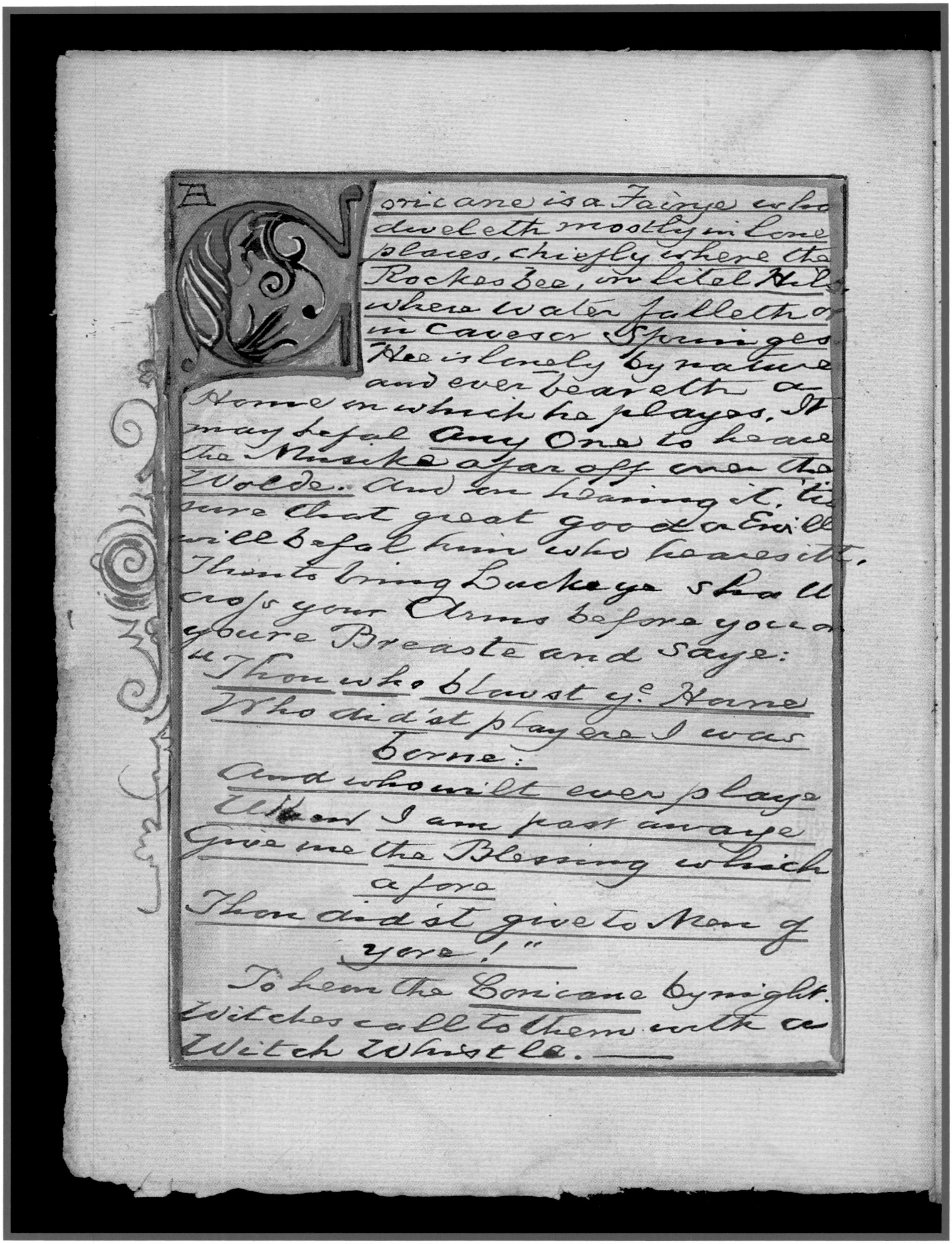

A Corricane is a Fairye who dwelleth mostly in lone places, chiefly where the Rockes bee, or litel Hils where water falleth or in Caves or Springes. Hee is lonely by nature and ever beareth a Horne on which he playes. It may befal Any One to heare the Musike afar off over the Wolde. And on hearing it, tis sure that great good & Evill will befal him who heares itt. Then to bring Lucke ye shall cross your Arms before you on youre Breaste and saye:

"Thou who blowst ye Horne
Who did'st playe ere I was borne:
And who wilt ever playe
When I am past awaye
Give me the Blessing which afore
Thou did'st give to Men of yore!"

To heare the Corricane by night. Witches call to them with a Witch Whistle.

Dwerfs or Dergs are Manikins of the Elf kinde; dwell in Hills, Mountaines Barowes or Hillockes And Rocks. They mostlie wone wher Metalls be, as of Tinne Iron or Coper. Silver. They are little very Strong and mighty in all Magic. They doe make Jewells and wonderful Swordes which give Victory and slaie so many men as are apointed to their Weirde. When such a Sworde is once drawn it may not bee regained till itt has killed a man. Yet there ever goeth some Evil with their Gifts. Soe itt befel a King who by force made a Derg smithe for him a Sword with golden Hilt and Gaine which shulde slay Twelve Men, but by itt were his owne Sons slaine.

Unto Thee, Lord,
I give the Sword
Of great Victorie,
Yet shall thy Sons
All perish anones,
And therewith be slee.

Which came to passe tho' he threw itt into a Sea but when founde in after time itt still did wake its Weirde.

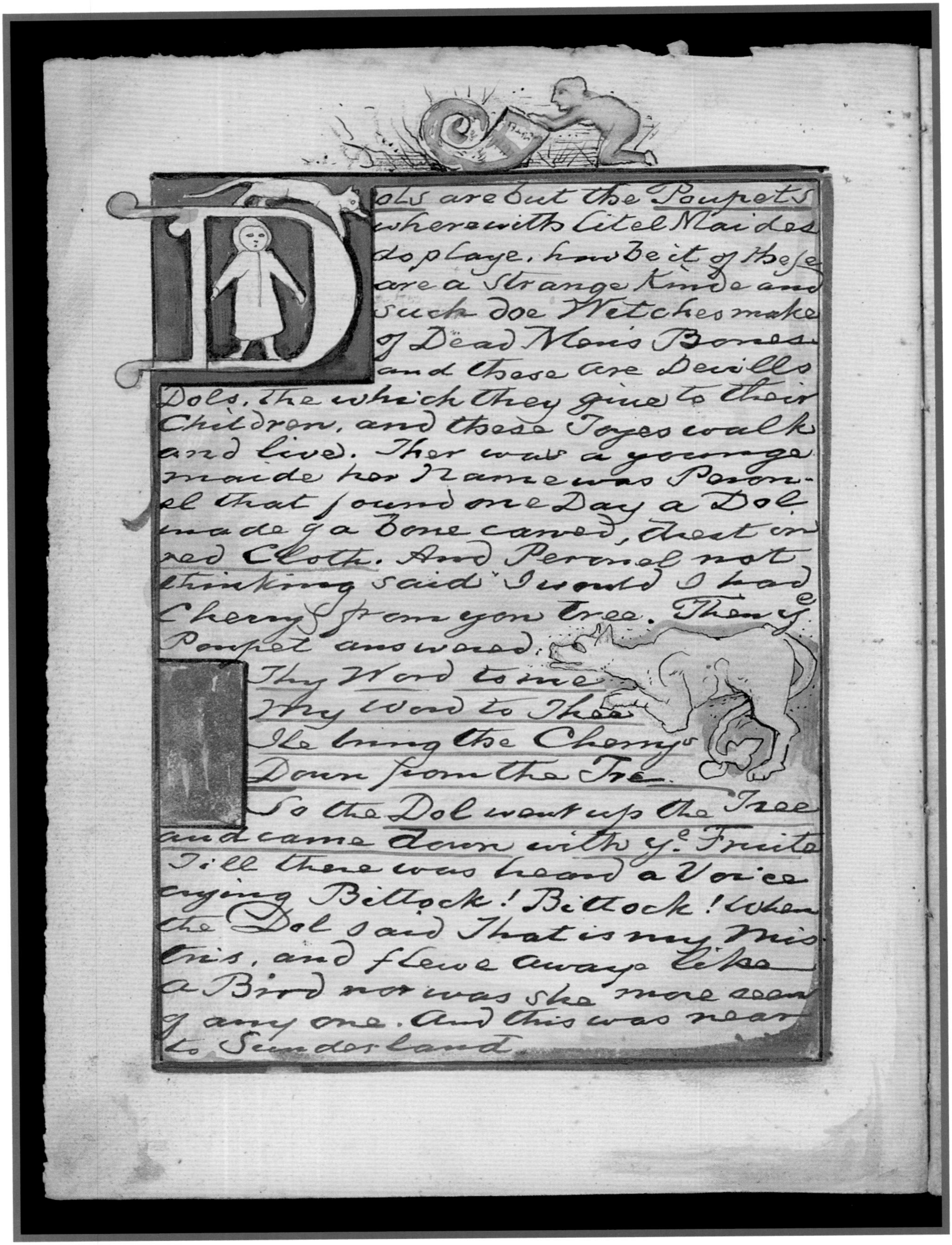
Dols are but the Poupets wherewith Litel Maides do playe, howbeit of these are a Strange Kinde and such doe Witches make of Dead Men's Bones and these are Devills Dols, the which they give to their Children, and these Toyes walk and live. Ther was a younge maide her Name was Peronel that found one Day a Dol made of a Bone carved, drest in red Cloth. And Peronel not thinking said "I would I had Cherrys from yon tree. Then ye Poupet answered:

Thy Word to me
Thy Word to Thee
Ile bring the Cherrys
Down from the Tre.

So the Dol went up the Tree and came down with ye Fruite Till there was heard a Voice crying Bittock! Bittock! When the Dol said That is my Mistris, and flewe away like a Bird nor was she more seen of any one. And this was near to Sunderland

1. Diccon is but ye Name
of a merrie Devilkin
who danceth, yet is
hee so well knowne
that many crie
out The Dickons as if
he were ye Divell.
He cometh ever wher
Folk dance and disporte themselves
And the Dryed Leeves and the dead
Leef which clingeth to ye Tree
yet ever fluttreth in ye airie
Wind, spinning rounde and
round, and those that flie
away before the Storm as iff
they were Wood are Diccon
his Children or Litel Diccons.
There was once a young maid
who having had some intuse
a Hurte of her Legg, could not
dance. Therewith she sat ones
by the Wall looking on while
others danset, staring like a
Dazzed Larke at a daring Glosse
to her came a merrie littel
wonkand man with a queint
Visnomie, who saide Maiden
Why do not danse? To which

She answered Truly tis not
of my own wil kind Sir that
I bide here on my Bace like
a Brake by a Bourn seeing the
water run by whyle I byte
and can only swaie my heade
to the Sound." "Bellabone," an
swered ye Manikin, "What
aileth thee?" "What aileth is
that my Lag faileth else
would I fain dance forever."
Therewith the littel man betook her Legg in his hande
and stript up her Juppes
and Kirtel, nor cared she say
him Naye! Therewith the
prene Man dyd frote her
naked Lag as yf it were
Froze. and itt became warm
and was heled and saine
So she danced all night with
the Stranger, as they were
imbayed with Love, There
with the wall did seem to
open unto the Landwide or
Champaygne and the Fay went
dancing and caroling awaie
behind Bush and Copsefole
and they vanisht dancing in y^e^
moonlighte.

Dream Holes. Thes be ye Sterrs, and how the name cam was thus. Ther was of olde ere yet ye worlde begun a Gyant in whom were al Things And hee said to himself Loe I am all alone and onlie One it wer beter gif ther were many insted of me. So he gave himself to Deathe. His bones became ye Rocks, his Flesh Earth his Bloude the Sea, but of his Skul a Brain pan Heaven was made and theye capt itt over ye Earth like a Lidd on a Pott. Then was the world without Lighte — save for ye Moone. So did a great Gyant he took a greate Pine tre fo a Lance and prickt holes in the Skye a Skul so that ye Lighte came thro. and men hed the Sterres whiche are onlie holes as some think to this day.

Now Dreames are a kind of Elvs that dwel in the Light and when they saw that Holes

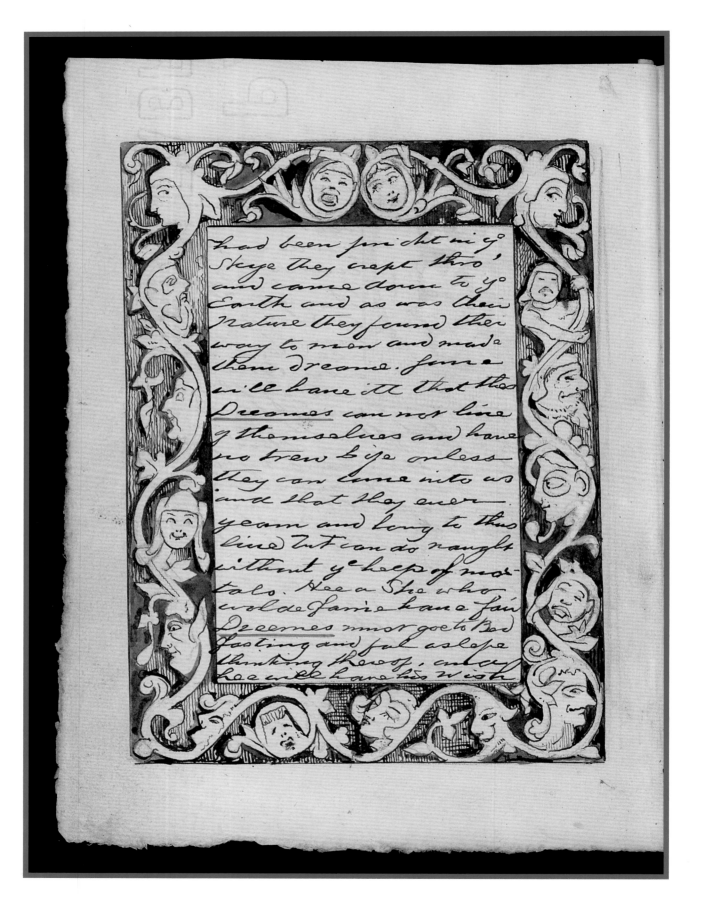

had been pen'd up in ye
Skye they crept thro'
and came down to ye
Earth and as was their
Nature they found their
way to men and made
them dreame. Some
will have itt that the
Dreames can not live
of themselves and have
no trew Lyfe onless
they can come into us
and that they ever
yearn and long to thus
live but can do naught
without ye help of mor-
tals. Hee or She who
wolde fain have fair
Dreames must go to Bed
fasting and fal aslepe
thinking thereof, and so
hee will have his wish

Dule is the Devil I doe
thinke it is an Irish
word. There be men
who are carneyed
by the Dule or Dule
carnies, that is
tricked or entysed
by him. So is dule
what is double
for y^e^ Devil is ever
double-faced and
lined with scin.
Dule Crooks are
evill men ther is a
Flye hath the same name all
Flys are of the Devil Dame Danell
saith Beelzebub is the devil of Flys.
and y^e^ Like, itt may wel bee.
Dule is Dole or Suffering.

And itt soundes to me y^t^
a Dule may bee as a
Doll that is to say an
Idoll that men worship
even as Childer doe theyr dols
I trow tis all one and y^e^ Same
all Idollatrie. And this mind
me of a strange tale ther was
a yoman who lived in
this good man ones day in
his plowing did turn upp a
littl image or Figure itt
was of baket Clay or stone
had two brite Eyen likewise,

Hee knew not verily itt had been an Idoll of ye old Heathen folk that woned here afore tymes so hee gave itt to his Children to play wi, for a Dol. One day as they played there with came in they had set it upp for a Sainte and were play ing att praying to itt. Then there

came in a preest a very wise and learned Man who saide: What doe ye a praying to this accursed Dole, itt is a devill and no Seynt. Theron he stamped itt beneathe his Feete and broke itt. Out came from itt many brite and shining stones o Gemms. There yee have hee said whatt wil doe ye more good. As in trouth it did for the Yeoman sold them for solid golde and grew riche. Truly many men do worship in this world, many an idle or idoll Thing which were it broken would be better for them. For in many an old folly there is a dolly which when itt is broken giveth gold token.

rum is a Devilkin who sets at naught the Saying that little Children should be seen and never heard for he is oft tim heard playing on a drum or Tabor in the Forest or green wood Which he is mostly in the Autumn. But few have ever sene him and some declare that those who say theye did, lookt at him thro' a Horne, or that I maye not lye, thro' a Quarte Pott, which those who doe, doe in faithe see wondrous Thinges, specialie Faerys. Some say that to hear Drum is a sign of War, others that a King is to die.

Drum is like all his kin and kind, sometimes honey and sometimes harsh as his fancy goeth. Howbeit I have known a man of York, one Stephen Carr, who would hear no ill word spoke of Drum, and all for this that ones by Night when

he was in sore travall and hard
stead, Drum helpt him out of
it. And it twas this. Stephen
was coming home from a Fair
with a great bag of gold, having
sold and that merrily well
all his Cattle, and with him
were his three knaves, but he
was beset by six Theeves with
every strong Theef a sword
a Pike, while the Knaves
had but their knives and
staves. However Stephen and
his men fought well, "to hand
hold hand won Gold," as the
Millers rhyme says, yet were
they about to yeeld a dye when
there was heard the rattle of a
Drum close by and the sound
as of many men. Whereat ye
Theeves verily believing that
Soldiers were at Hand ran
for their Lyves, as if the divell
were lose. And so perhapps
he was for devil a soldier
or any other man could

Stephen can see a fiend, far or near. Therefore all said 'twas Drum the devill who had drummed away the Theeves.

Druides are only Witches among our common folk, but some say they haunt Oak Trees or use acorns in sorcery. And a man who was learned said to me they should not be called Druides but Dry-ads, because they were a kind of Elves, born of the dryed Leaves which fall from Oakes, but of all this there is no word among the common folk. But the Witches called Druides are known by the mark of their feet; 'tis said they can jump a mile but not fly and so it is they flee apace and afar. Anatol

ow it oft haps that on
Trees but most ly on
Oakes ye may see great
Knuels a Lumps which
some cal Boles and from
these Mazer Bowles are made
which is the cause why they are
cal'd Bowls. But some do cal
them Witchs Heads for it tis
said that Druides a Oak Witches
seek to be buryed nere Oak Trees
Than is their life, aner Soule
drawn into the Tree, and as their
Heads grow outwards, And
of yare there were fine Conjura
tions and Spels to make them
speak. but these be nowe lost.
Yet can ye drawe from Aye a No
and the manner to do itt is this.

The manner to make a Bole answer.

Take Seven Oak Leefs and
a powder of Thyme. and I thinke
it is for Time long past. As I have
found Itt in other Spels for Past
Time of old dayes for such Words
have mostly a meaninge inside of
them. And ye shall burne these
must together to the Bole and saye

Drude, Drude, Drude
Tho now thou art rude
Once thou wert faire
Joly and debonair.
Let this be thy Taske
More I doe not ask
Unto what I pray
Answer Yea a Naye!
So shalte thou be
Ever dear to me
And may ye Woodman never
fell thy Tree

Thenn will ye hear in the Leeves of the Tree Yea a No. according to your Question. And I have heard that not far from York there was the ruine or wals of a littel old church in which grew an Oake on which was a Drude or Bole very like a womans head, on which were all that pertains to a face, such as Eyes, nose, mouthe, very marvellous to behold this Heade had a neck, it came forth oute of the Trunke as a Woman who lookt from a Windew. And this Drude it was told would talke at the Full of the Moon. unto all who told the charme: Erebon.

t came to pass that the Bishop having heard this gave order that the Tree should be felled and burnt. Which was done but a workman stole the Drude and sold it to a certain witch and as I have heard it yet talks. And thus much of the Drudes, of which I have writ so much because they are so litel known though they be common in every wood.

Now will I speak of the Eager or Eiger. He is a Spirit of the water, some do say he is a wild rising tide which comes in a hasty rage, others call the third wave which is mighty an Eger or Eagre. But it is a torrent or swash or great gurge ye can understand in which boats and men often perish. So the fisher wives do sing to him or Higre.

Eagre take the wicked man,
Let the canny folk alane.

Elves be Fayries without doubt or of Fairy kind yet there are Fairys who are not Elves. Elves be light and dark, the Fairys are only light. Elves be ever small and I thinke them to be one with the Dwergs or Dwarfs. Dame Darell thought them to have come sooner into the world Faerys did not come out of the Light Sky World till men grew larger and better al beit there were Gyants in those dayes and many Drakes or Dragones. And of these too wil I speak anon. All that is prime shall come in time. And Thyme is the bed wherein man was bred when we tell children that Babes are found in Bedes of Thyme. Yea and all Things mortal do come thro that Portal. Mon amy ie vous le dis as we did say in Jersey. In Frenche. La verite com l'amour vient tojors au jour. —

The Ellwives I think like the Ell men are Elves of the water. For there be Fishes which are called Ale wives but they are Ale-wives. tho in sporte men call women who sell Ale by that name. Because they putt Water into ale. The Ellmen are their Husbon Does.

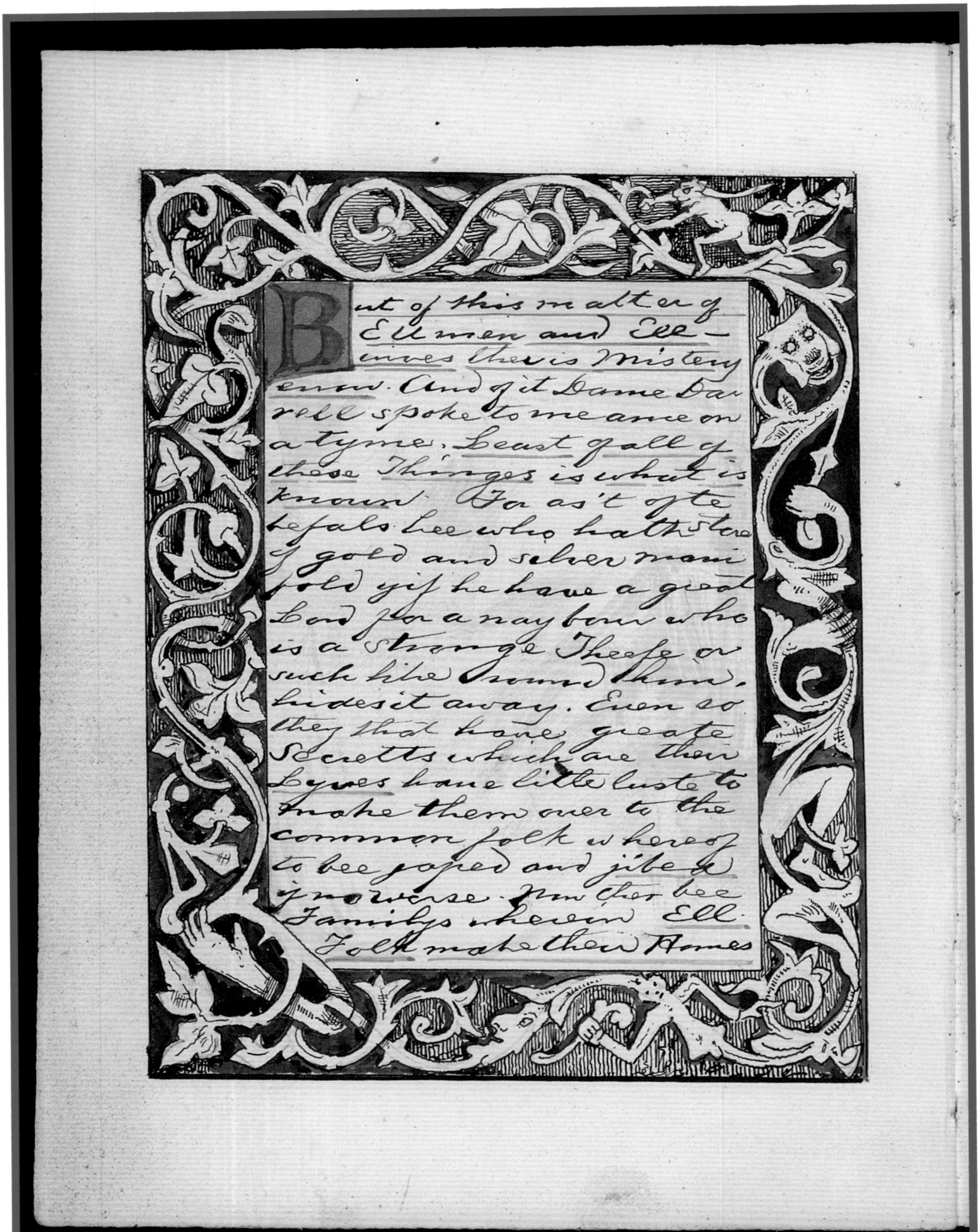
But of this matter of
Ell men and Ell-
wives ther is Mistery
enow. And of it Dame Dar-
rell spoke to me ance on
a tyme. Least of all of
these Thinges is what is
known. For as't ofte
befals hee who hath store
of gold and silver mani
fold gif he have a great
Lord for a nayboure who
is a strange Theefe or
such like round him,
hides it away. Even so
they that have greate
Secretts which are their
Lyves have little luste to
make them over to the
common folk whereof
to bee gaped and jibed
if no worse. Now ther bee
Familys wherein Ell
Folk make their Homes

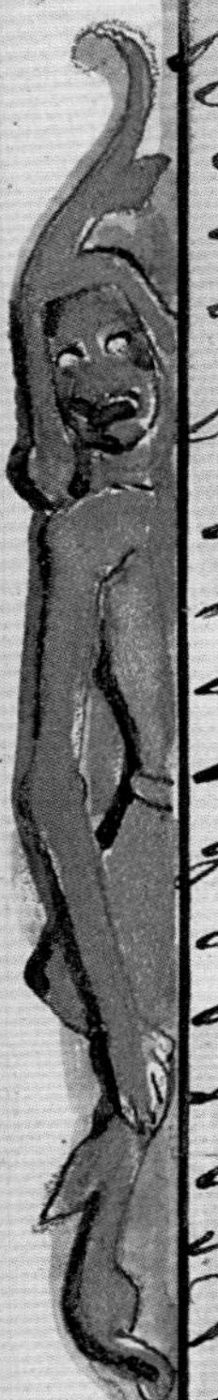

and live in Peace, and no Mann
a Woman knoweth thereof, save
the Master or his kin, and there
feare to tell as twere come Deathe
& stopp Breath, lest the least fly
thou shalt surely die. And these
folk be mostly Sakin or sib to the
Ell men. For in the old time the
Ell men often lay with the daughters of those who were wizards
and witches or of the old faithe
of hethens Idoles, or the Ell wemen had joye in Men, and so
were borne full many who
had strange giftes. Tis saide
they could talke wit the Deade,
with Druides Heades in Okes—
yea, with Streames and the Wind
and old Head-Stanes and with
all Images, with Spirites in ye
Lakes and Hils. That was no
true Ell man's son who could not
with a Witche Hasel wand or
Rod, find him a hidden store,
nay 'tis said this Folk could see
through Wals and Rockes, Ther
dwelt in   in Yorkshire, such a Family in an old
House far and lone, little did they
see of other People, no one kenned

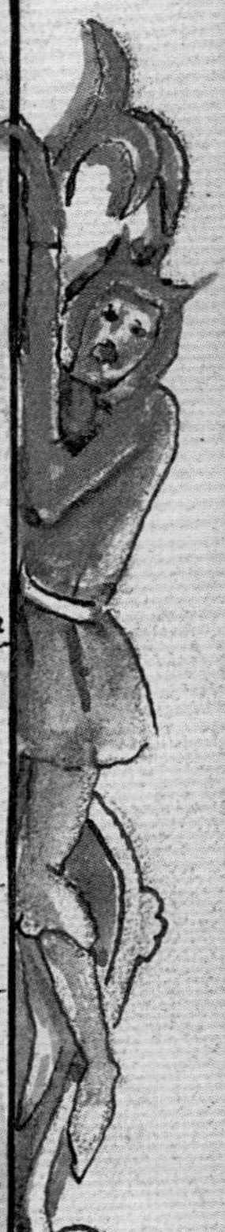

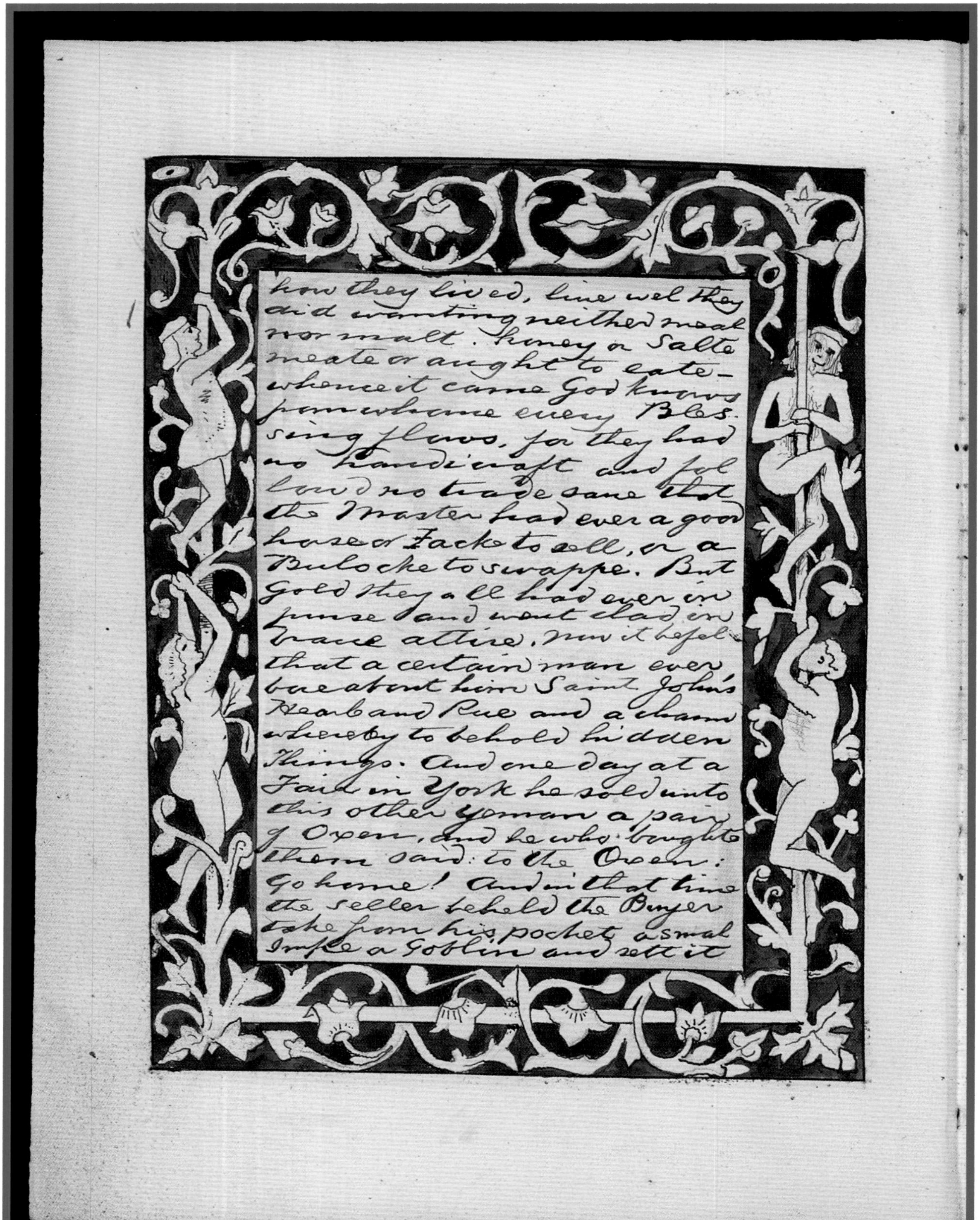

how they lived, live wel they
did wanting neither meal
nor malt. honey or Salte
meate or aught to eate—
whence it came God knows
from whence every Bles-
sing flows. for they had
no handicraft and fol
low'd no trade save that
the Master had ever a good
horse or Jacke to sell, or a
Bulocke to swappe. But
Gold they all had ever in
purse and went clad in
brave attire. Now it befel
that a certain man ever
bare about him Saint John's
Hearb and Rue and a charm
whereby to behold hidden
Things. And one day at a
Fair in York he sold unto
this other yeoman a pair
of Oxen, and he who bought
them said: to the Oxen:
Go home! And in that time
the seller beheld the Buyer
take from his pocket a smal
Impe a Goblin and sett it

on the Ox's neck. And he warned that the other saw itt not, howbeit by the Virtew of his charmes he saw all and knew that the other dealt with Ell-folk, where Ell wives and ell-men bide, the house is aye kept clean, the cattle cared for and all the work done. In olde Familys they nurse ye Childrene that no harme befal them. There was an Elf was wont to carry a babe to the top of a very high tree, this was not far from Bernicke, there he would sit for Houres rocking up and down on a bough, singing Rock a by baby upon the Tree top, I have heard that the song came from this, I cannot believe it. the Mother took no feare, but only said —

What to my grandsire's great
grandsire was done
May hapen I owe to the Elf
and my son.

So there be full many Familys wherein Ellmen dwel and none know it, because when tis tolde they go awaye. As Dame Danell said Plura latent quam patent. More thinges hidden be than ere are sene by mortall Eye. —

f Friar Rush
I telle you ther
be more merry
Tales than are true
since everie
Gammer in
the Land hath
one and the
beste a Jeste.
However what hee is is a
Goblin that is hight
Good Fellowe Robin.
and his Crafte and Cal-
ling, that is to play
Trickes and Jeste Japes
on Travelers or any
other man or mayde
and iff he findes none
of Them, since maydes
have growne rare of
late here abouts, he
mocketh any Women.
Thus the Fyer or Lighte
which is seen in marshy
places, which some doe
call Will of the Wispe
which leadeth men astray
is tolde Friar Rush
with his Lanthorne, a
rushing here and there in the
nighte.

ays is naughte but the Frenshe for Fairys as I well know. Once in the Isle of Jersey where I was borne theye did call them so. But some Folk will so have itt that Fays are the Bubbels or Blubbers or Buls which rise and fall and dance and burst on running water like little Heads which are alive. And Dame Darell told me that when you see a Bubbel-Fay or Bulle floating, if you bee a mayd and counte, one two three, so many Numbres as ye can count ere it burste so many Loves shall you have, or iff you like itt better, so many Lemans ere you dye. I knew one who thus counted to a thousand for it was a very stiff Bulle when shee walkt away and said "Goddes mercie — that is enough for any Woman!"

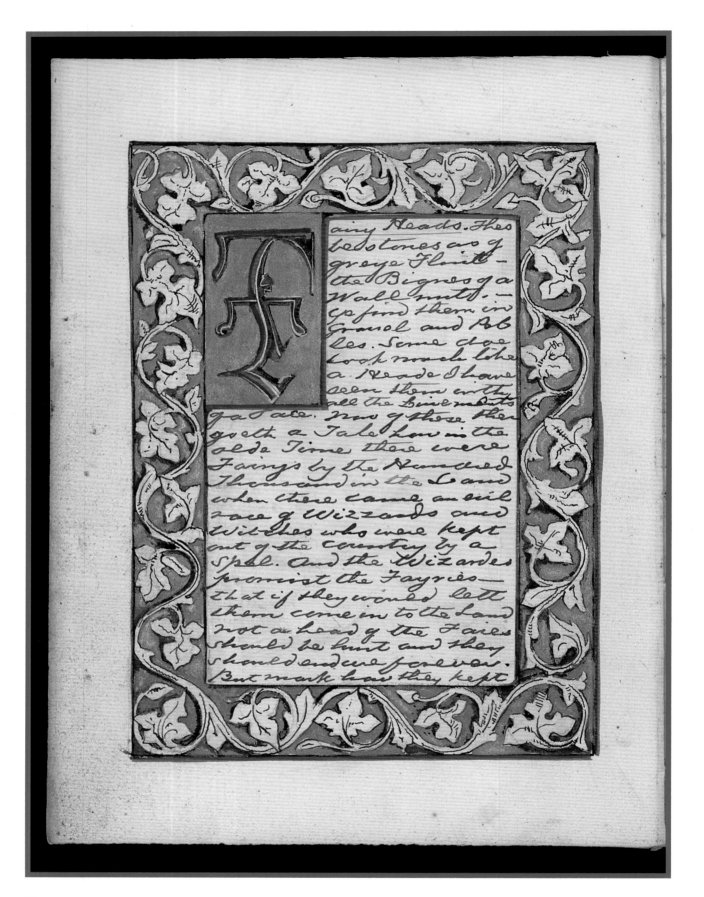

F*airy Heads*. Thes
be stones as of
greye Flintt —
the Bignes of a
Wall nutt. —
ye find them in
Gravel and Peb
les. Some doe
look much like
a Heade I have
seen them with
all the Lineaments
of a Face. Now of these ther
goeth a Tale how in the
olde Time there were
Fairys by the Hundred
Thousand in the Land
when there came an evil
race of Wizzards and
Witches who were kept
out of the country by a
Spel. And the Wizardes
promist the Fayries —
that if they would lett
them come in to the Land
not a head of the Faires
should be hurt and they
should endure forever.
But mark how they kept

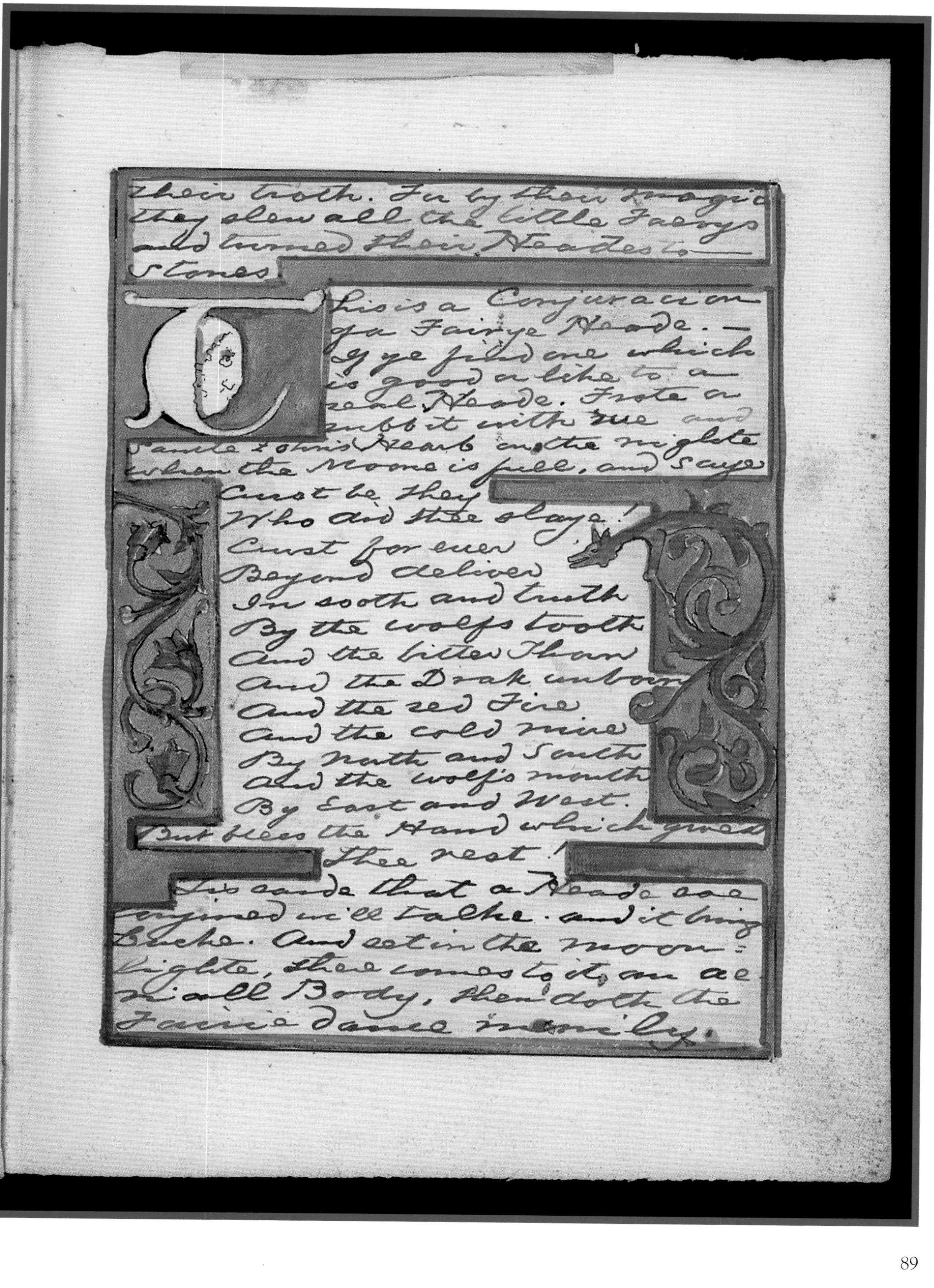

their troth. For by their magic they slew all the little Faerys and turned their Heades to Stones.

This is a Conjuracion of a Fairye Heade.— If ye find one which is good a like to a real Heade. Frote or rubb it with rue and Sandle to this Heart on the nighte when the Moone is full, and saye

Curst be they
Who did thee slaye!
Curst for ever
Beyond deliver
In sooth and truth
By the wolfs tooth
And the bitter Thorn
And the Drak unborn
And the red Fire
And the cold mire
By North and South
And the wolf's mouth
By East and West.
But bless the Hand which gives
Thee rest!

Tis saide that a Heade soe conjured will talke. and it bring Lucke. And set in the moon-lighte, there comes to it an a-small Body, then doth the Faerie dance merrily.

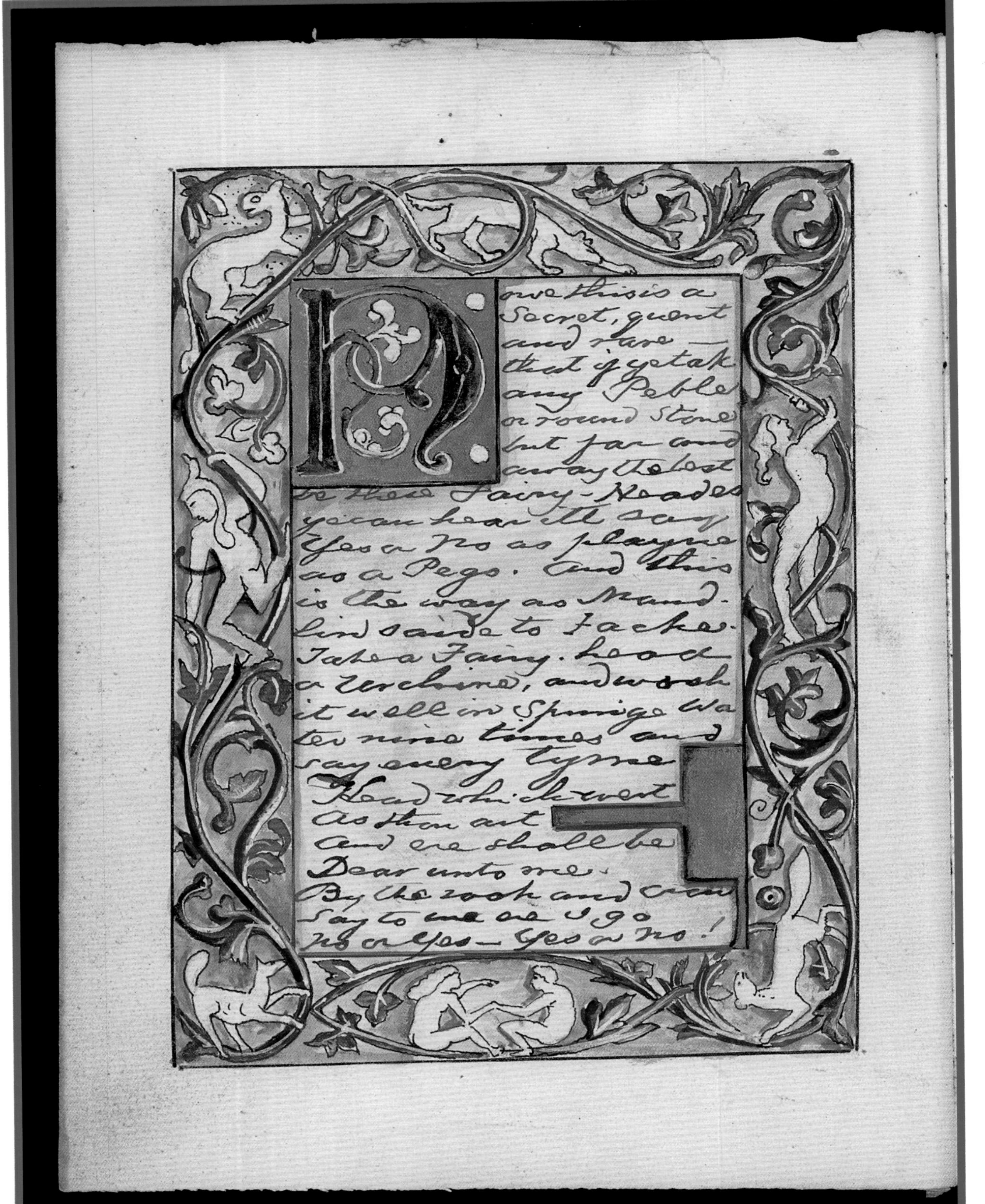

Nowe this is a
Secret, quent
and rare —
that if ye tak
any Peble
or round Stone
but far and
away the best
be these Fairy-Heades
ye can hear ith say
Yes or No as playne
as a Pegs. And this
is the way as Maud-
lin saide to Jacke:
Take a Fairy-head
or Urchine, and wash
it well in Springe Wa
ter nine times and
say every tyme
Head which wert
As thou art
And we shall be
Dear unto me.
By the rock and [illegible]
Say to me as I go
No or Yes — Yes or No!

This shall be done by nighte, under a full Moone, by a Wel or Pool or such Water, but it must be depe and Stil. Than throw the Stone upp, so that itt fall into the Wel, and as itt plumpes in ye can it say Yes or No. There was a merrie girl who had one of these Fairie Heads which lookt like a Damsel's face, or that of a little Virgine, and one day she threw it into a pool, and got her answer, but when she sought to finde the Stone in ye water shee could not reach itt. So she went to a House neere by and askt for a Rake. For as she saide she had loste her little Mayden-Heade. To which a wise man made reply that he had often knowne a Rake to tyne a maydenhead, or lose one, but never to finde such a Thing.

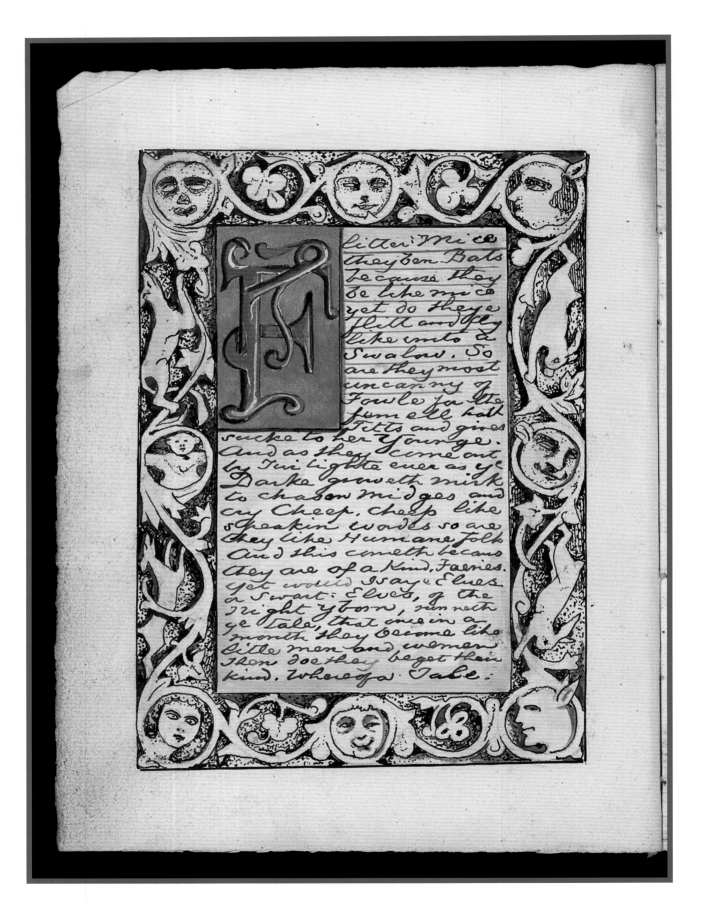

Flitter Mice
they ben Bats
because they
be like mice
yet do theye
flitt and fly
like unto a
Swalow. So
are they most
uncanny of
Fowle for the
femell hath
Titts and gives
sucke to her Younge.
And as they come out
by Twi lighte ever as ye
Darke groweth mirk
to chasen midges and
cry Cheep, cheep like
speakin wordes so are
they like Humane Folk
And this cometh becaus
they are of a Kind, Faeries.
yet would I saye Elves
a swart: Elves, of the
Night yborn, runneth
ye Tale, that once in a
month they become like
little men and women
then doe they beget their
kind. Whereof a Tale:

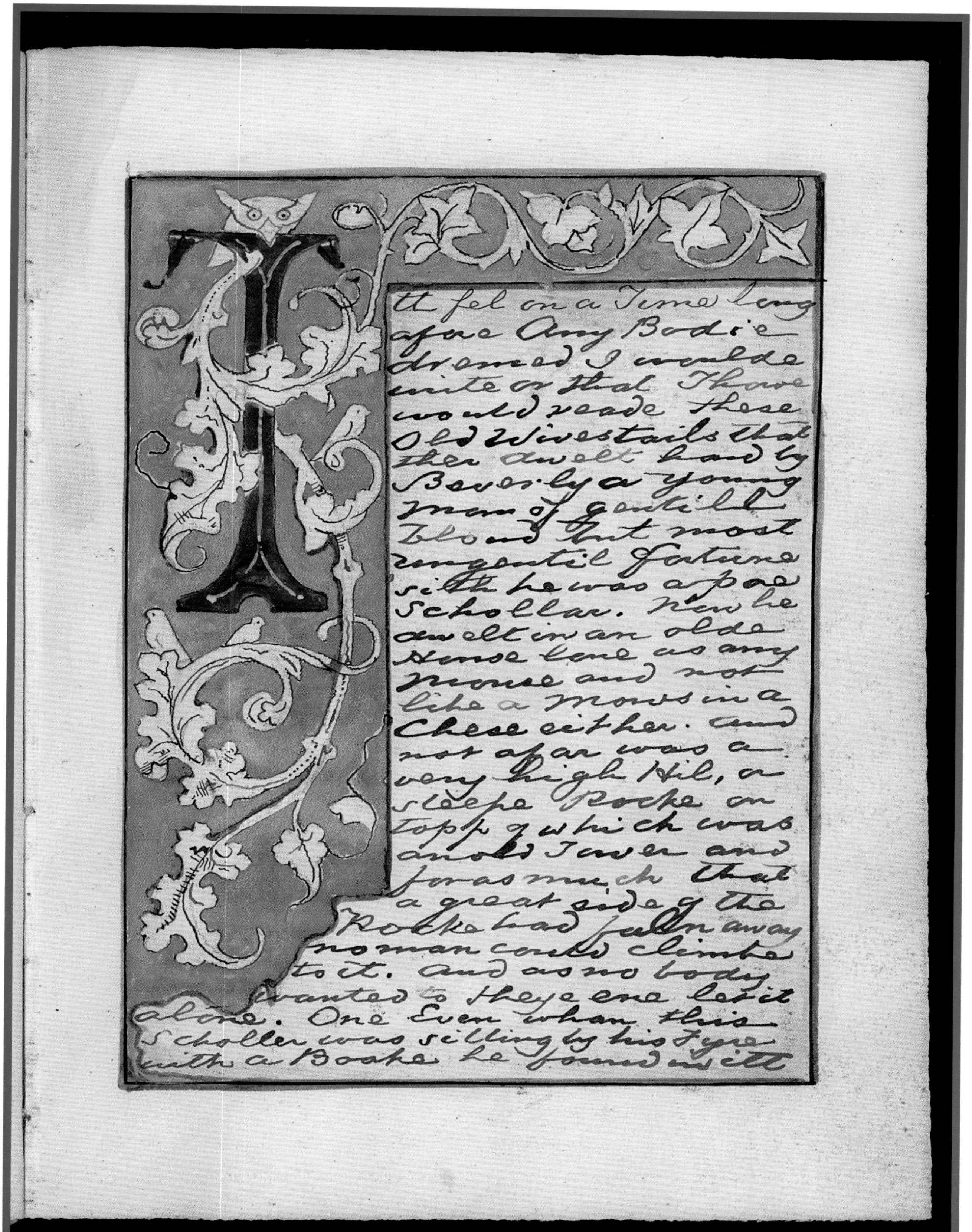

It fel on a Time long afore Any Bodie dremed I woulde write or that Thave would reade these Old Wivestails that ther dwelt hard by Beverly a young man of gentill bloud but most ungentil fortune sith he was a poore Schollar. Now he dwelt in an olde House lone as any mouse and not like a Mous in a Chese either. And not afar was a very high Hil, a steepe Rocke on topp q which was an old Tower and forasmuch that a great side q the Rocke had fallen away no man could climbe to it. And as no body wanted to they ene let it alone. One Even when this Scholler was sitting by his Fyre with a Booke he found in itt

a Spel whiche all unwytting
hee reade alowde and itt was a
Corporacyon by which any animal a Birde a suche Beinge
hearing of itt could become
Humane according to itts kind
male a femell. And when
he had done this he heard a
crye as of Chepe, chepe, here
I am as the Lamb to yͤ Ram.
So he Ealld "Come in," and lo
there entered a verie litt la-
but comely maide. all [illegible]
in soft furr. And she made there
& she stayd by him and layd
by him as Gilian did to Jocke
until one nighte she sayd to
him. I have Something be-
neath my Smocke. What is
that sayde he.
" And she answered soothe and
faire:
Well I have
That thou shoulst knowe
Sith thou didst putt it there
And this Thinge was a
Babe. So time past and shee
was lighter for the Babe was
y-born. Now the mother was
ever wilde as a hawk and

full of capriccios, oft time
she sprang and leape aboute
like mad, running after
Flys, ever merry. When
one Evening they heard from
without in the Mist a cry
of Fleta, come!" and she said:
That is for me. here can I no
longer stay, my time is ore
I cant delay. But if thou
shouldst ever bee in dire
nede, to ye childe make
thy Rede. She will holpen
thee in Dede.

here with off she
ran and was no
more seene. But
the Childe who
was now a twe
lmonth olde
spake to his won
der, and saide
Dere Father doe not greve
for my Moder has left me
her Voice seems that shee
hath no use for it mare.

ow itt befel on
a Tyme that ye
Scollar was so
poorlee made
his mone to the
Childe

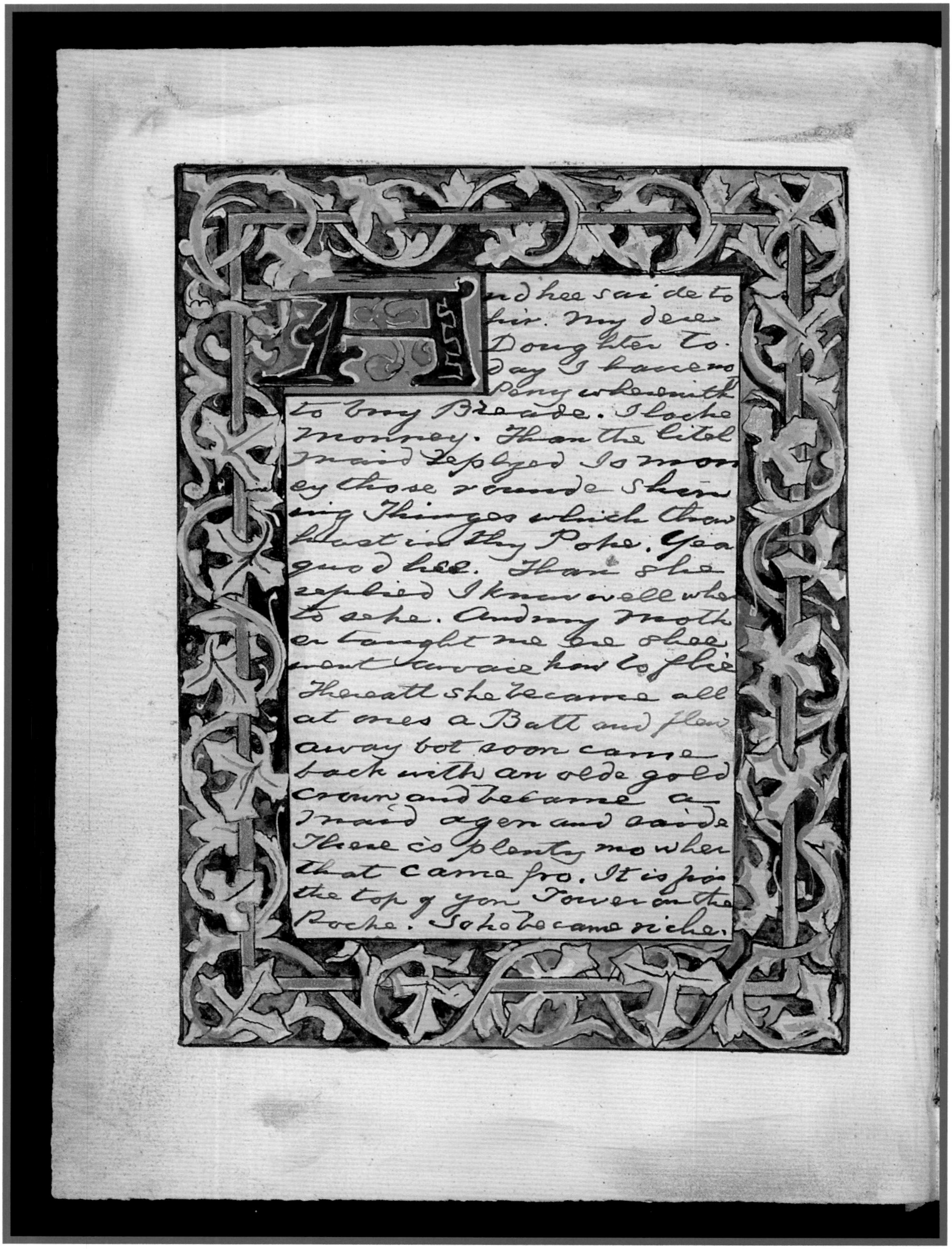

And hee saide to hir. My dere Doughter To-day I have no Peny wherewith to buy Breade. I lacke Monney. Than the litel maid replyed Is money those rounde Shening Thinges which thou hast in thy Poke. Yea quod hee. Than she replied I knew well wher to seke. And my Mother taught me be sheewent away how to flie Thereath she became all at ones a Batt and flew away bot soon came back with an olde gold crown and became a maid agen and saide There is plenty mo wher that came fro. It is in the top of yon Tower on the Rocke. So he became riche.

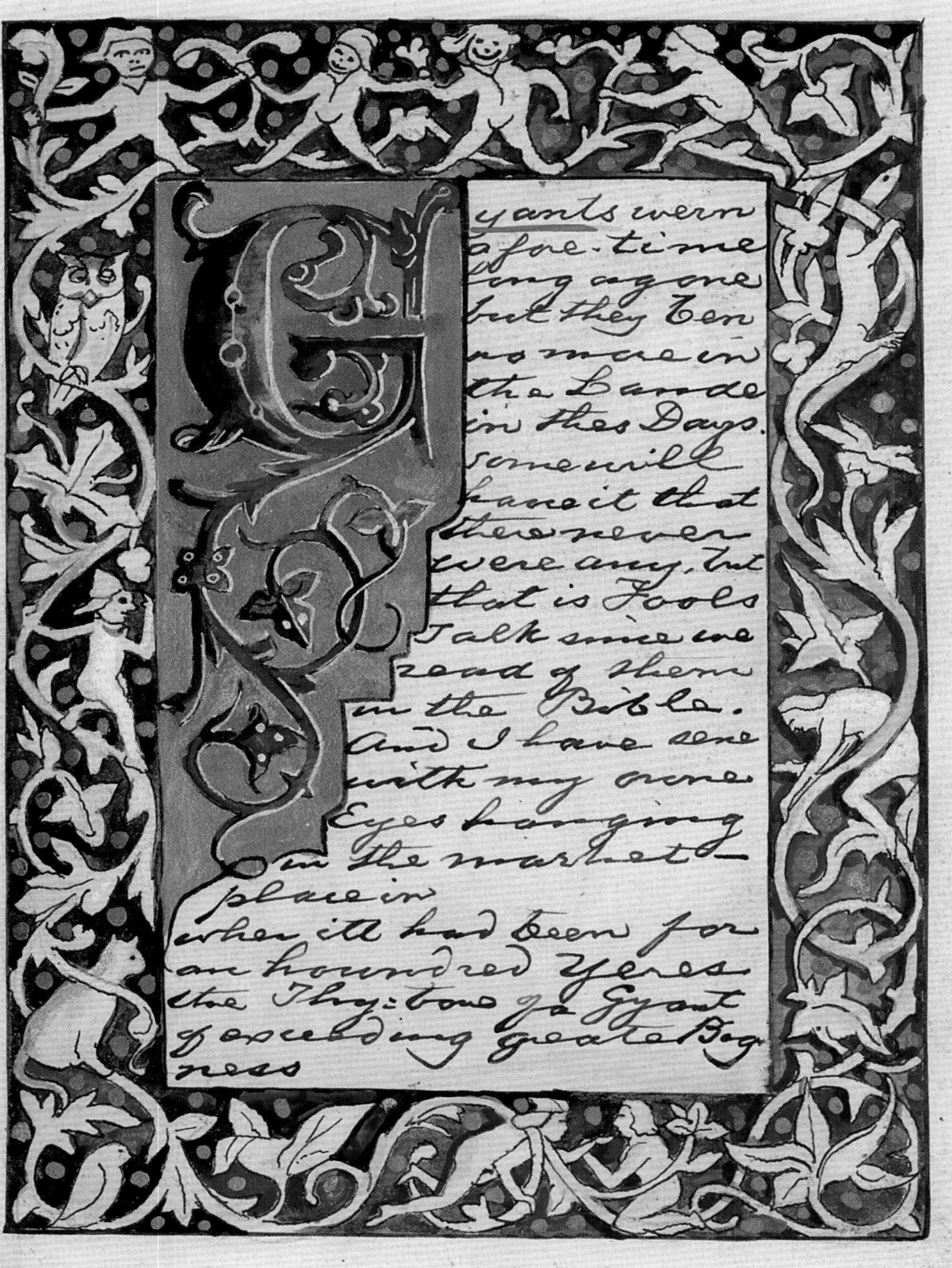

Gyants wern
afoe-time
long agone
but they Ben
no mare in
the Lande
in thes Days.
some will
have it that
there never
were any, but
that is Fools
Talk since we
read of them
in the Bible.
And I have sene
with my owne
Eyes hanging
in the market-
place in
when itt had been for
an houndred Yeres
the Thy:bone of a Gyant
of exceding greate Big
ness

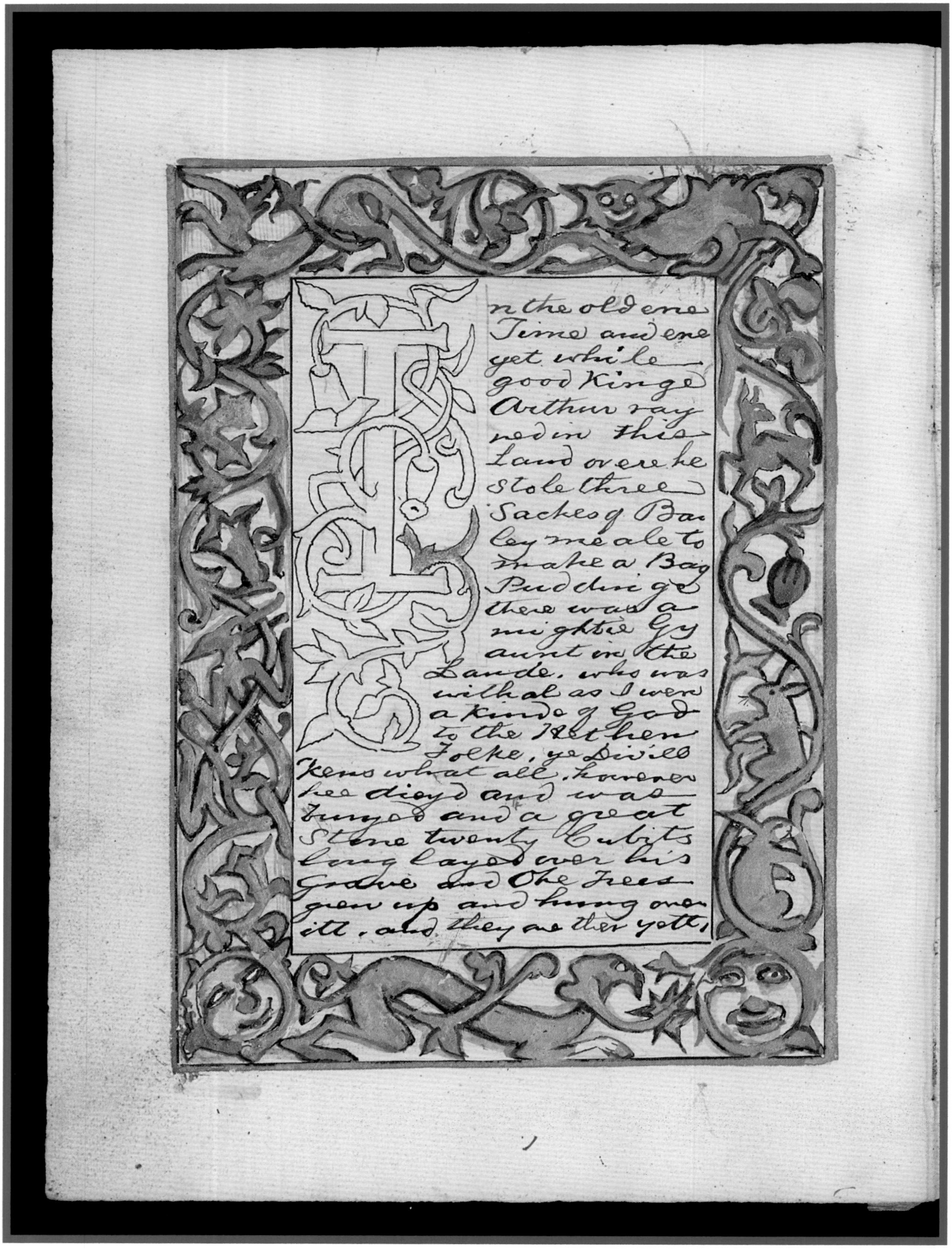

n the oldene
Time and ere
yet while
good Kinge
Arthur ray
ned in this
Land or ere he
stole three
Sackes of Bar
ley meale to
make a Bag
Puddinge
there was a
mightie Gy
aunt in the
Lande. who was
withal as I were
a kinde of God
to the Hethen
Folke, ye Divill
kens what all. however
hee dieyd and was
buryed and a great
Stone twenty Cubits
long layed over his
Grave and Ohe Trees
grew up and hung over
itt, and they are ther yett,

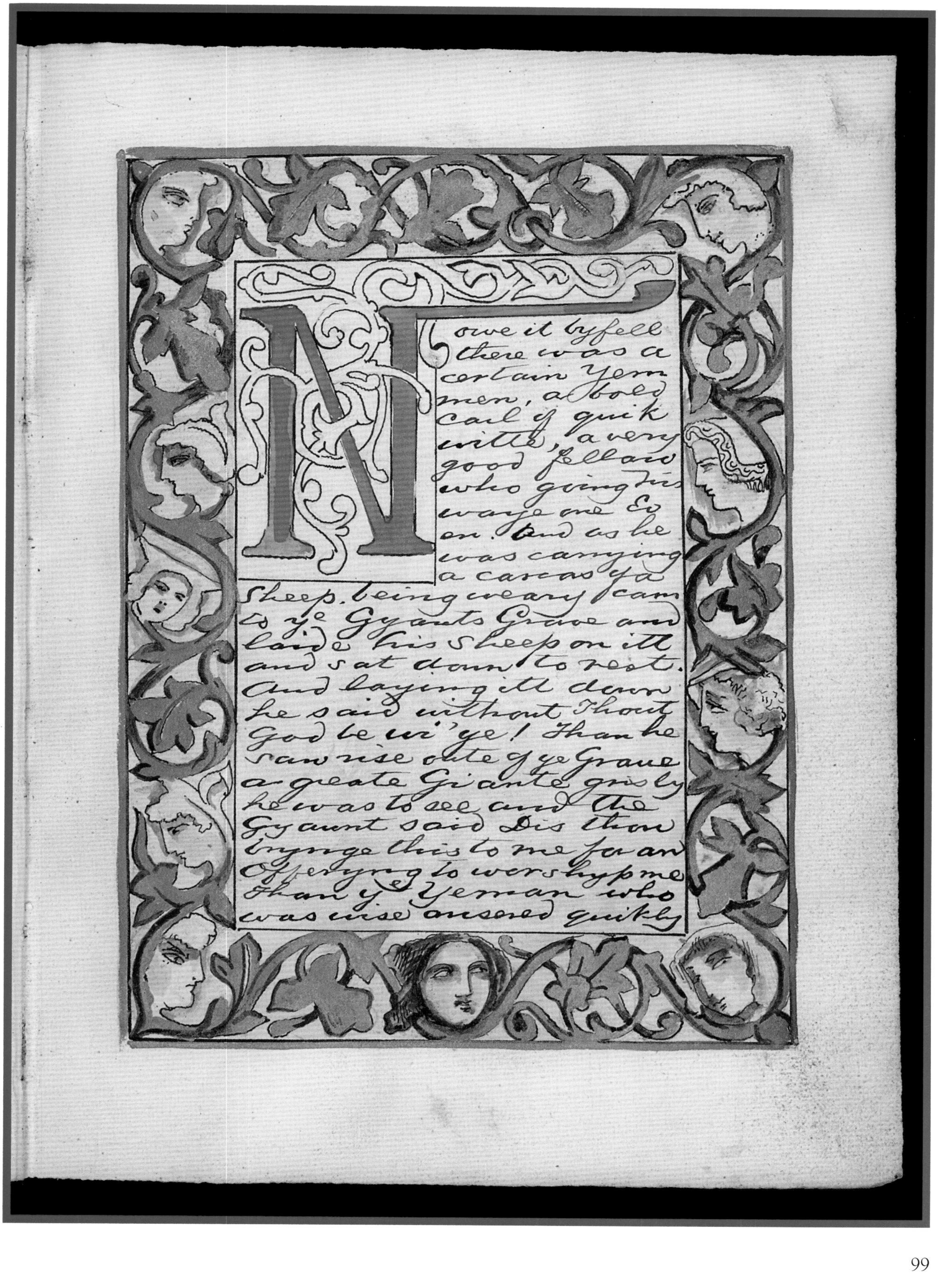

Nowe it byfell
there was a
certain Yeom
men, a bold
carl of quik
witte, a very
good fellaw
who going his
waye one Ev
en. And as he
was carrying
a carcas of a
sheep. being weary cam
to ye Gyants Grave and
laide his sheep on itt
and sat down to rest.
And laying itt down
he said without Thout
God be wi' ye! Than he
saw rise oute of ye Grave
a greate Giante grisly
he was to see and the
Gyaunt said Dis thou
brynge this to me for an
Offeryng to worshyp me
Than ye Yeman who
was wise onsered quikly

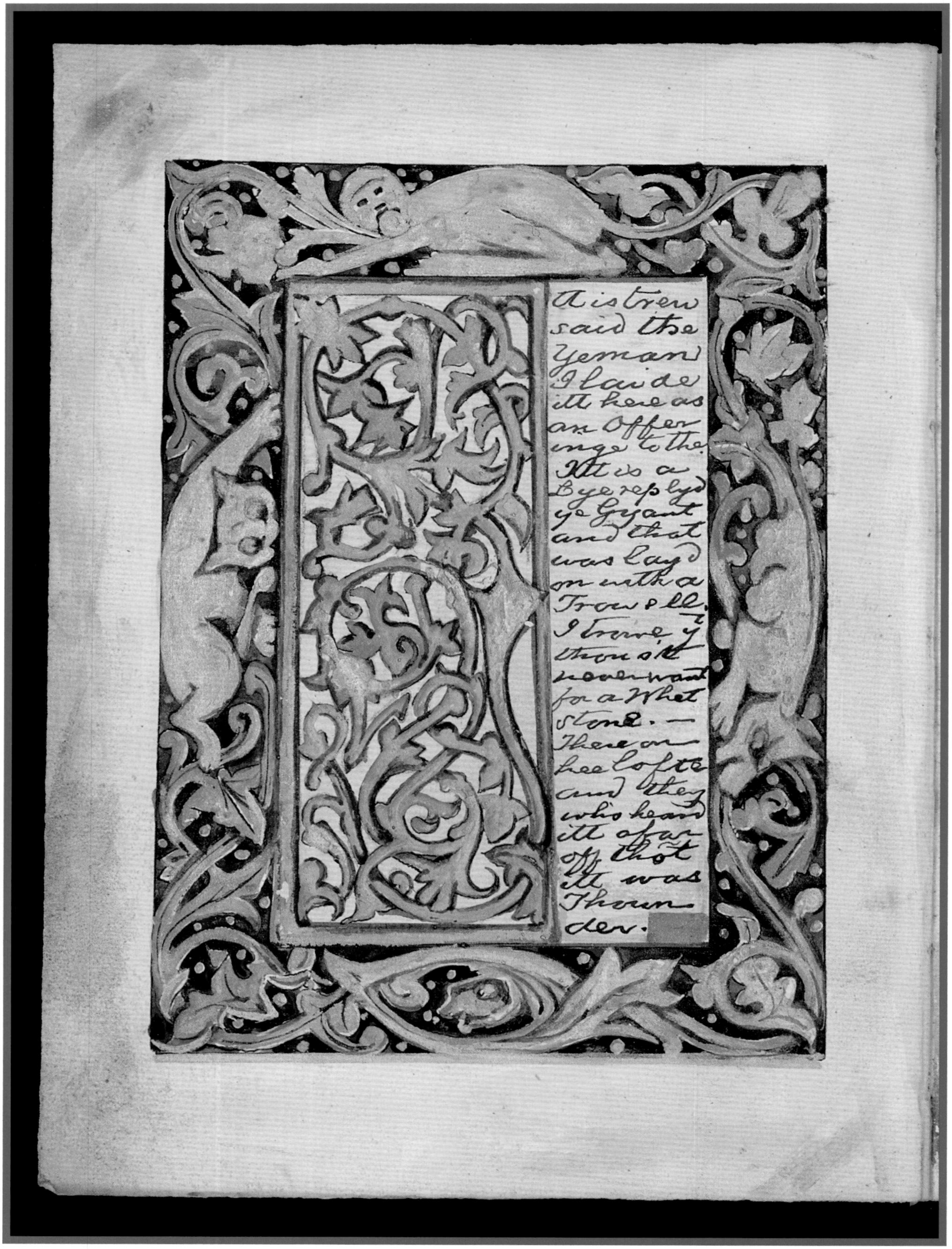
It is trew
said the
Yeman
I laide
itt here as
an Offer
inge to the
Itt is a
Lye replyd
ye Gyant
and that
was layd
on with a
Trowell.
I trowe, y
thou sht
neuer want
for a Whet
stone. —
There on
hee lofte
and they
who heard
itt afar
off that
itt was
Thoun
der.

Gally-Bird is one whiche maketh gret feare the Wodewale or mad bird is like it, both are witches. Gale or gally giveth drede as doth the Nightingale tho its song be swete it singeth Woe, these be all strange thinges. So is a Galleytrot, a thinge like a Barghost very fearsome to beehold some call itt Gallows bird it beth not that. for as are things mixt. He who meets a Galley-trot, should say:
Ab-ba-acca-adda
Affa Agga!

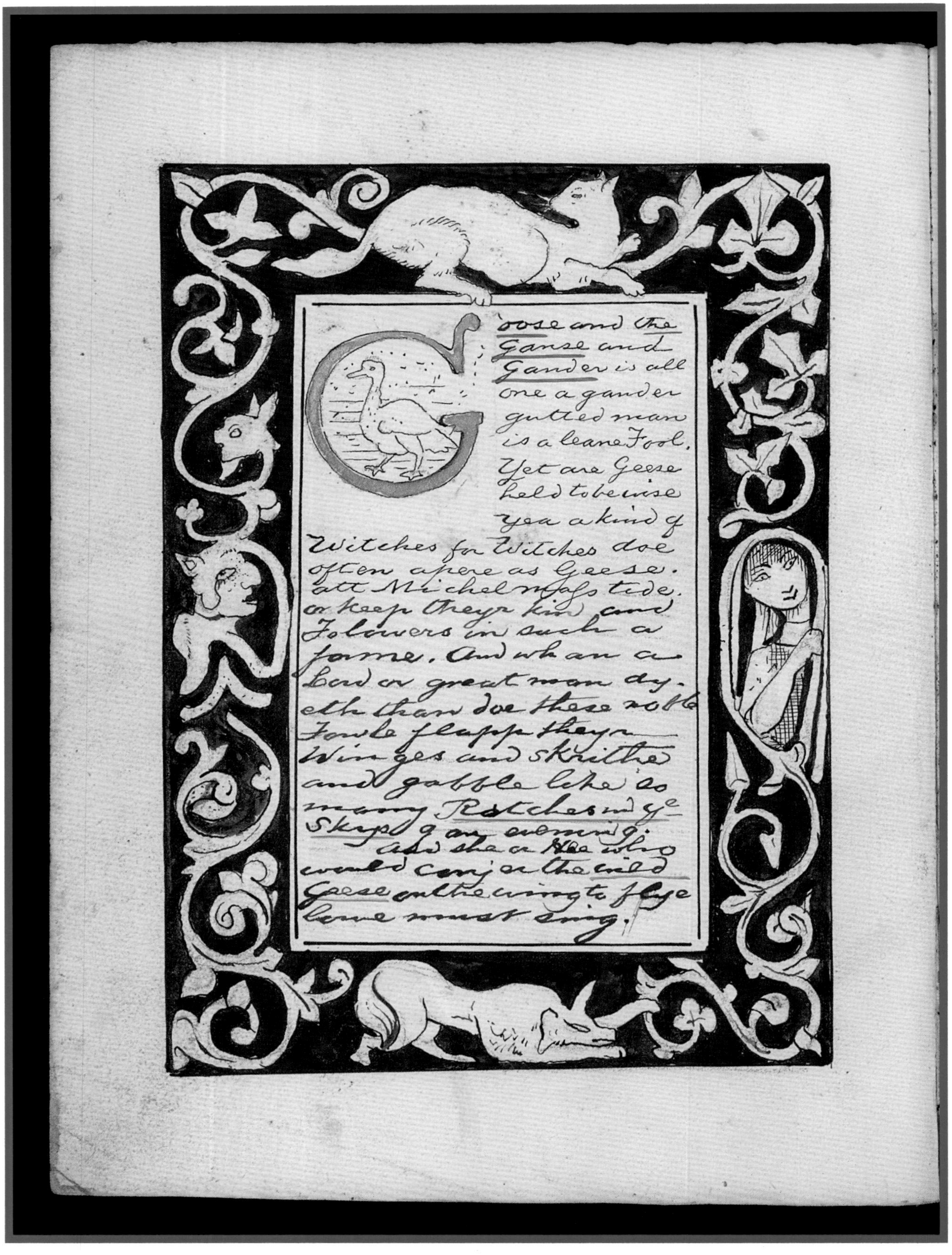
Goose and the Ganse and Gander is all one a gander gutted man is a leane Fool, Yet are Geese held to be wise yea a kind of Witches for Witches doe often apere as Geese. att Michelmass tide. or keep theyr kin and Folowers in such a forme. And when a Lord or great man dyeth than doe these noble Fowle flapp theyr Winges and Skrithe and gabble like as many Ratches in ye Skys a an evening.
Ass she or Hee who would conjor the wild Geese on the wing to flye lowe must sing.

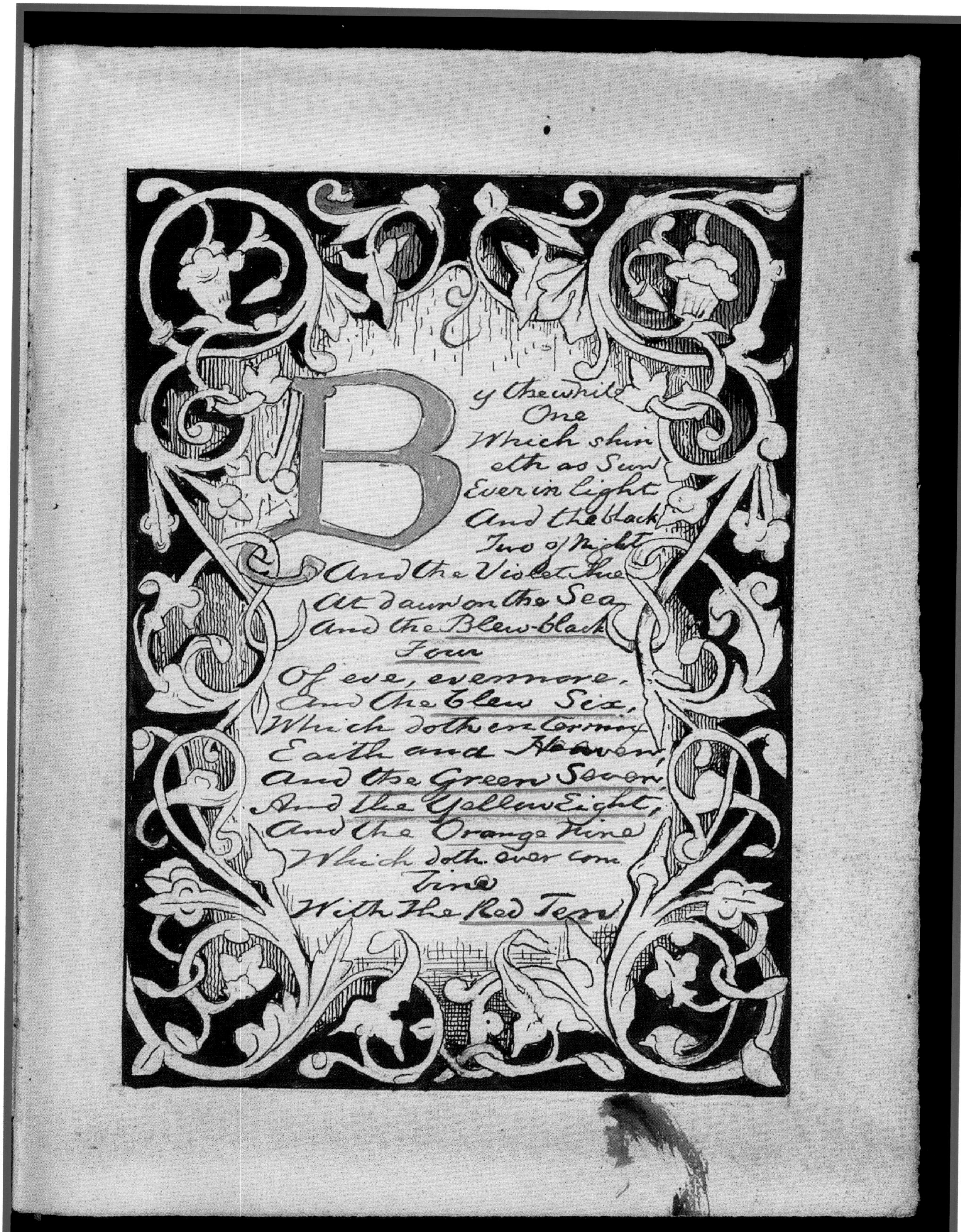
By the white
One
Which shin
eth as Sun
Ever in light
And the black
Two of Night
And the Violet Three
At dawn on the Sea
And the Blew-black
Four
Of eve, evermore.
And the Blew Six,
Which doth entermix
Earth and Heaven,
And the Green Seven,
And the Yellow Eight,
And the Orange Nine
Which doth ever com
bine
With the Red Ten

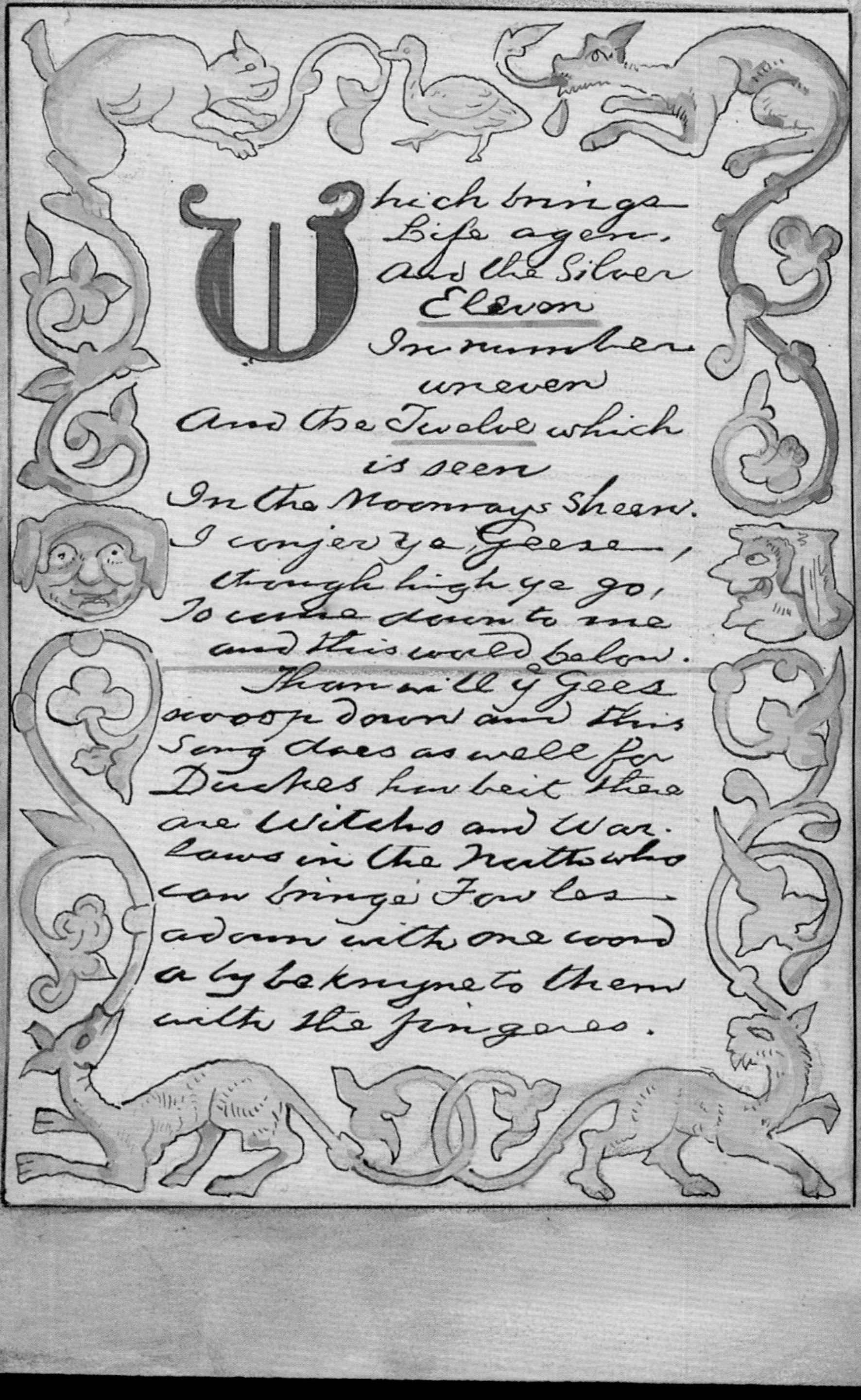
Which brings
Life agen.
and the Silver
Eleven
In number
uneven
And the Twelve which
is seen
In the Moonrays sheen.
I conjer ye Geese,
though high ye go,
To come down to me
and this world below.
Than will ye Gees
swoop down and this
Song does as well for
Duckes howbeit there
are Witches and War-
lows in the Northe who
can bringe Fowles
adown with one word
a by beknyne to them
with the fingeres.

Nowe I have writen of the Spel to call Geese and this minds me of a folish littel Song which Childern singe to a Goos but and yet Dame Davel wold have itt and so put up, that itt was a Conjeration to plese and charm the Fowle. And itt is this.

Goosey Goosy Gandere!
Whedere dost thou wandere
Upp Steyers, doun Steyers,
In my Ladis Chambre;
Ther I mett a litel Boye
Who wolde nat say his
Preyers.
I tooke him by th left Legg
And strake him doune ye Steyres,

Howbeit there were of yore som kinde of Heretikes or Lolards in the Land who did worship both a Goos and a Pigg, and Dame Davell said they sware in the name of a Bore which they cal ye Gulenbarst, or Borstle which is golden Bristels att New Years tide and sware what they wold doe the Coming Yeere.

Gaster or Gaste is a spirit which causes exceeding great feare yet will I not say it is a comon Ghost, but rather any Bugg or terrible thing because as men say they are gastered or agast at a Gastne which is a specter of any kind, the Lord keep us all therefro, and all hawkit thinges!

From the night mar and ye Gobin
Which is hight Good Felawe
Robin:
And all which wandereth by
night
Between the duske and morning
light.

Ther was a Gentleman who lived neer in a large Manor, therein woned a Gaster very horrible to behold one daye the Gentleman saw the Gaster and conjered it with a strong spel so that the spirit was agast him self and said Now I feare thou will conjure me out of house and home and lse I have dwelt here this fower hundred Yeeres and done no harme. Thy re-

plyd the Master, I do rather
conjer the to remaine an thou
wilt doe somewhat for me what
wilt thou haue quoth ye Gas
ter. Only this that whan my
men servantes or Maids would
steale aught from me or doe
aughte Amiss that thou
fray them. That can I well
do said the Gast tell they fal
down in a fullock. So he
went his way and I trow from
that day the Lord lost little.
So the Gaster served as a har
row and a Scar to the Crows.
(Illegible).... Jankin who
made a <u>Scar for Crowes</u> so
terrible..... he was wel-nye
scart to death of Itt him selfe
Truly ther be armany thinges
which are all Funk or Gam=
en and Gillor as old folk say
yet which doe good, for what
is a holy besant to the wise and
learned may be a holy Sainte
to Another. Eagles fearen
naught Scarcrowes. And so
a Bull-beggar is a Begger to a
Bull and this ends my discourse
on the Gaster.

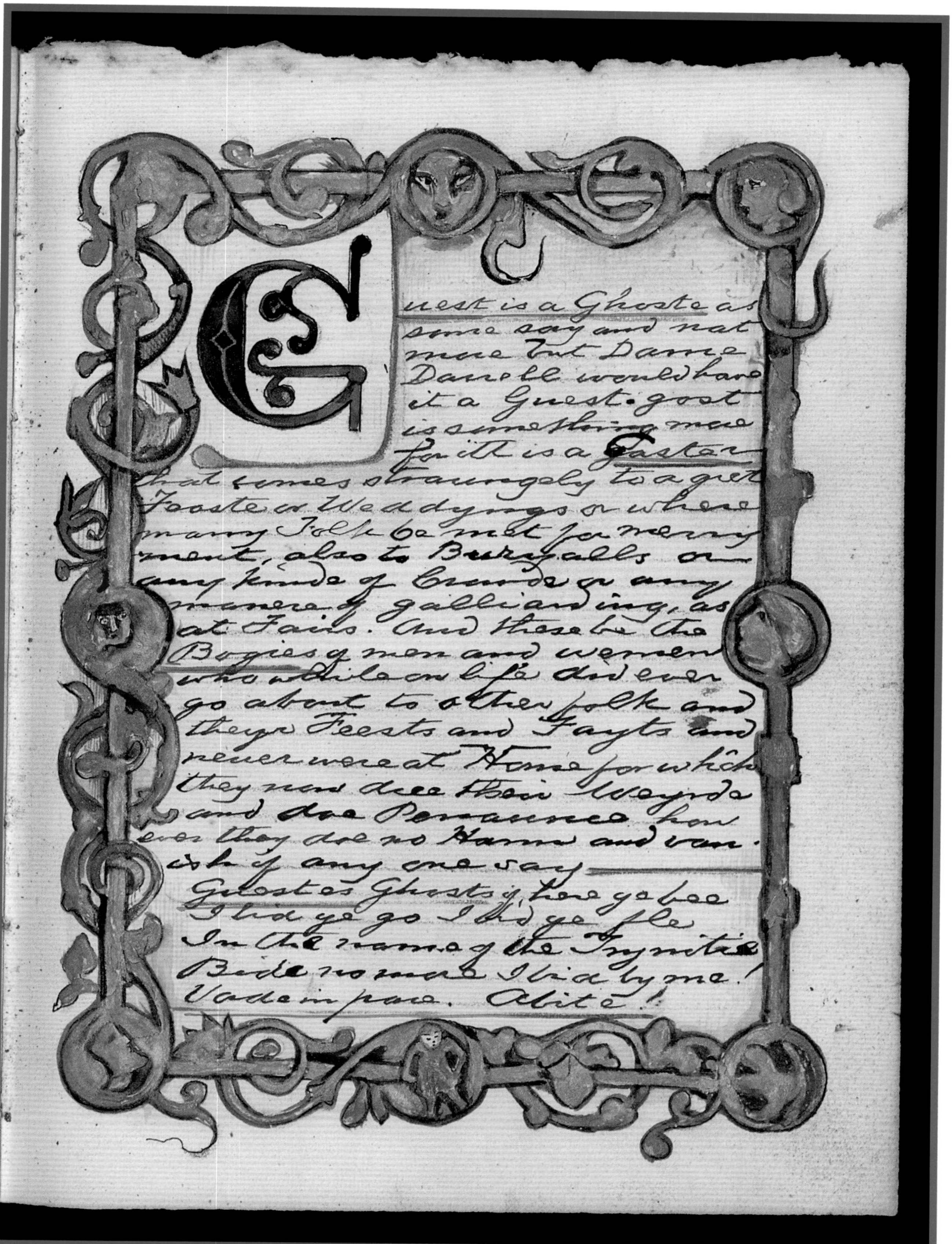

Guest is a Ghoste as
some say and nat
mare but Dame
Darrell would have
it a Guest. gost
is somethinge mare
for itt is a Gaster
that comes straungely to a gret
Feaste or Weddynges or where
many Folk be met for merry
ment, also to Buryalls or
any kinde of Crowde or any
manner of gallivanting, as
at Fairs. And these be the
Bogies of men and women
who while on life did ever
go about to other folk and
theyr Feests and Fayts and
never were at Home for which
they now dree their Weyrda
and doe Penaunce how
ever they doe no Harm and van
ish if any one say
Guestes Ghosts if here ye bee
I bid ye go I bid ye flee
In the name of the Trynitie
Bide no mare I bid by me!
Vade in pace. Abite!

avel is ÿ Slough or Skin of a Snake which itt casteth off. Let those who find 'Em guard 'em with care for they doe bringe good Fortune but they are beste when found by chance and nott when sought after. Those who will never kill a snake nor make any pain or tormente to Man or Child or anie of Gods creatures or in killing aughte doe gett great good Luck fro such Havels Ther was a vene poore man of that ilk who had such Kindness that he spared all Snakes ther Lyves. So one Daye hee found a Havel and on the next there came to him a greate Estate of which he had loste al Hope and so itt ever went wi hym. God grant us in his Grace all the same!

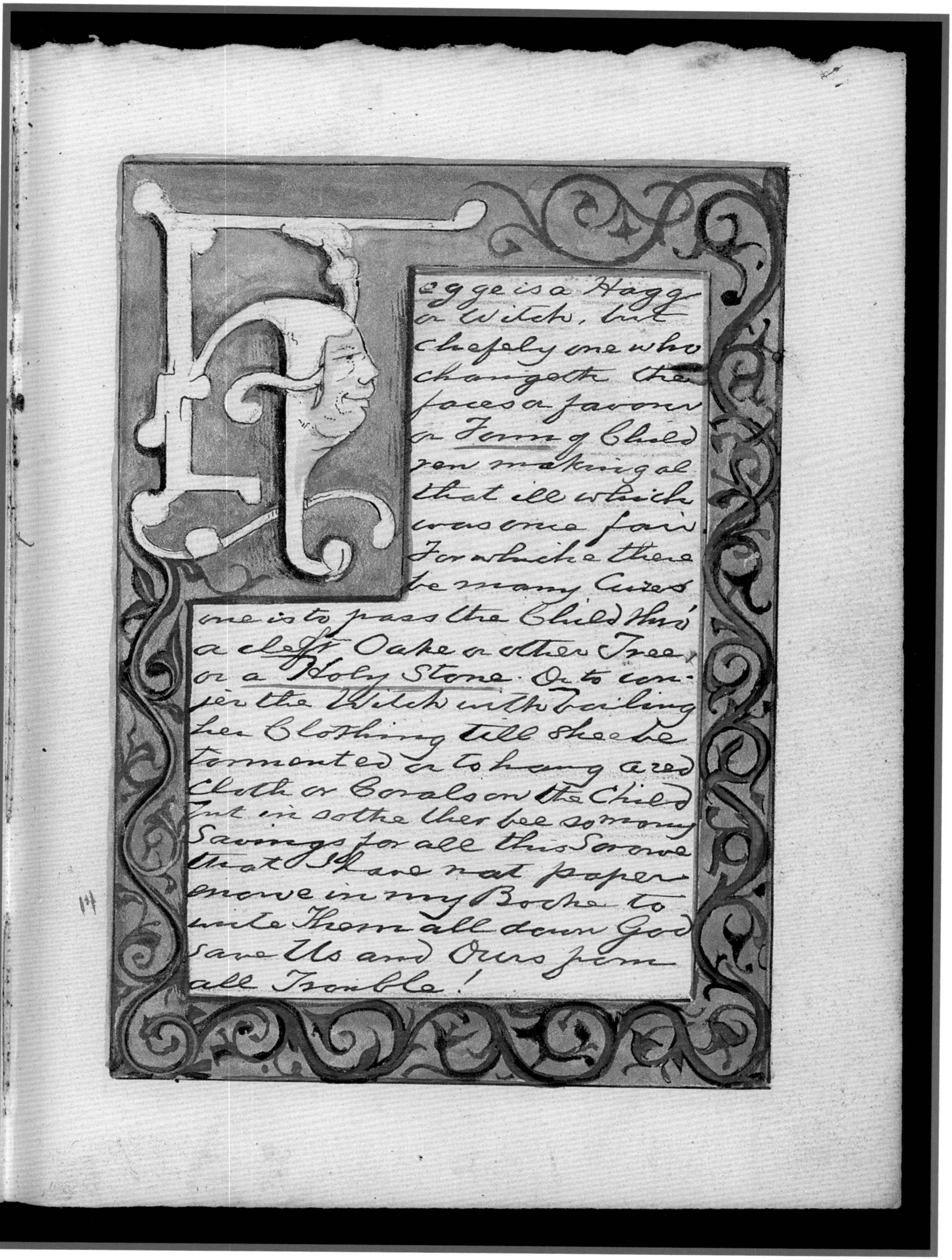

Hegge is a Hagg
or Witch, but
chiefely one who
changeth the
faces or favour
or Forme of Child
ren making al
that ill which
was once fair
For which there
be many Cures
one is to pass the Child thro'
a cleft Oake or other Tree
or a Holy Stone. Or to conjer the Witch with Tailing
her Clothing till shee be
tormented or to hang a red
Cloth or Corals on the Child
but in sothe ther bee so many
Sayings for all this Sorrowe
that I have not paper
enowe in my Booke to
write Them all down God
save Us and Ours from
all Trouble!

ella is the Nighte Mare Shee that was aforetime ye Queene or Lady in Helle of all the Witches and sent forth her Witches & Bitches to torment Christen Folk in ther Dreames by Nighte howbeit, Mare is not a Horse but as I thinke either Mère, a Mother, as we doe saye in Jersey, or as many say Mare for any Whore or Shee-Devill, or Impe or Hagg. Itt is said the Hella hath such madd delite to bee the Nightmare as Menn have to enjoy Wemen, and Wise men have Devices to intrap them and bring them to repent anone. Yea and itt often haps that there be Nightmares among our Gossipes and Nyghbores, tho no one wetes thereof ne of theyre Sinns and Subtleties.

Hell wain is the
greate fiery wain
a wagon which
is seen in the sky
a nightes in whi-
che witches doe
ryde with theyr Queene, and of
which are manye old Tales
Hob goblin is soe cald
from Hobb as one
says Jacke O Lan-
tern, and in sooth
the same is often
y-cleped Hobby
Lanthorn, and
it meneth wel ny any Fende
or Goblin which playeth and
frighteneth
Hob Thrush is a gob
lin, but not so
euill. Hee is a
merrie Sprite who
maketh Mischief
and Sporte, but sel
dom great Scathe.

Hoodkin a Hodekin a Hotkin tis al the same and meaneth a merry Impe though a Lether bottel is also so called. Hotkin is al one with Robin Good Fellow, but he wereth a Hoode. It is a merry Tale that once on a time a good man who was going a long journey left his Wife who a Loose Piece to the care of Hodekin to keep Men from lying with her - and this hee did but had so muckel Trouble to drive her Lemans away that when ye Husbond returned he said: "Never again Robin, for I had leefer drive a thousand wode Swine thorough a Forest, than have the care of one whore."

Jemmy Burty a Berty which means one who sweats and is a heat is al one with the Will o the Wisp and Jack o' Lantern and is so cald because he maketh men to Bert or puff and sweate who do tyle after him: There was on a tyme a man who had been lyse misled by a certaine Goblinn, and so going to a Wise Woman or Warlok he gott a magicke Lanterne with which he went forth to the marish and when the Burty would faine delude him he saide:

"By the Starres so brite
Which are the Dream-holes
of Night!
Go thou into my Lanterne!
There shalt thou forever burn
And for Wonder unto all
Caste thy Image on the Wall!"

And Dame Darell tolde me she had truly seen this miracle with her own Eyes how that the Impe did shewe himself in Light, I trowe itt is trewe.

A
Kern baby is
a Dol or Im-
age made of
Strawe, which
at Harvest tide
the Country folk a Reapers
doe make of Straw, on the
fielde when all is in-
gathered, of the last She
af. Than they beare itt
before them, and singa
Song untoe ye Harvest
Supper. But iff ye ask mee
what it al meanes I think
Kern is Corn. And itt was believed of old that this was a
living Elphe a Ouphe who
made ye Corne grow, and gave
good luck wherefore they
still worship
its Image with
greate Merri=
ment, Finis.
to ye Knacke.

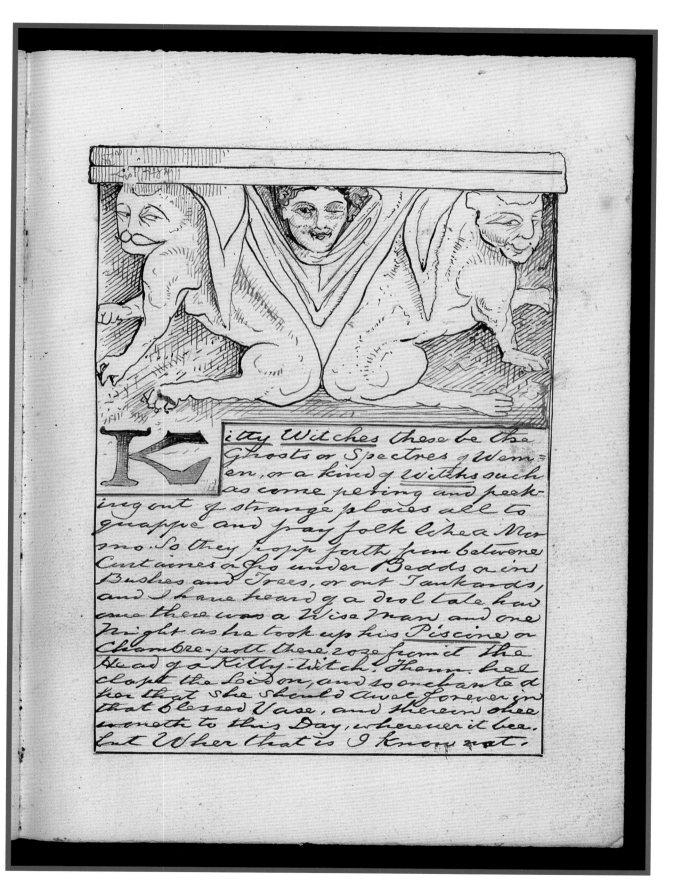

Kitty Witches these be the Ghosts or Spectres of Wom=en, or a kind of Witchs such as come pering and peek-ing out of strange places all to guappe and pray folk like a Murmo. So they popp forth from betweene Curtaines or fro under Bedds or in Bushes and Trees, or out Tankards, and I have heard of a drol tale how one there was a Wise Man and one Night as he took up his Piscine or Chambre-pott there rose from it the Head of a Kitty-Witch. Thenn hee clapt the Lid on, and so enchanted her that she should dwel forever in that blessed Vase, and therein shee woneth to this Day, wherever it bee, but Wher that is I Know not.

averock is a Larke that is a Birde yet it is of Faery kind, and bringeth good Lucke and a merrie Heart to all who never doeth harm but tis bad lucke to kill it. And I thinke yt. ye name is from ye Frenshe word Laricot or Lark-o which is a pipe a flute which soundeth like a Larke Songe when tis as played. And tis saide the Larke flieth in the morning upp to Heaven and asketh in its Singing Is itt time meaning Is it time for me to come in? And a Voyce answereth Not yett. Then the Larke in sorrow fal leth adown to Earth. Of the Larke is a folish little ditty

Tiri liri lor peine ye Laverok song
So merrily pipped ye Sparrow.
The Cow brake loose and ye Rope
ran home
Syr, God give you a good Morrow!

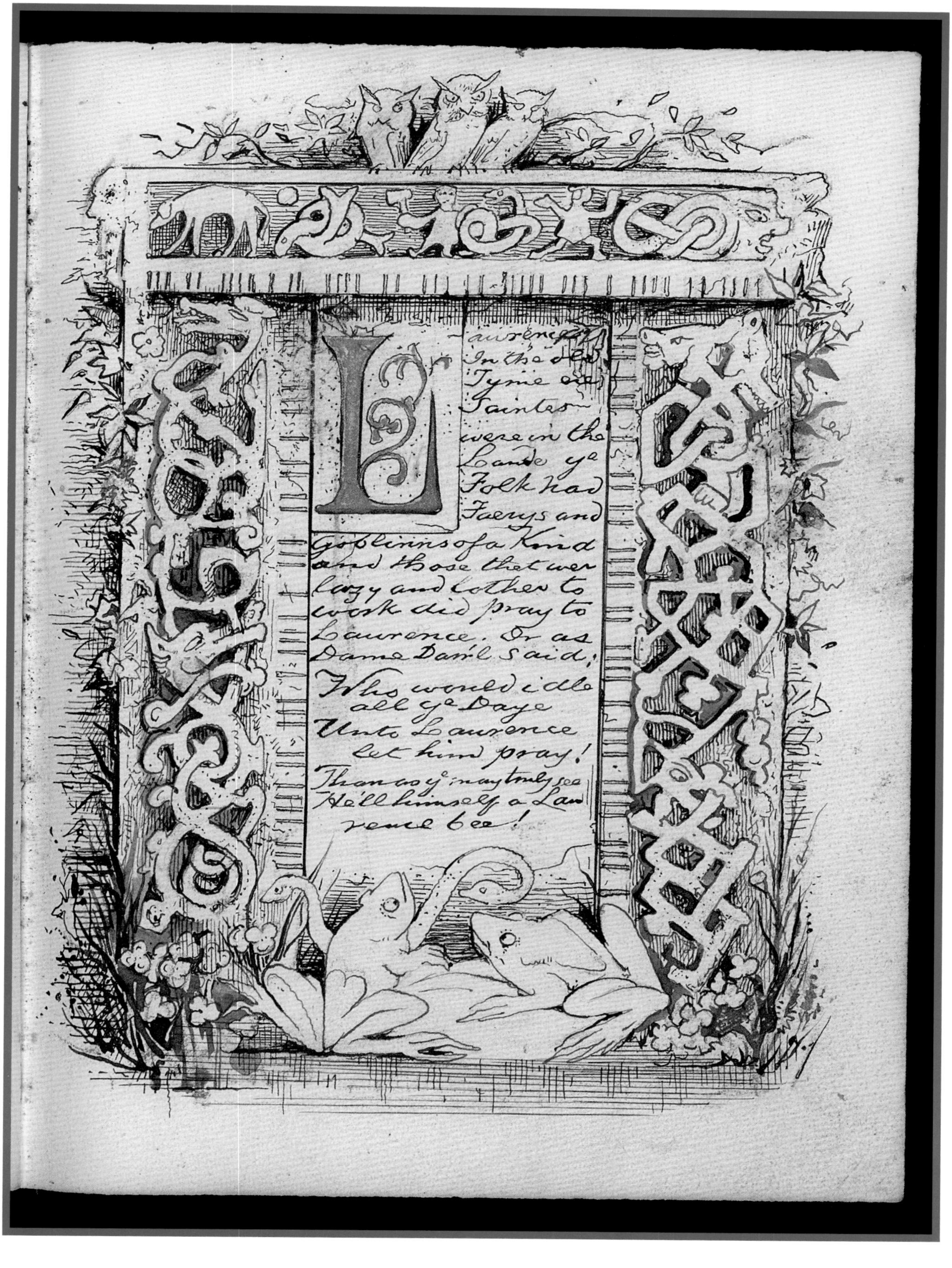
L
aurence
In the
Tyme
Saintes
were in the
Lande ye
Folk had
Faerys and
Goblinns of a Kind
and those that wer
lazy and lother to
work did pray to
Laurence. Or as
Dame Daril said;
Who would idle
all ye Daye
Unto Laurence
let him pray!
Than as ye may truly see
He'll himself a Lau
rence bee!

Ludlam. This I learned from a man who came fro the South he was from Surry. There is a great Caverne called Ludlam's Hole in which whilome dwelt a Witch called Dame Ludlam a white one who harmed none. When a man or woman had nede of aughte They went to the Hole and walkt thre times round itt making theyer prayer. And the morowe morn what they prayed for was ever found in the Entry to ye Caverne, Thus they did borrowe all they wanted. But one time a man borrowed her Kettle or Iron Pott, and did nott returne Itt. And She was so angered that from thet Day forth Mother Ludlam wold never lend or give aughte to Anybodee

Loterie is ye telling of fortunes or Divinatione in any Way and a Lott wife or Lott ollere is such a Witch for Lots be Fortunes and a Lote bye is a Lemman or Lyer-bye.

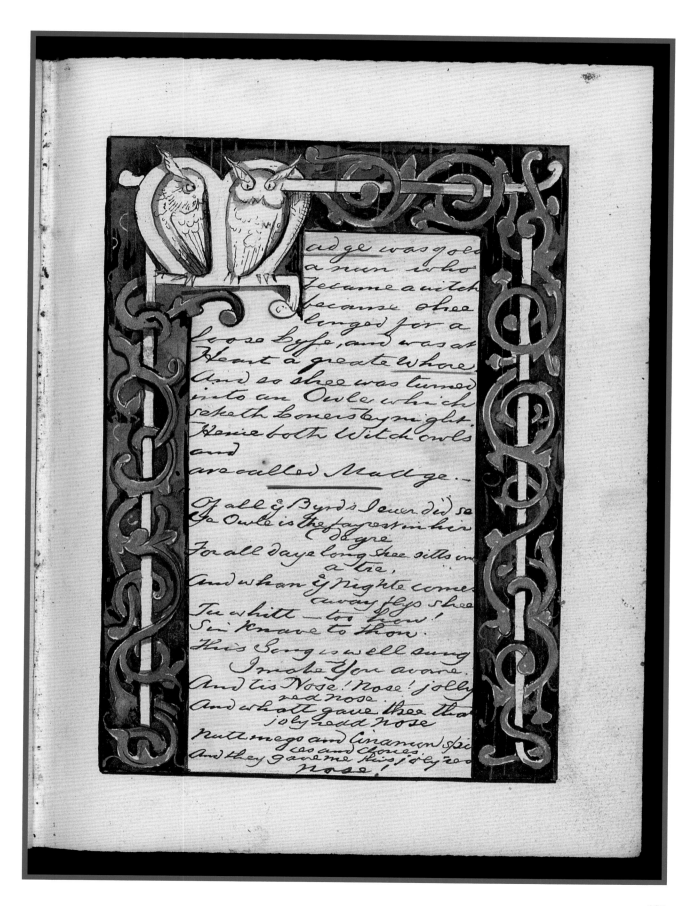

adge was once
a nun who
became a witch
because shee
longed for a
loose Lyfe, and was at
Heart a greate Whore.
And so shee was turned
into an Owle which
seketh Lovers by night.
Hence both Witch owls
and
are called Madge.—

Of all ẏ Byrd's I ever did se
Ye Owle is the fayrest in her
(degre
For all daye long shee sitts in
a tre,
And when ẏ Nighte comes
away flys shee
Tu whitt — too hoo!
Sir Knave to thou.
This Song is well sung
I make You aware,
And tis Nose! Nose! jolly
red nose.
And whatt gave thee that
joly redd nose
Nuttmegs and Cinamon spi
ces and Cloves.
And they gave me this joly red
Nose!

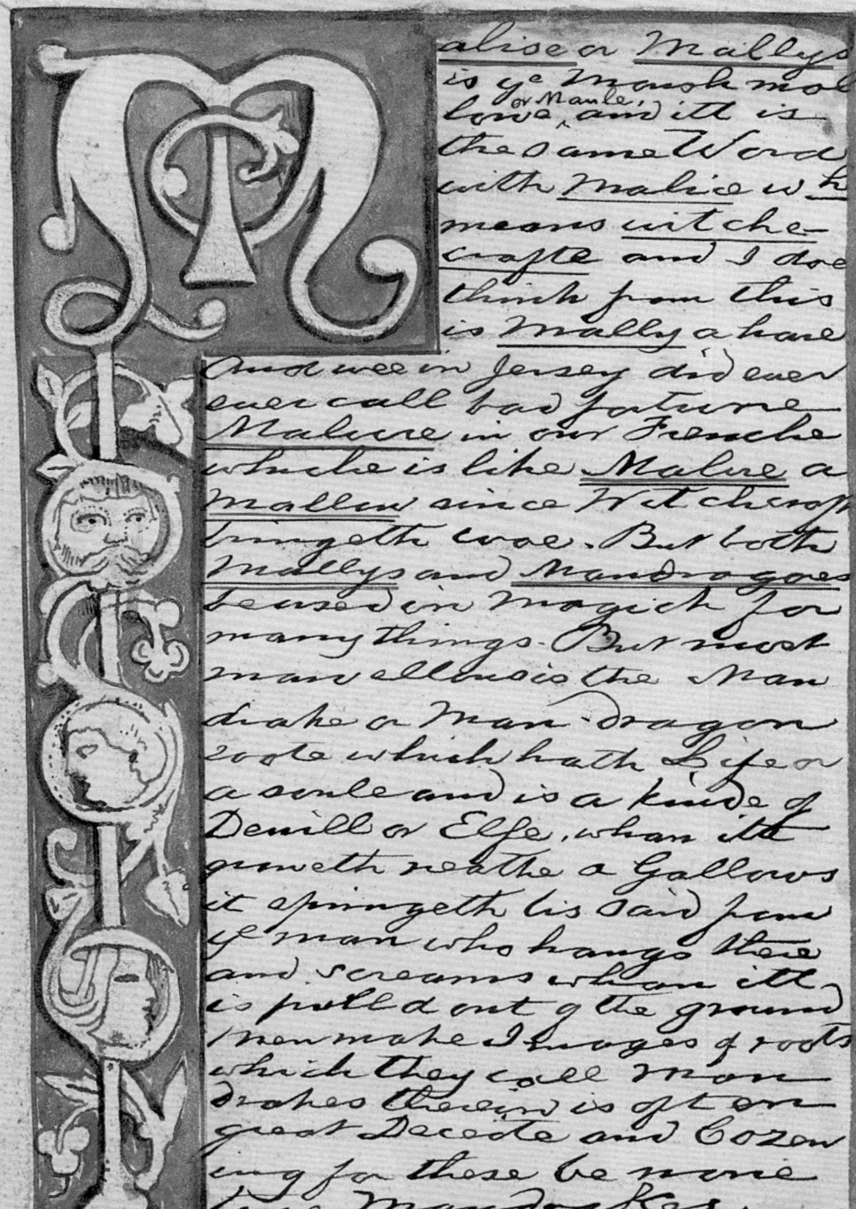

Malise a Mallys
is ye Marsh mal
lowe, or Maule, and itt is
the same Word
with Malice wh
means witche-
crafte and I doe
think from this
is Mally a hare
And wee in Jersey did ever
ever call bad fortune
Malure in our Frenche
which is like Malue a
Mallow since Witchcraft
bringeth woe. But both
Mallys and Mandragoes
be used in magick for
many things. But most
marvellous is the Man
drake or Man-dragon
roote which hath Life or
a soule and is a kinde of
Devill or Elfe, when itt
groweth neathe a Gallows
it springeth tis said from
ye man who hangs there
and screams when itt
is pulled out of the ground
Men make Images of roots
which they call Man
drakes therein is oft on
great Deceite and Cozen
ing for these be none
true Mandrakes.

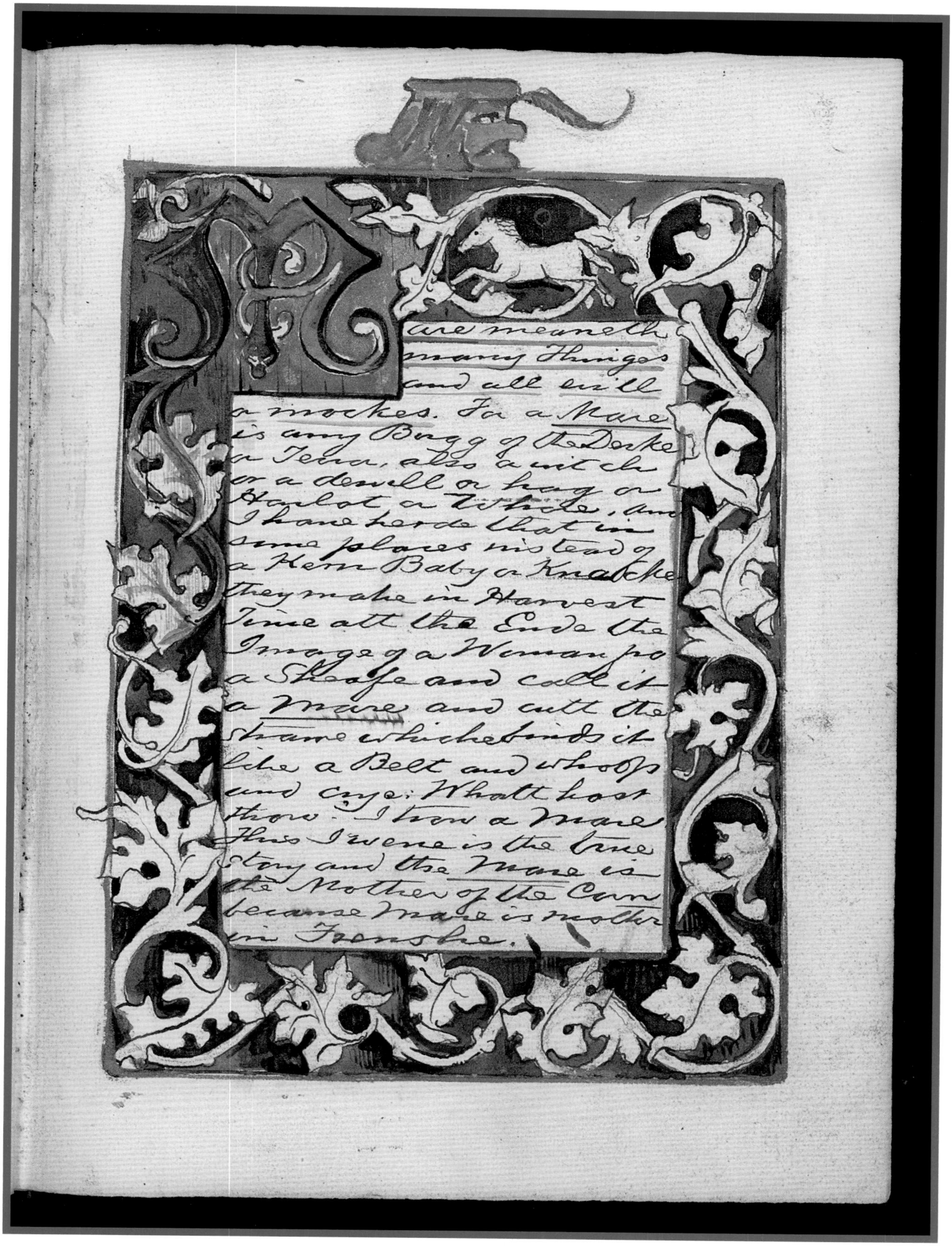

Mare meaneth
many Thinges
and all evill
or mockes. For a Mare
is anny Bogg of the Derke
or Terra, also a witche
or a devill or hag or
Harlot or Whore, and
I have herde that in
some places instead of
a Kern Baby or Knacke
they make in Harvest
Time att the Ende the
Image of a Woman fro
a Sheafe and call it
a Mare and cutt the
strawe whiche binds it
like a Belt and whoops
and crye: Whatt hast
thou - I have a Mare
This I wene is the true
story and the Mare is
the Mother of the Corn
because mare is mother
in Frenshe.

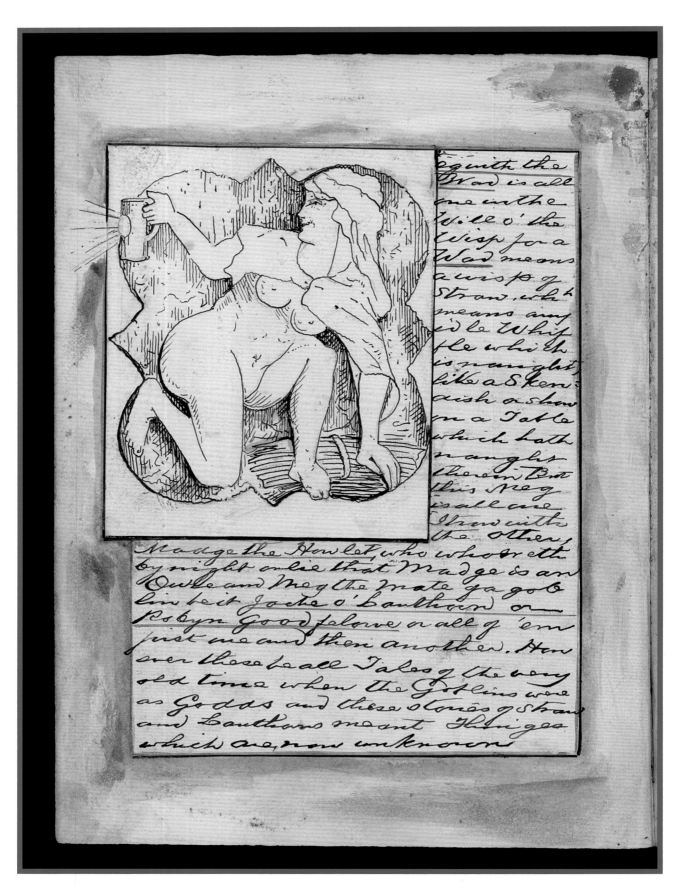

eginith the
Wad is all
one in the
Will o' the
Wisp for a
Wad means
a wisp of
Straw, wh[ch]
means any
idle Whif
fle which
is naught,
like a Sken=
dish a straw
on a Table
which hath
naught
therein But
this Meg
is all one
Straw with
the other,
Madge the Howlet, who whoreth
by night onlie that Madge is an
Owle and Meg the mate ga gob
lin be it Jocke o' Lanthorn or
Rsbyn Goodfelowe or all of 'em
just one and then another. How
ever these be all Tales of the very
old time when the Goblins were
as Godds and these stories of Straw
and Lanthorns meant Thinges
which are, now unknown

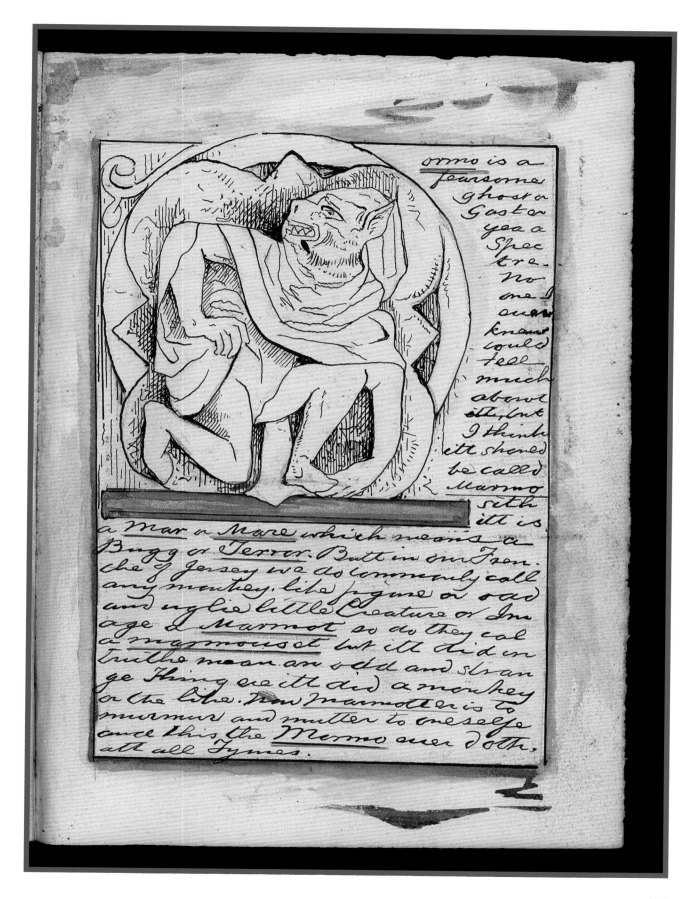

ormo is a fearsome ghost or Gast or yea a Spec-tre. No one I ever knew could tell much about itt, but I think itt should be called Marmo sith itt is a Mar or Mare which means a Bugg or Terror. Butt in our Fren-che of Jersey we do commonly call any monkey. like figure or odd and uglie little Creature or Im-age a Marmot so do they cal a marmouset but itt did in truthe mean an odd and stran-ge thing ere itt did a monkey or the like. Now marmotter is to murmur and mutter to oneselfe and this the Mormo ever doth att all Tymes.

Murch meneth a very little Man or a Golin but more a Devilkin because Murchy is also mischief hence men say The old Murchy! which is the old Devill and some say Mischty these Zee Southern folk. And some call the Devill. Mischief

Nick is a name for ye Devill yet it cometh not as Fooles say fro Seint Nicolas but from Nick or Neck a Spirit of ye Water who lives in Rivers or the Sea and was greately feared of old time. He was also called of old Nikir Hee dwelt in the cold sea I doe thinke that Nikkle as many doe cal Iccles, that is Ice Candles or Ice-shockles or Shoggles is all att one with Nickel the Spirit. He singeth often and men who have herd him say his Song is sad and sweete. He riseth up from the Water like a round Bulle or Bubble which is called a Nick, as is the round and rising Bottom of a pott or Bottel

The Night-bat or Night Mare tis all one and the same It is a woman Mare or Terror shee hath Winges of a batt some did call it the Night Raven which hath Feadthers. Of all which there be soe many tales and rimes that I might wel fill all this Booke with them as if it semed that all Bugges were Night mares

And of all Spels yt ever were spelled there is not one which is oftener said than one of the Night mare, to Sainte George al be it manne do maken itt Some to one Sainte and some to Another. And itt is thus. Firste ye shal say

In nomine Patris et Filii et Spiritus Sancta!
Sainte George our Ladys Knight
Hee walked by daye and eke by nighte,
Untill ye Night mare he found
Her hee beate and Her he bound
Till her Troth to him shee plite
Neer to come within his sighte
Thereas Sainte George our Lady's Knight
Named was three times thatt nighte.

And like unto this is another
" Sainte Wittold footed thrise ye Wold
Hee mett ye Nyt-mare and her 9 fold:
Hee bade her alighte
And her Troth plite
And aroynt thee witch, aroynt thee!
Aroynt means may thy necke be twistyd!

Noah's Arks
These be Clou-
des which do
seeme like
Arkes or Boats
or Shipps in
the Sky they
come before Raine or a
Storme. Itt is sayde how-
ever that they are truly
Shipps made by the
Witches and Warlaws
who lade them with
Hail Stones or Snow
and then caste itt adown
and all to shente and
spoyl the Corne and
Graine. There is a Tale of
a certain gentlyman
who was in a Castle by
a magnel which shotes
great stone balls. And
seeing above him a Noe's
Ark he with a Chalke
drew on a stone ball ye
Signe of a Cross and sayd
In Nomine Domini
and so shott at ye boat.

Then beholo ther fell
down from the Aire
a Witche, a faire
yonge Woman and
hee knew her for a
Ladye of greate Re-
noun shee begd him Nisen corde
being thus miscreed beggd Him
nat to mistreat her. And he sayd
Ile lett the goe and say naughte
iff thou leave thy Witchcrafft
and Become a Christene so must
thou now say a Paternostre so shee
ayd when all at ones there came
from the Boat above a Skelpe or shott
of Lightening and a bolte but itt
turned fro her and hurted her
not as she made the sign of the
Croſs. So he made her his Wife
and all went wel with them

Nut-Hake or Nutt-hàck
This name is by right
Nutt Hag, for it is
of a Bird which is
comonly held to bee a
Hag or a Witch for
a Jay is a whore and
a Jay pia or a Nutt
hacke is a chattering bird and eke a
woman who jaweth over much.
And I thinke that itt is also cold
a Jay-hawk, one who maketh
mischief. And whenn one will
say You Lie he cryeth Nutt
Hook, tis all ondamd y^e Same
for as all Roads lead to Rome all
these words meane Evil report.
Tis all one with a Night Hawks name.

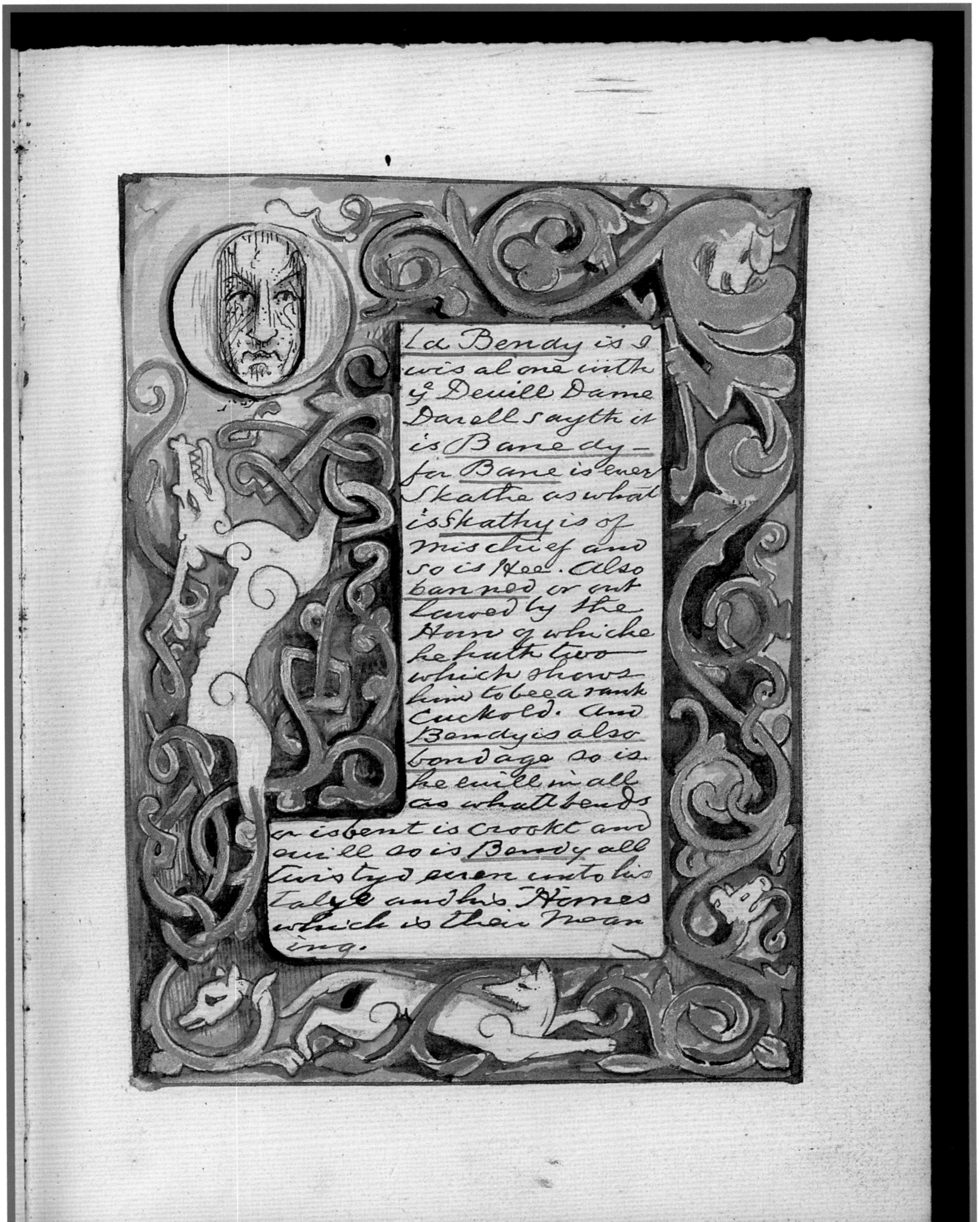

Ld Bendy is I
wis al one with
ye Devill Dame
Darell sayth it
is Banedy—
for Bane is ever
Skathe as what
is Skathy is of
mischief and
so is Hee. Also
banned or out
lawed by the
Horn of which e
he hath two
which shows
him to bee a rank
Cuckold. And
Bendy is also
bondage so is
he evill in all
as what bends
or is bent is crookt and
evill so is Bendy all
twistyd even unto his
Tayle and his Hornes
which is their mean
ing.

Old Shock is a
gobblin who is
is strange to see
very rough and
covered with long
Haire like a dog
or some say a
calf, so do many
call a hairy dog
a Shock. But
this is no good
Elfe, so do we call a man of bad
fame and Name a Shocker.
and a Good-for-Naught a shack
who is a ragged and worthlesse
felowe or Wafy. And this is one
with Shag or Shake as when one
hath to do with Werren, and a
lewde fellawe is a Shag-ragg.

There was a man of Beverley
who was ill treated by his
Town-folk, and all for nowt.
They cald him ye Shagg.
And it misliked him sore. One
night he mett with a strange
hairy kinde of man brute who
askt him: "Why so sadd?" He
answered "And why not, sith
all the Folk curse me and cal
me Shagg, and God wot I have

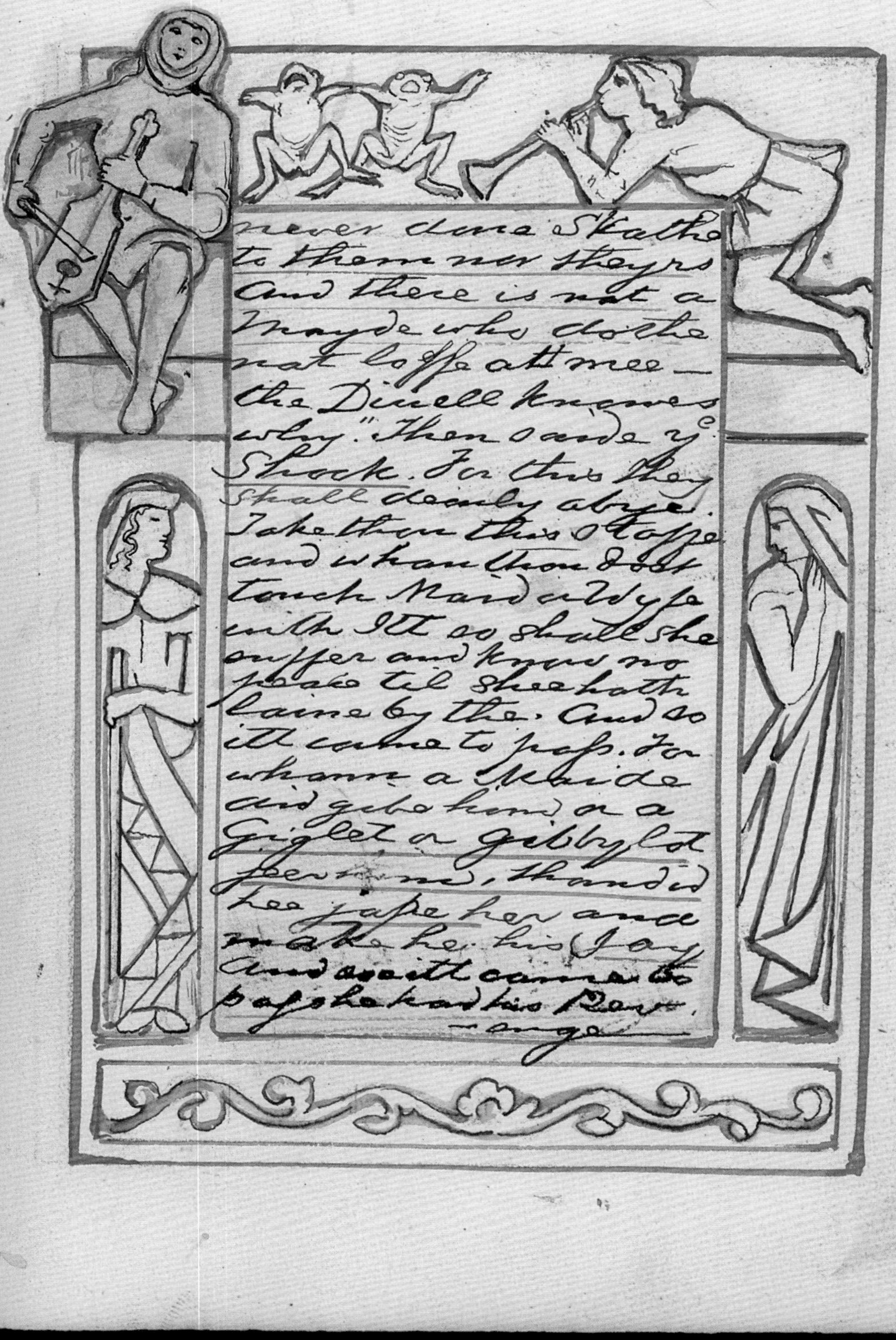

never dure Skathe
to them nor steyrs
And there is not a
Mayde who dothe
not loffe att mee —
the Divell knowes
why." Then sayde ye
Shook. For this they
shall dearly abye.
Take thou this Stoffe
and whan thou doest
touch Maid a Wyfe
with Itt so shall she
suffer and knowe no
peake til shee hath
laine by the. And so
itt came to pass. For
whann a Maide
did gibe him or a
Giglet or gibbylot
fleer at me, than did
hee jape her and
make her his Jay.
And as itt came to
pass he had his Reve-
-nge

Ouphe is an Elfe a Sprite or Faerie but many take it for a clumsie Goblinn like the Shack since we doe call a rude Fellow an Oafe. as if it were the Oneliest and Chief of Fools. But these bee of the Folke to whom all that is not an Angel is un-good and all Fays devills, which is to say that God filled all the Aire and Skye and Earthe yea and the Watres and Woodes with Devills and Hellikins, and all to worke Evill. Which the thing Dame Darell woulde in no wise believe, altho' common folke in theyr Faithe have twenty Bogles and Terrors for one Good Fairy. Which did but stablish as shee said yt ther was twentie times as much evill in Burrel Bulfinche and common Bors as in gentle Folke for the beter people be the betre do they thinke of all.

Phasmation
is all one with the a
Fantome or anye
Thinge that is fan-
tastic or fancical a
fantomy some call
em Fantasmes and
say they aren Ghosts
of Dead. This Dame
Damel did not alow
Shee held them to bee
born in many Wais
even from the idle
Thoughtes of Menn
which escaping take
on thin bodies of air
or thick vapour of po
Dreames of Love
making or are begotan
by Elves on Mayds
in Sleepe, or by the
Elves on one ano
ther. For al kind of
Life passeth into
Life anew as vapour
is born of Water —

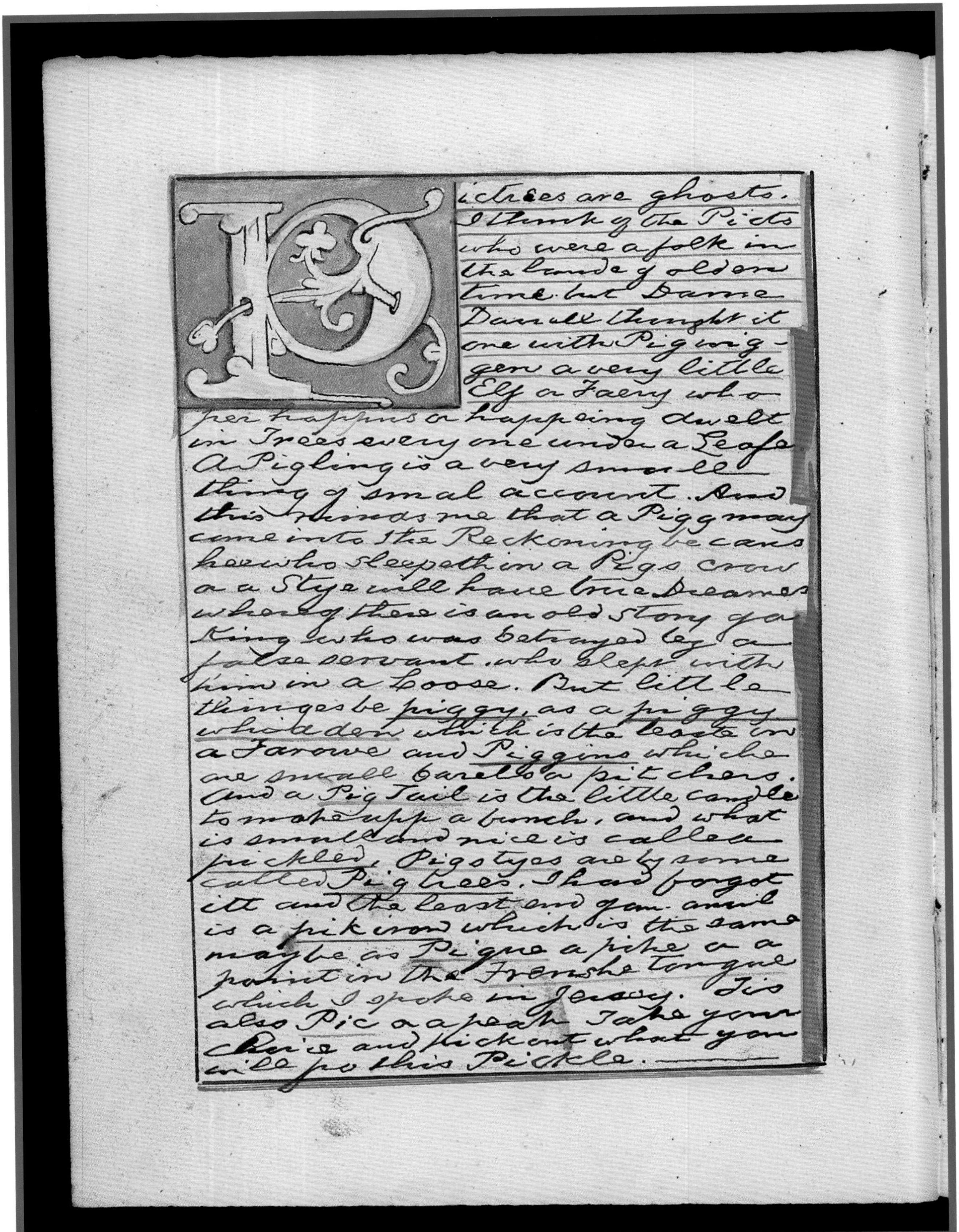
Pictrees are ghosts.
I think of the Picts
who were a folk in
the lande of olden
time but Dame
Darrell thought it
one with Pigwig-
gen a very little
Elf a Faery who
per happus or happening dwelt
in Trees every one under a Leafe
A Pigling is a very small
thing of smal account. And
this reminds me that a Pigg may
come into the Reckoning because
hee who sleepeth in a Pigs crow
or a Stye will have true Dreames
whereof there is an old Story of a
King who was betrayed by a
false servant, who slept with
him in a Loose. But little
thinges be piggy, as a piggy
whidden which is the leaste in
a Farowe and Piggins which
are small barells or pitchers.
And a Pig Tail is the little candle
to make upp a bunch, and what
is small and nice is called
pickled. Pigstyes are by some
called Pightees. I had forgot
itt and the least end of an anvil
is a pikiron which is the same
maybe as Pique a pike or a
point in the Frenshe tongue
which I spoke in Jersey. Tis
also Pic or a peak. Take your
choice and pick out what you
will for this Pickle.

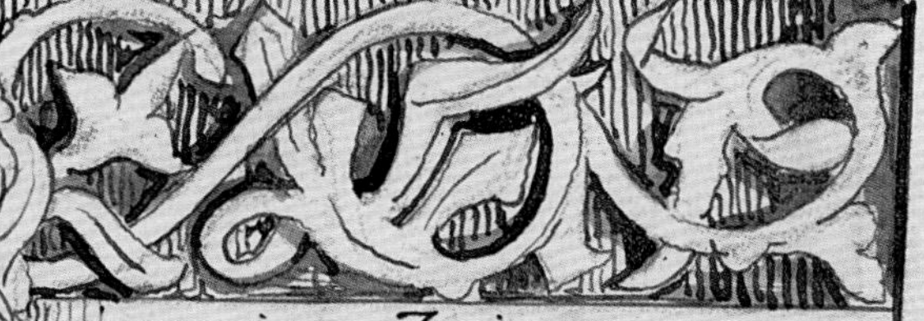

Pixy is a Fairey sume
haue itt of any kind
but they are I weene
of the Elves who
make Sporte and
Mischief with Men
I thinke they are of
the Pictes and
Piguiggem by the
Name. Some
feare to name
them. They often
rob orchards, a pick
fruit, that is pike
itt and then Pyke
away a pack off.
They lead folk as
tray and wilder
them than must
yee turn yer Cap
a your Coyve off
yee be a woman,
a your Coate off
year a Manne.
So from this are
men called turn
cotes who change
their minds for
Feare as many do
when are bested.

here is a litle folish song
known to all yett it is
a Song of a Pixy. that
is ———

Litel Jacke Horner
Satt in a Corner
Eating a Christmass Pye
He putt in his Thumbe
And puld out a Plumme
Loe whatt a good Boye
am I!

Now the Pixy hath hornes or
long Eares: tis all one, and the
Devill is calld Old Hornie
but the Pixy in a corner eating
a Pye or whatever the Housewife
giveth him is Jacke Horner
and of thatt yee may be sure
and lett on itt a Sixpence iff
ye have one.

illicock is a lewd and foul word, but I trow that ye al knaw whatt itt means, al ye Same. Itt is the Cockrel without ye Cobbs, or the Pipe ye Cornemuse without ye Bag. Dam Darell often said 'twas that which every Man had, and every Woman fain wold have. But Pillicok is in-deed not Arbor Vitae itself, but the Elfe or Faery or Sprite which dwelleth therein and inspirith it. Yee have heard a song which every graceless and lewde Garson and Bordjor in the Land can sing, how Pillicock sat upon Pillicock's hill, so that I need not give itt. But Dame Darrel wold have itt that this balade was a Conjuration or spel, tho' altered.

Pucke. Men thus call a merrie litel Elfe or Faery and Puckrels be verie smal Pucks which appeare in Glasses or Cristalls or Rings. But old Dame Darrel woued haue none of this, for she said that of later times Elues and Sprights and Goblins which were of yore all different are now all called one by the others' name as some were that all Buggs be Nightmares

Nowe al of this is as greate folye as to thinke that a Corn Bogle or any such Fantomy is a true ghost. For the true Pouk or Poorka as hee was of the olden time was a terrible Spirit, whom men did feare, more as a Fraying Devill than a joly merrie Elfe, and one who smelt more of brimstone then of Roses. And I have heard that there is a fearfull Spirit who liveth in ye Sea, and in great Waters, hee is named Phouka, and lieth in wayte to drowne all men. Also any ghost or Spectre is called a Puckle. I think this is to doe with Puckey, a marish or Quakemire a muddy swampie place where they wone, where there be polkes or pools. There bee many who wil aske mee what is the devill use in thus proking about among old gobs and rubbage words, and I reply, None at all to folke who have no name of any account, butt Gentil folk with faire Nomes or Nomina recken otherwise. And itt mostly befaleth that unlearn and lewde men be al one with Piggs.

Quede or Kwade wh
meaneth Evill is al
one and ye same
wi ye Devill. So
is a woman wi an
Evil Tongue who
bewrayeth and
scoldeth, sour as
sour, a Qued. For
shee maketh 'em
all queader and
Shake. And some
call a Prison a Quod all
because tis a bad place.
I doe thinke that a Qued
may be a Goblin who
is right grum or grumpy
ever griffling and
grugging for such ther
bee among Elves as among
Menn and Wemen too
God wot. I would that
I did not know itt to
my Sorowe. Now I know
that I have but littel Lea
rning, but whatt I have I have
got as Dickon said of his Sheeps.
and this I doe beleeve that man
or woman who has Lere tho' itt
bee never so little is beter than
any Lorde who can not reade or
write for Lorde folk who knowen
naught of Letters must take all
they know from Clerkes and beleeve many a Lye. as it is sayd
the Blind eten many Flyes
and he who can not reade is
as blind as a Batt.

Quimby is I wene ye Elfe who dwelleth in every Quim, and a wanton and lewde Sprite itt is which doth more mischief than all others put togeder. Now this word quim as Dame Darell told me is Welsh or Cwm which meaneth a clefte in a Bank, or a Gulley through which mostly runns a littel Streame. Some do call it Quem, and others also Quent or Queint, also another word which is kin to Quent. Now Quimby is to a Woman what Pillicock is to a Man, They seeme to me to be like the Paddocks or Froggs which ye see in Churches Hee and Shee gaping one another in Sinn with Leacherous Eyes.

R
agamoffin is commonly enow heard yt is a poor devill all in rags. But Dame Dard wold have itt she had heard there was y olde a certain devill or a Impe who was so-cald because he did ever goe about in raggs shee sayd to rag meant to beg or goe a tramping, and maffin a Moffin a simple fellowe. There y all, I saye naughte but truly I have heard a story which semeth to fit into this.

There was an honest
Jankin a good fel
lawe it befel that
one night late when
riding home by ye
Light o ye Moone
hee was throwne
into a river and
well-ny drowned.
So down streame he
went swimmyng but just as he
deemed he should sinke hee saw
on the shore a man who putt
forth his Arme till it was
as long as a church steaple
it may be a hundred yards
and caught holt of hym
and drew him ashore. Then
he saw that ye Man who
had rescowed him was all
in Rags unkempt and
a Ragg Robin indeed. Then
he thought the Ragamuffin
and said Wilt thou have
my horse, it is all I have to
geve thee. Nay answered the
ragged man but if thou
wilt change thy Coat wi'
me Ile be well Contented.
But sweare to me that thou
wilt weare my coate till
thou art in thy House. Ay
Ile do that said Jankin —

o hee set forth too walk homeway but at every Step his Coate became so heavie that he could hardly stand, till he was in his house and his wife cryed, Jesus! who hath shente thee so Beest thou been pilled by Theeves, nay he replyed but I met with a man who hath played a jape upon me and made me swere to weare this Coate home I thinke it wayes a hundred pound. As he tooke it of there heard something jingle jingle and loe the pokets were all full of coine in good money but all very old. So hee became very rich, and a Knight and hee put a Ragged Robin flower into his Shield. This tale hath a fine moral which is that a tattered coate may cover a good fellow.

alpho or Ralph.— This is a Goblyn of whom wee know but littel hee maketh noyses in ye Houses when ye Children heare a tapping and rapping in the walls they saye: That is Ralph! Dame Darzell saide that of Olde Ralph or Rolfe did mean a lustful Wolfe or one who was mad to couple with the Shee-wolfe in the tongue of the people gold. And Ralfe was I wene whatt we call in Jersey a Loup garow or a weer wolf. sith he is called to frighten Children. It is I do think a strange name to give to Chrisom Children and call em Leacherous Wolves after a devill but many doe it here in Yorks.

Riding Hagg. That
is a Night mare
Some doe call it
the Witch's Riding.
Yett do these troub-
les and deadlie
Dreames not al-
wayes come fro wit-
ches. There is a merrie but unseeme-
ly Tale how a certain Gentilman
who had a faire and very lusty
Wife who was always maris
appetens, did suffer from ye
Nightmare every nighte and
naught could rid him there
from tho' he went to the doctor
or the priest every day for
possets or prayers. But one day
hee came as crous and fryke
as a friskin and cride in joy
to the Frere. "Wish me joye
for I have found out whatt
ailed me and 'twas neither
my Belly riff nor my Brain yt
were in Faulte. And whatt was
it than asked the Frere in grete
merveil. "Truly replied the
Husband. "It was naught but
my wife Jeaneton who while
I slepte did helpen herself
to a ride. For she was Salt.—

obyn Good fellow, his name is soe
wel Knowne that for many Folk
itt is the Same with every Kind
of Faery and Elphe or Goblin. —
Dame Darell did say that hee
was of the newer kinde for Rob
or Robin is a name for any
Good felowe who loveth a Pott
and a Paramoure, but shee did
thinke him one with Duse or
the Deuce who is a merrie litel
Elfe who mockes Maides and
Lies wi' 'em. So They say.

Rana is the Latin for a Frog or a Paddock as some do call a Toad. But a Paddocke is trewly a Frogg and Ile tell yee why. For a pad or pat is a foot as in Frenshe it is spied and ther is among us a Frog Goblin called Pad-foot who liveth in marishes and by water. Howbeit all Frogges are Goblins. Iff ye never hurte a Frog and will kepe one in your House by you, in a Piggin or Jar of Water, all Winter, itt will be well contente and bring you Lucke above all in Love and with faire Women. Try itt quod Shee.

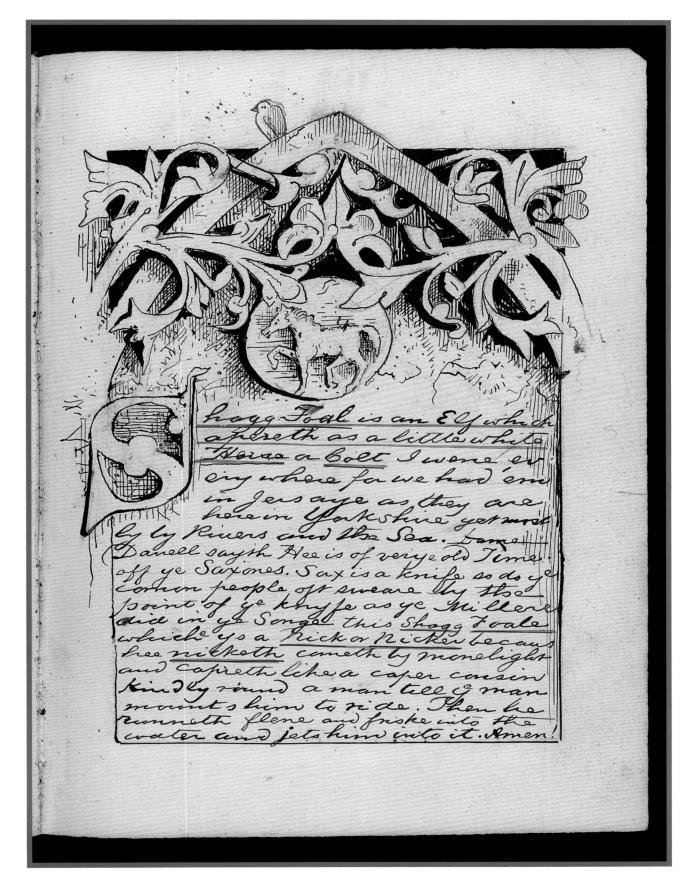

Shagg Foal is an Elf which
apereth as a little white
Horse a Colt I wene ev
ery where for we had 'em
in Jersaye as they are
here in Yorkshire yet most
ly by Rivers and the Sea. Dame
Darell sayth Hee is of verye old Time
off ye Saxones. Sax is a knife so do ye
common people oft sweare by the
point of ye knyffe as ye Millere
did in ye Songe this Shagg Foale
which ys a Nick or Nicker becaus
hee nicketh cometh by monelight
and capireth like a caper cousin
kindly round a man till ye man
mounts him to ride. Then he
runneth flene and friske into the
water and jets him into it. Amen!

Sooner is a kind of spectre or a ghost. It is not a worde oft ene heard. Dame D thinks it is a kind of Visione seen by them who are in a Soone or Dreame as the Scotch see them in second sighte. It may be for at such times as in a Dreame wee can behold strange things such as live betweene this Life and the next or as it were in the Hall, or the Entree Porche betweene Out doors and In-doors and of this kinde I weene is the Sooner.

Spellicoat is a kind of
ghost but iff ye will
have my Mind o't,
it is the Same as the
Shelly-coat who is
a Goblin of the Sea or
Waters thereby, who,
is all overgrowne wi'
shels and scales
and the like such
as gather on Ships
botomes. Dame Darel thinkes it
may be Pelle coat or a coat of
sheeps pelts for there are many
tales of wild folk and goblins who
ever apeare in such a garb and
soe the two names were mixt
and no wonder sith it is all
among ignorante and unlered
Folk that these Names are moste
And the reason is that such people
live more in the Wildernesses or
Forestes, or by the Sea where the
Fairies and all theyr kinde doe
most abounde, so itt cometh
to pass that they knowe more
of such lore: be seen things than
any (as cept a He-witch) who lives
in Citys. For such Uncouthes
love best lonelie and darke
places afar from Townes. ___

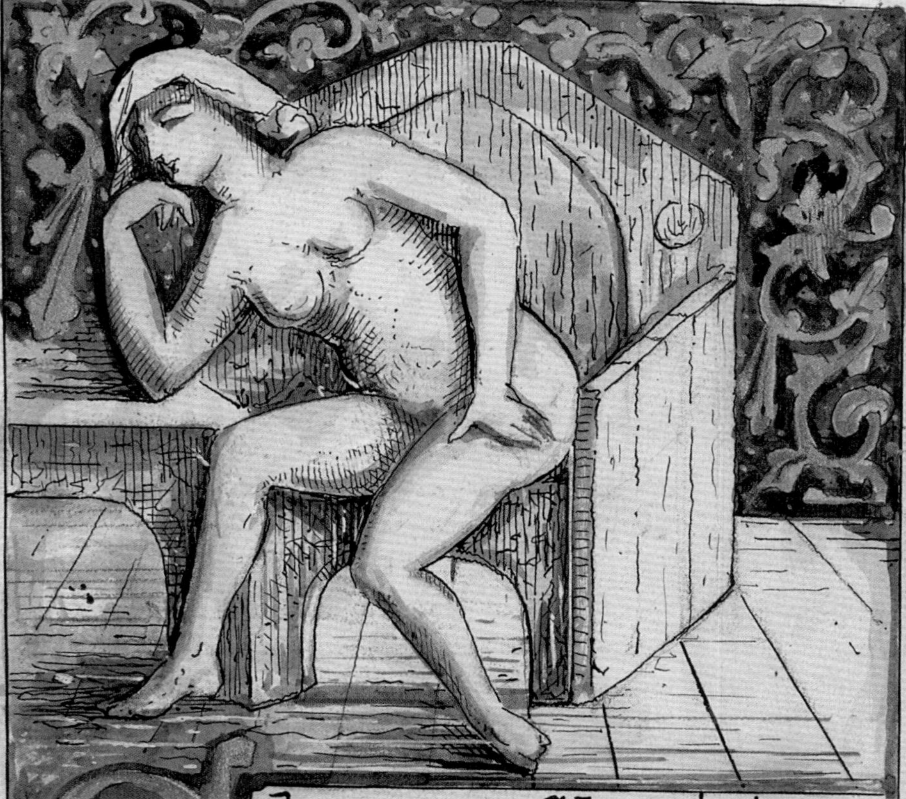

Spoorne or Sporn 'tis all one that is a Spret or a Sprite seldome seene by any save in its tracks a Spur which It leaveth in duste in Sommertime but in the Snowe in Winter. And in summere these tracks be like those of Geese tho there bee neer a Goose in the land, but in Winter they are like ye printes of Asses hoofs and are comon enow.

Stry is a witche just to an inche. A learned man told me thatt it was a Latin word cut down a litel for use as on trims a collop of meate to eate and that ye Worde was Strygga. Itt may be buth as to stry is to distroy and spoile. I thinke with Dame Dazel that the Folk who call'em Strys meaned that and no more. How ever iff any one will believe that the 2 wordes together made a third even as a man and a woman make a Babe Ile nott saye that he hath not reason. And yett againe to Strye is to cure tho' itt be none so comon a word hereabouts, and manye Witches do cure the Sicke with theyr Medicaments and that so well that most Folk putt more Faithe in them than in all the Phisitiouns also doe they coste far less Expenses as ye Saw is:

Doctors be Angels when they come to thee:
But are as Devills when they want theyr Fee.

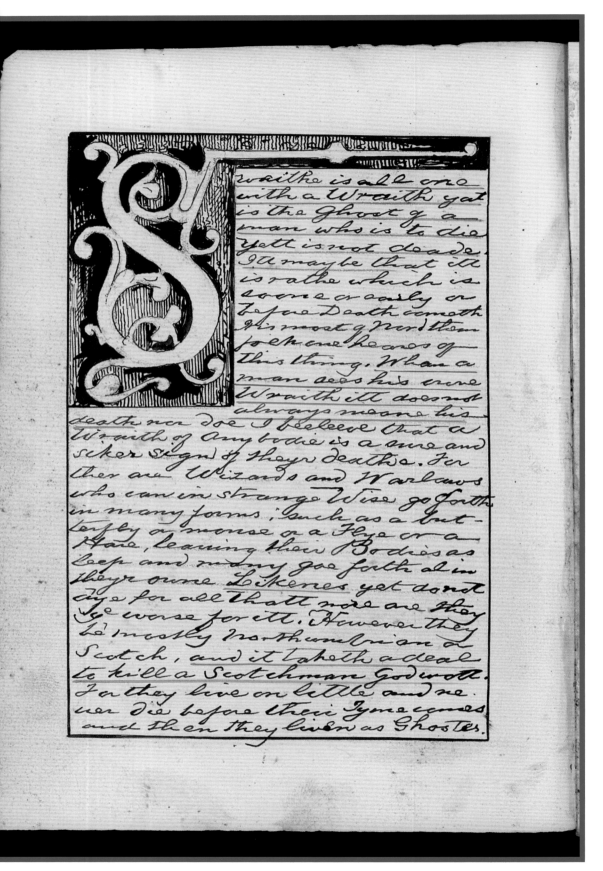

Swaithe is all one with a Wraith yat is the Ghost of a man who is to die yett is not deade. Itt maybe that itt is rathe which is soone or early or before Death cometh. Itt is most of Northern folk one heares of this thing. When a man sees his owne Wraith itt doesnt always meane his death nor doe I beeleeve that a Wraith of anybodie is a sure and siker signe of theyr deathes. For ther are Wizards and Warlocks who can in strange Wise go forth in many forms, such as a butterfly or a mouse or a Flye or a Hare, leaving their Bodies asleep and many goe forth al in theyr owne Likenes yet donnot dye for all thatt nore are they ye worse for itt. However they be mostly Northumbrian or Scotch, and it taketh a deal to kill a Scotchman Godwott. For they live on little and never die before their Tyme comes and then they liven as Ghostes.

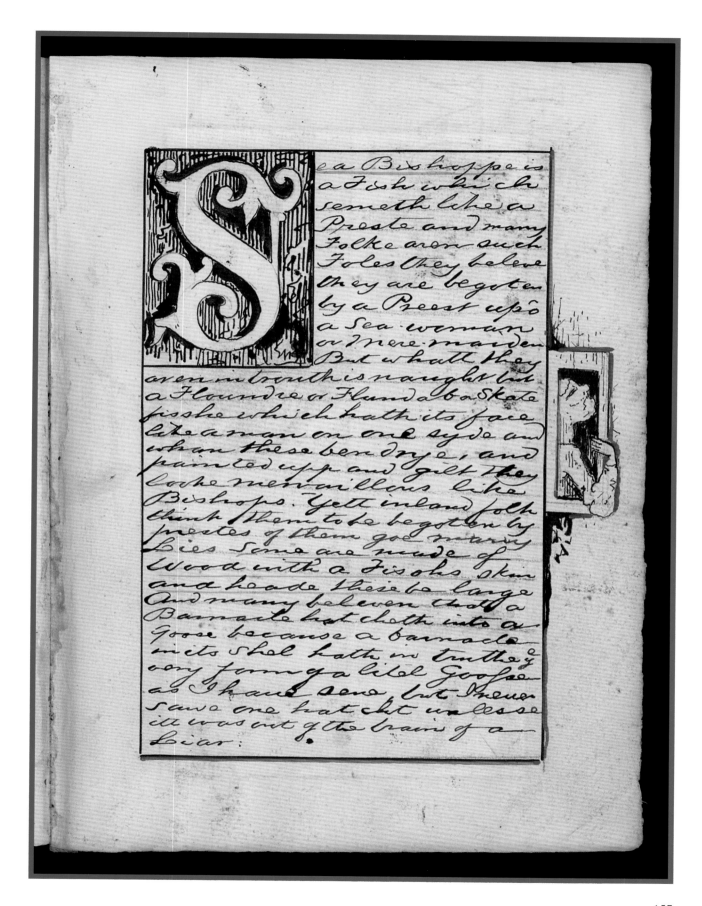

Sea Bishoppe is a Fish which semeth like a Preste and many Folke aren such Foles they beleve they are begoten by a Preest upō a Sea-woman or Mere-maiden But whatt they aren in trouth is naught but a Floundre or Flunda ba Skate fisshe which hath its face like a man on one syde and whan these ben drye, and painted upp and gilt they looke merveillous like Bishops. Yett inland folk think them to be begotten by prestes of them goe many Lies Some are made of Wood with a Fisshs skin and heade these be large And many beleven that a Barnacle hatcheth into a Goose because a barnacle in its Shel hath in truthe ye very forme of a litel Goose as I have sene but I never sawe one hatchit unlesse itt was out of the brain of a Liar:

T hrumcap
or Thrummy is
a drole and wan
ton Impe or Gobb
lin or Elfe, but
a Jackanapes sat
allone with Faerys
in this kind doe haunt
old Ruines and abene
all old Castles. Dame
Darel said twas Hodekin
and that theye ghosts of
pore Children who were slain
afore time of old when a Castle
was builded to bringe good For
tune to itt Twas a Sacrifice to
their Goads I feare itt was only
too true. Thrum seemes an old man

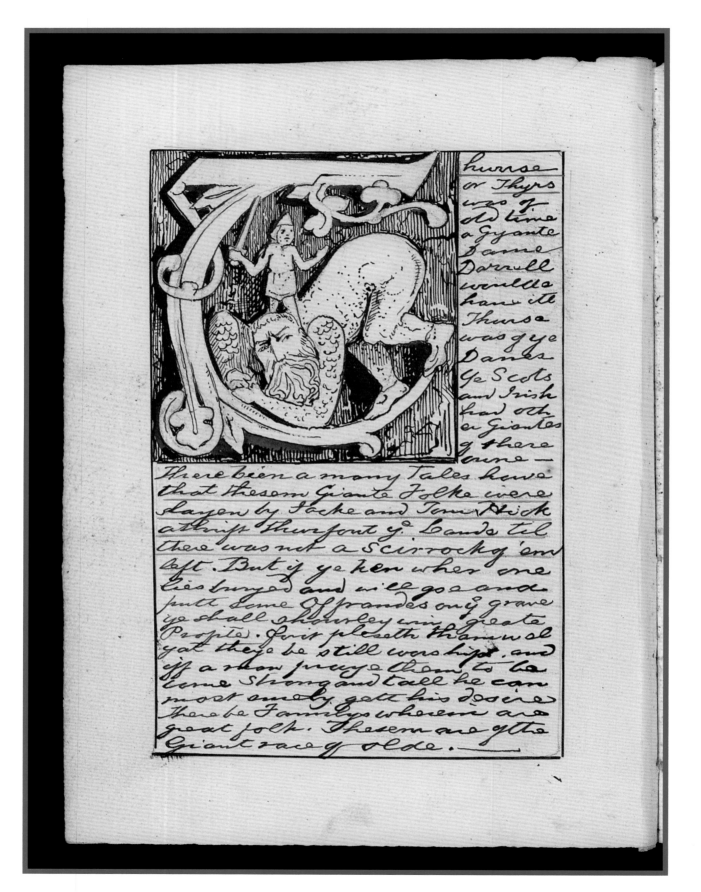

hurse or Thyrs was of old time a Gyante Dame Darrell woullde have itt Thurse was of ye Danes ye Scots and Irish had other Giantes of there owne—

There been a many Tales have that thesem Giante Folke were slayen by Jacke and Tom Hick atthrift thurfout ye Lands til there was not a Scirrock of 'em left. But if ye ken wher one lies buryed and will goe and putt some Offrandes on ye grave ye shall shourley win greate Proffite. For it pleseth themmsel yat theye be still worshipt, and iff a man preye them to become Strong and tall he can most surely gett his desire there be Familys wherein are great folk. Thesem are of the Giant race of olde.—

hirce a Thurce is
I wonse all one in
Thrisse a giant
yett many have it
tis a goblin or an
Elfe or a mischevi-
ous kind or kin —
Or else tis a ghost
or a Duse or the Deu
ce himselfe, lest him
who knows speak out tis a pin
which I can not unravel. I
weene twas all the same as
Tib and Tom among 'em.

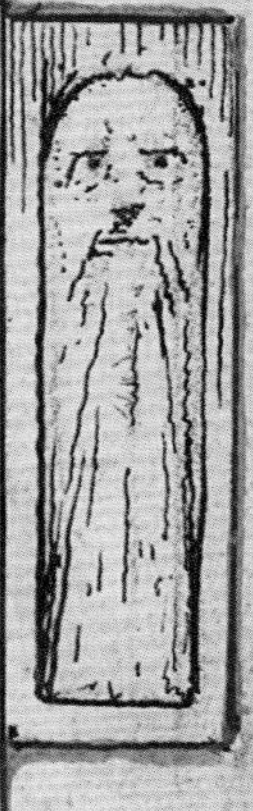

ilsterre is a negro-
mancer a sorcer
a magician one
who maketh his
living and layeth
his hunger by rai
sing the deade.
Some of these m bee
wise men and
as many more greate Knaves
and cozeneres, truly they will
coze with any one like a cosin
cossing and costning him but
in the end the pore fonde who
hoped to have ye Devills
treasoury of golde findes him
selfe with devill a Penny.

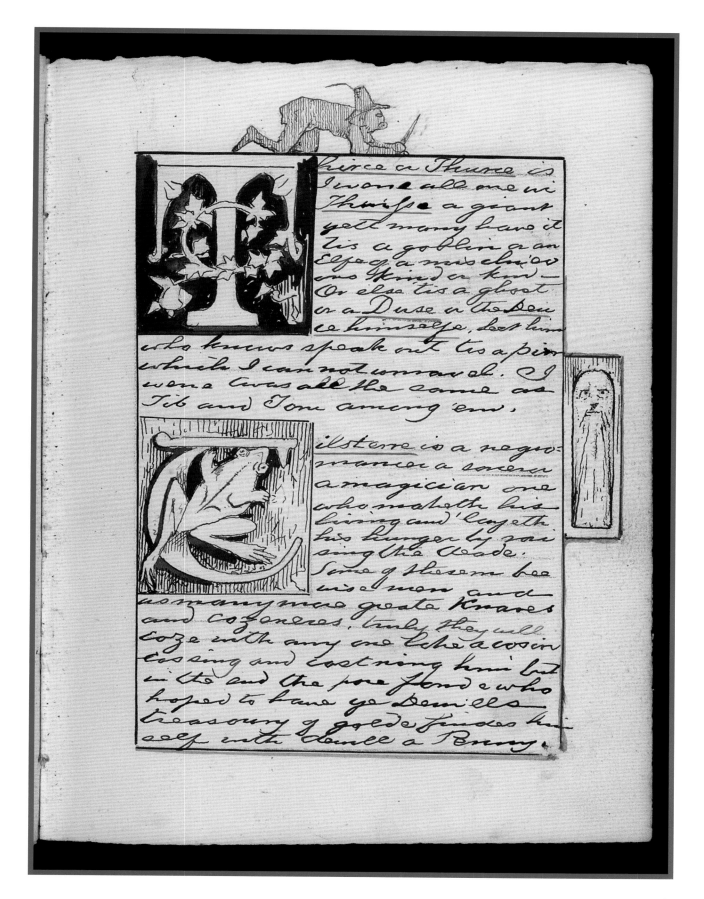

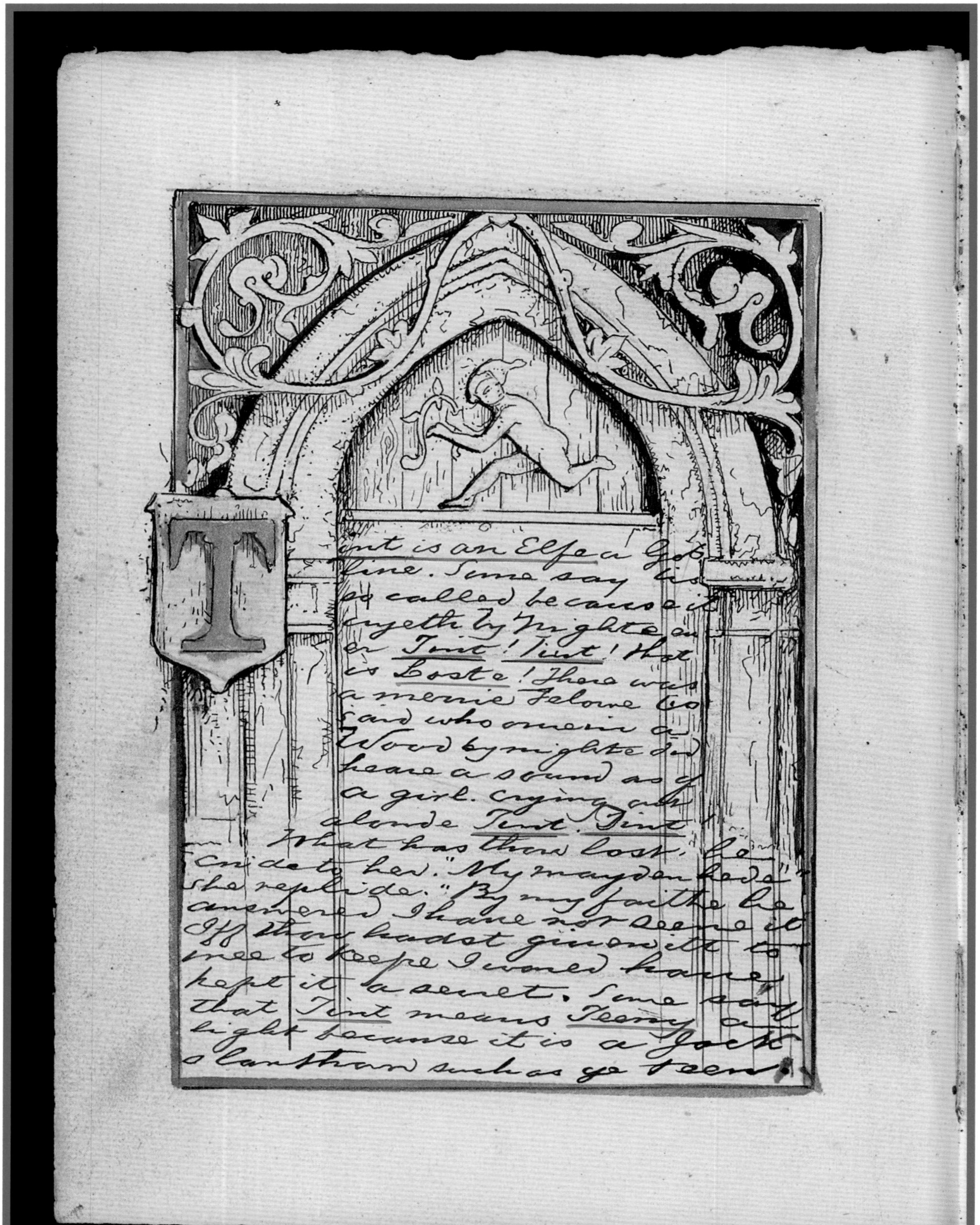

Tint is an Elfe a Gob-
line. Sume say tis
so called because it
cryeth by Nighte ev-
er Tint! Tint! that
is Loste! There was
a merrie Felowe lo-
sand who [illegible] a
Wood by nighte did
heare a sound as of
a girl. crying al-
aloude Tint. Tint!
What has thou lost, he
cride to her. "My mayden hede"
she replide. "By my faithe he
answered I have not seene it
Iff thou hadst given itt to
mee to keepe I would have
kept it a secret. Sume say
that Tint means Teeny a
light because it is a Jack
a lanthorn such as ye seen.

od Lowry. This is a
dismall sprite a
Bugg. Dame Dar-
zell explaned that
itt is a death gob-
lin. Tod is a word
for dead and Larr
a sprite who ch-
feareth men and
skereth them awaye. Larren
are Ghosts of ye olden Time they
are oftenest sene in ruines
of olde dayes where Romanes
dwelt for Dame Darzell said
ye Name was Latine. A tod
is an Ivy bushe therein Owles
and Elves do comonly en-
habite as doth the Ivy girle
of whom I forgate to write.
Shee is the Sprite a Faerye
of the Ivy bringeth Lucke to
those who spare her Bines
Tis wel to plant them as they
growe those who have them
will be protectede and favoured by their Lades as the
Ivie protecteth away the
Raine and Hail. The Ivy lefe
hath five points when it is ful
younge but only one when
olde so man loseth his 4
Senses till only one is lefte.

Tom Tumbler and Tom Poker are ye Names of a Goblin or Fandey whom I knowe littel save that hys name is uset to fretten Childre, and that ther are Men who swere by the Roley poly and the Tumbling Tom. This is as I deeme a fantom who appears tumbling Head over heels as hee goes on, or rolling over and over, like a bird which pretendeth to be wounded and goes lame to make men chase her, to get them afar from her young ones. Or a Tumbler-dogge.

Toot is the Devill I ween hee is so-called because Hee is ever tooting about and prying here and ther. I did here this word fro a Scotchman wheder itt bee right I will not say. Toot is to blow a Horne and the Devill hath Hornes so is hee the Tuter of all Sinners.

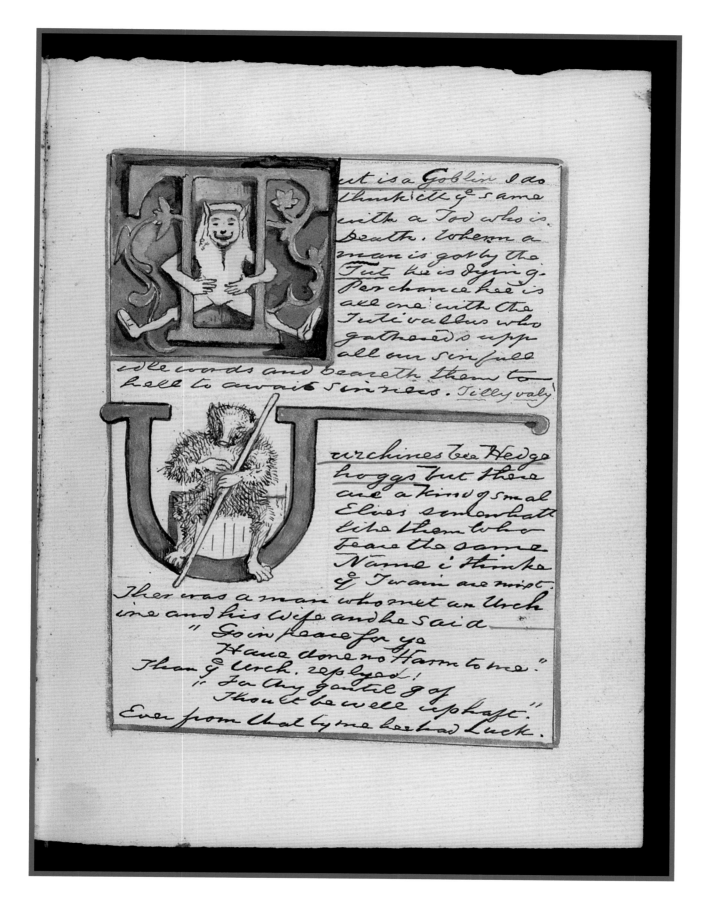

ut is a Goblin I do think ye same with a Tod who is Death. Whenn a man is got by the Tut he is dying. Perchance hee is all one with the Tutivallus who gathered up all our sinfull idle words and beareth them to hell to await sinners. Tillyvaly!

rchines bee Hedgehoggs but these are a kind of smal Elves somewhatt like them who beare the same Name i thinke ye Twain are mixt.
Ther was a man who met an Urchine and his Wife and he said

" Go in peace for ye
Have done no Harm to me."
Than ye Urch. replyed:
" In thy gentil gof
Thou'lt be well uphapt."

Ever from that tyme hee had Luck.

Waff is a sperit or ghost, I trow tis all one with an Ouphe or Oaf. but there is ye same word for ye Flame of fire when it is blown and moves like a living being. This brings itt to one with Hob Thrush or Jack o' Lanthorne, which is like a living and moving Flame. Waff is also a foul earthly smel, as in a church-yard or a Vaulte. Tis I thinke an evill spirit of ill smels if not of magic spels. But the word cometh from waving by a wind or being puft up, as whatever moves about is a waff and so these sprites are ever on the go and swepen here and there sans repos, volant tojors.

Waith semes to be all at
one with Wraith sens
it meanes the same
Thinge which is the
ghost of anie one not
as yett deade, however
tis an old worde that
straying away or a:
bout losely is wathe, even so
do waiths stray, as men say
Wathes walken wyde for when
ye Soul goes out of ye Body
itt strayethe fast and farre in
wyld places by lonely water
fals and woody Torrents, and
a Waithe is also any Evill
and itt may bee anie Evill
Sprite, a Esprit malin.

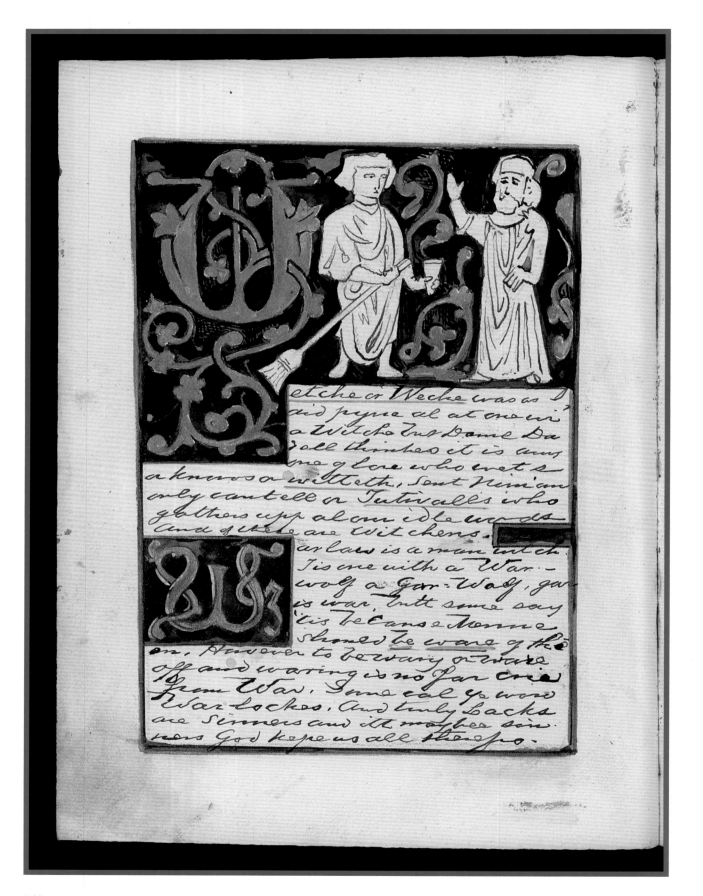

etche or Weche was as I
aid pyne al at one wi'
a Witche but Dame Da
ball thinkes it is amus
me of love who wet s
a knows a witteth, sent Nim i an
only cantell or Tutivalles who
gathers upp al our idle words
And of these are Witchens.

arlocs is a man witch.
Tis one with a War-
wolf a Gar-Wolf, gar
is war, butt some say
'tis because Menne
shoued be ware of the
m. However to be wary or ware
off and waring is no far crie
from War. Some cal ye wone
Warlockes. And truly Lockes
are Sinners and itt maybee sinners God kepe us all therefro.

Whit witch or White W[izard] is one who maketh his work without ye Devil or Sinne, as one that calleth Angells and not fendes doth al acordyn to Christen love. They doe make more accounte of their bookes and learning than doe ye black witches, for ye Divill loveth not Latin and the White wizzerd ever giveth him a Belly ful of itt. Hence itt came that the whit wizards were or are for the most, broken preests or some times whole ones. They make great accounpte to find treasures in old Ruines, things lost or Stolen, most of all to raise Spirites, and sell Religues, Charms, Amuletts, Luck-stones, blessed medals. Some are wise and many other wise, some good but more are whipp-Jackes and telers, cozeners and picaros. For many of them with all their Aves are but Knaves.

Wierde is the Fate or lucke or Un-lucke or Fortune to which a man is marked and apoynted. — So Witches and Dyviners are called

Wierde Women or Wyves because they tell a person his or her fortune: as Dame Darcell said what will be werdaned I knowe not ye Word, tis like ord=ayned. Now as a Wight is a Witch because she is wighty or strong and wise, so hath a Wierde — Wightness according as itt faleth to a man. So to Drie a Wiard is to suffer what penaunce one hath I thinke it is as if one were a-thirst or driend or dry. and must beare with it. and truly this is to many an old Trowl the Bowl or Tospott the worst penance which he knows of iff hee have no Beer.

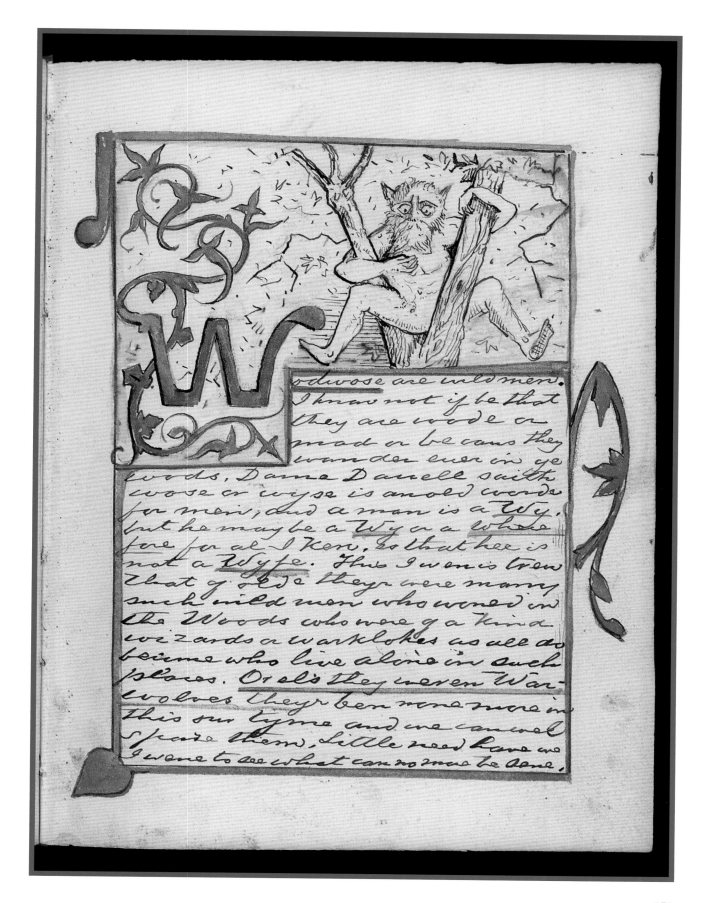

Wodwose are wild men.
I knaw not if be that
they are wode or
mad or be caus they
wander ever in ye
woods, Dame Darell saith
wose or wyse is an old worde
for men; and a man is a Wy,
but he may be a Wy or a Whose
fere for al I Ken, so that hee is
not a Wyfe. This I wen is trew
that of olde theyr were many
such wild men who woned in
the Woods who were of a Kind
wizards or warklokes as all do
become who live alone in such
places. Or el's they weren Warwolves theyr ben none more in
this our tyme and we cannot
speake them, Little need have we
I wene to see what can no more be done.

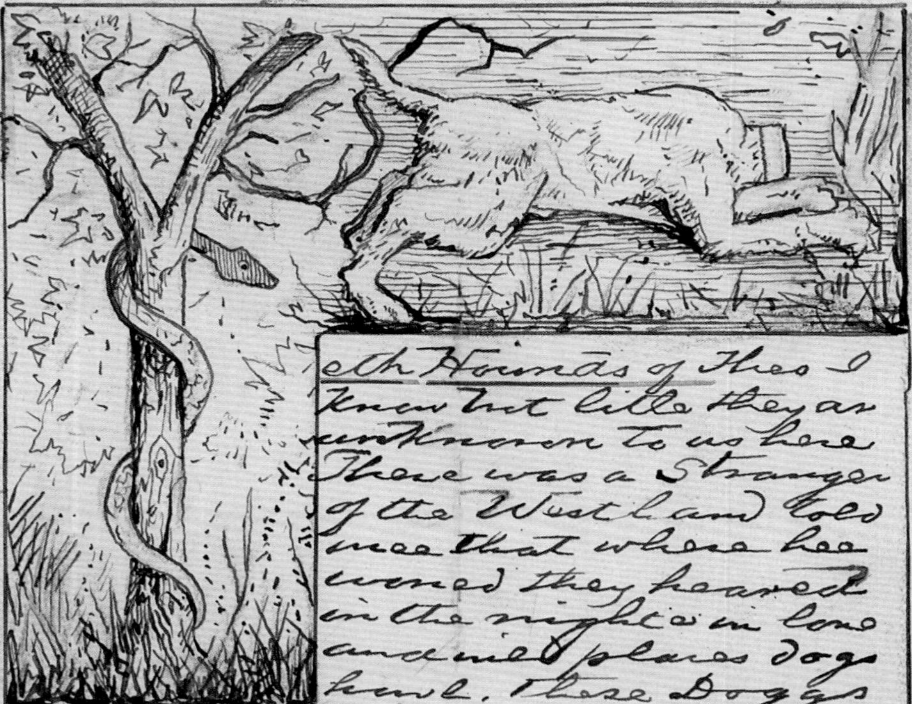

eth Hounds of thes I knew but litle they ar unknown to us here There was a Stranger of the West land told mee that where hee woned they heared in the night in lone and wild places dogs howl. these Doggs had no Heads. Also tis said the sprites of children who have mist theyr Baptism do so wayle and cry in the Woods, If they be of one kind I can not tell. Dame Darrell thinks Yeth is all the one with Sleuth Hound which is a dog that foloweth a track or slot as it dothe get or goeth. tis al one to mee.

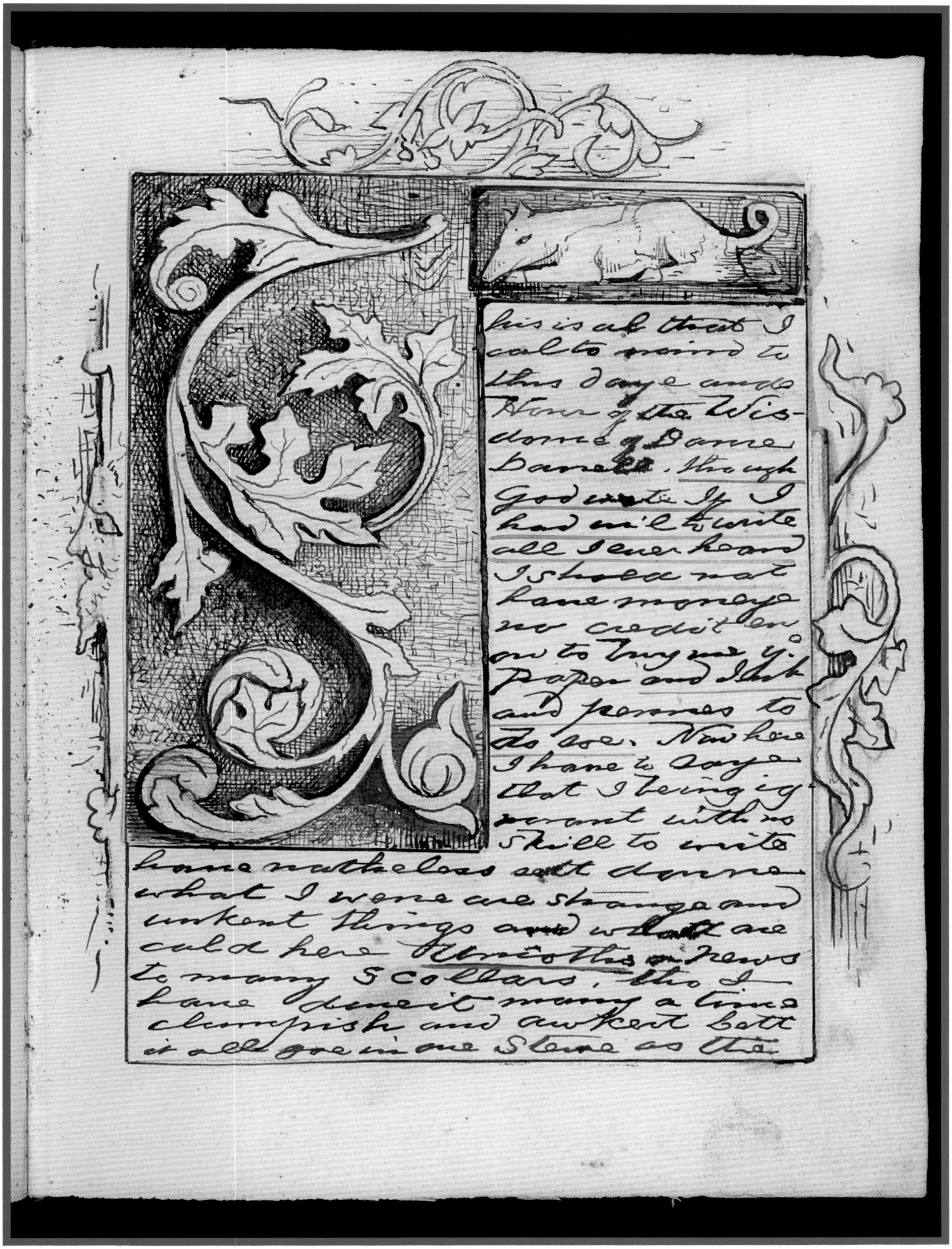

his is al that I
cal to mind to
this daye and
Here of the Wis-
dome of Dame
Darnell. though
God wote If I
had wil to write
all I ever heard
I sholde nat
have moneye
no credit en-
ow to buy me ye
paper and Ink
and pennes to
do soe. Now here
I have to saye
that I being ig-
norant with no
Skille to write
have natheless sett downe
what I wene are strange and
unkent things and what are
cald here Amerioths news
to many Scollars, tho I
have deme it many a time
clumpish and awkert batt
it all goe in one Steine as the

Good wyfe saide
wham she put meate
and fysshe cole and
coines and apples:
all to stewe in one
pott and make a
cockagnice whiche is a
dish that never cometh wise a-
like. Now tis a strange Thing yet
true that there bee
many unlered Folke
who are full of quainte
and rare Wisdom
who would be ale of a dither iff
made to write down what they
can tell and talke as wise-
ly and cannily as Hearte could
wish. And per contra I ever
find that those who learne
to write with Skil, as Scollars, when they get there have
nothing to saye a sett downe,
like Rob of the Greene who did
goe from York to London to
sell a wagon load of Stuff fa'
but whan hee got there the
wagone was bare, for hee had
traded away all hee had
on the way for Bait for him
and his horses. So that he had
learned muche yet loste more.

Or I may liken too
too many Scollers
to the man who
to jumpe over a
Dike did firste tak
a Runn ere hee
lepped, but runn
so long that ere
he gott to ye Ditch
was fain to sit down
and reste. And soe
itt is with Folke
who put all theyr
Will into learning how to write
well, soe that when tis learnt
they have no thing left to say
so there they sitt like so
many Dobbeys by the brook
which they dan't jump over
to ye other side where is the
House of Fame where all are
famoused who dwel therein

Wherein I tell you verily
We all of Us would like to bee
And wherein to fess it plain
Iff we could we'd ay remain.

Knowe this word Dobby
minds me that I for
gat to tell whatt a
Dobby is for it is a
Fool and yett no Fole,
At times itt is a folish doo
dering old Fathe or Gaffer.
but mostly a Goblinn who is
all one with Robin Goodfelow

Dobby like a Ratt a
Mowse
Cometh into many
a House
Castels and theyre
Towers by
On the Granes wh
round 'em lye
Sometimes to a
lonelie Mill,
Or a Ruine old and
Still:
But he loveth beste
to bee
Where there is a Fam-
ily,
And to serve 'em by the Night
Where hee's a Familiar Lite
All for naught save Breade
and Chese,
Hee will doe whatere they plees,
Milke ye Cows and kiss ye Maid
Half delyted half afrayde,
Cutt ye wood and swepe ye
Floor:
Just his Duty yett no more,
For tis ever his Intent
Faithfully to work his Stent.
So that none his Faith can blame
Fidelitev Do ye the Same.

Nowe if a Made bee named
Debora a Debby shee will
ofte be cald Dobby and she
need never be astonned if she should
meet this goblin for there bee
certaine folk with certaine

Names which Fairys and the
like loue. Of such names are
Gertrude loued by Witches and
Peronell a Perrel which is
my name loued by Birdes &
Sprites of the Aire. Mab or Ma
bel, and all in Bel, suche as
Florabel. Lucy, for it is Light,
shee is loued by ye light Elves.
Oriana getteth gold. Margaret for shee is a Pearle, Lisbeth shee is a Lis or Lilye this
is Frenshe. Fleur de Lys so
is Alys or Alice. Of which I
could write a book to shewe yt
a Good name is half the Game
but lett it be a Good Name
for more than that which the
youre Godparents gave Ye.

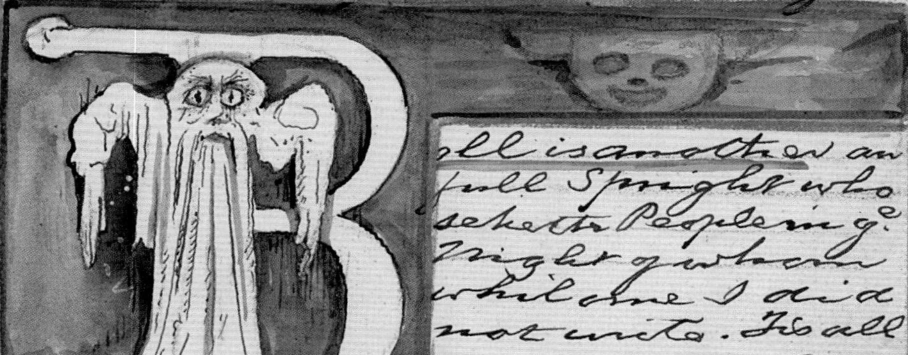

oll is another an
full Spright who
seketh People in ye
Night of whom
whilome I did
not write. Its all
one as some say
with a Balow, but
Dame Dorell says
nay, for a Boll is a ghost, as of
a man but a Balow is a Bo
ny and thin Bugge or Scare-
crow specter. And it was ever
used to frighten Bates, unto

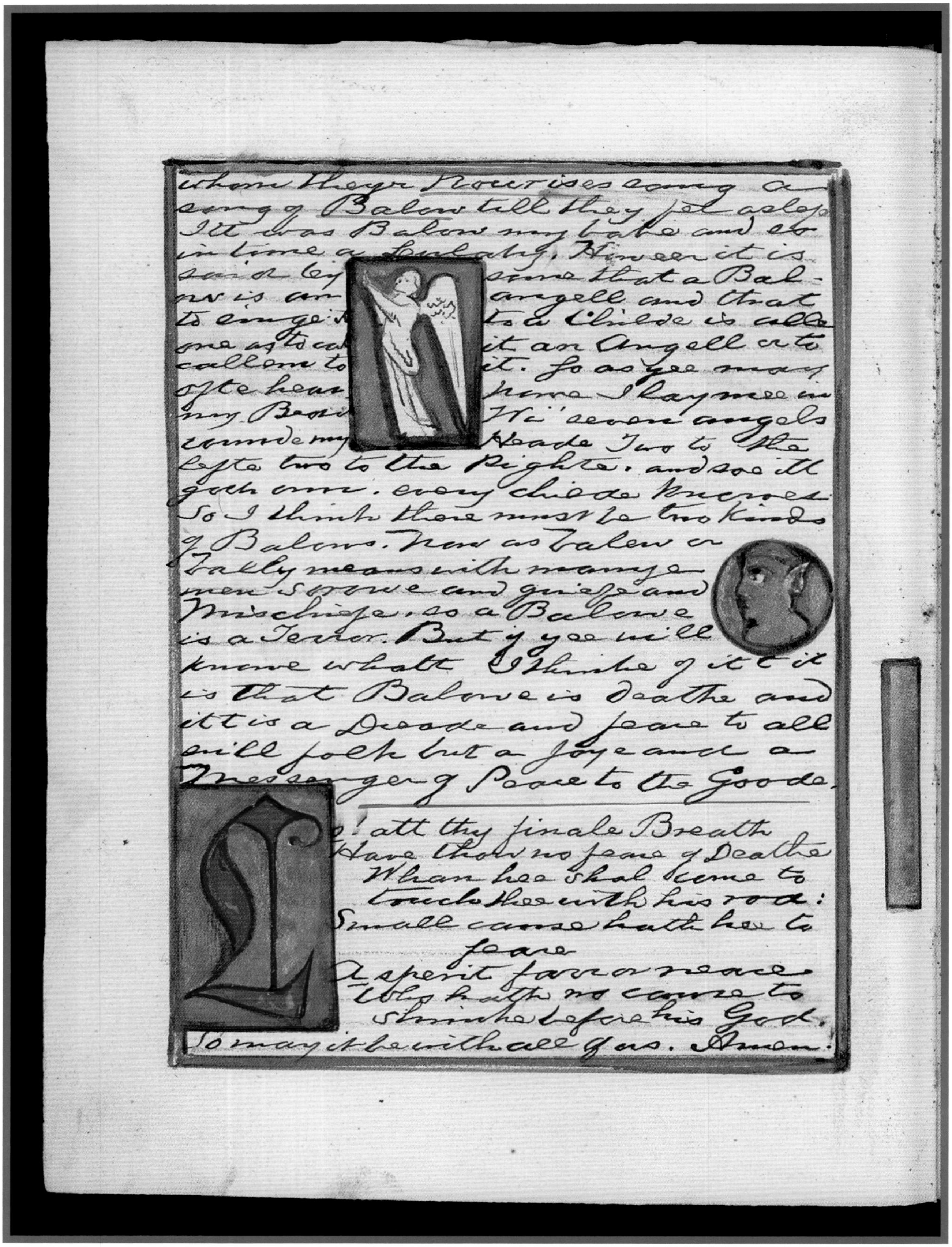

whan theyr Rocurises song a
song of Balow till they fel aslep
Itt was Balow my babe and so
in time a Lulaby. Hinsen it is
said by some that a Bal-
ow is an angell and that
to singe it to a Childe is alle
one as to call it an Angell or to
callem to it. So as yee may
ofte hear have I layme in
my Bedd Ther' seven angels
rounde my Heade Two to the
lefte two to the Righte. and soe itt
goth onn. every childe knowes.
So I think there must be two kinds
of Balows. Now as balew or
bally means with manye
men sorrowe and griefe and
mischiefe. so a Balowe
is a Terror. But if yee will
knowe whatt I thinke of it it
is that Balowe is deathe and
itt is a Dreade and feare to all
ill folk but a Joye and a
Messenger of Peace to the Goode.

Lo! att thy finale Breath
Have thou no feare of Deathe
Whan hee shal come to
touch thee with his rod:
Small cause hath hee to
feare
A sperit favor neare
Wh hath no cause to
shrinke before his God.
So may it be with all of us. Amen.

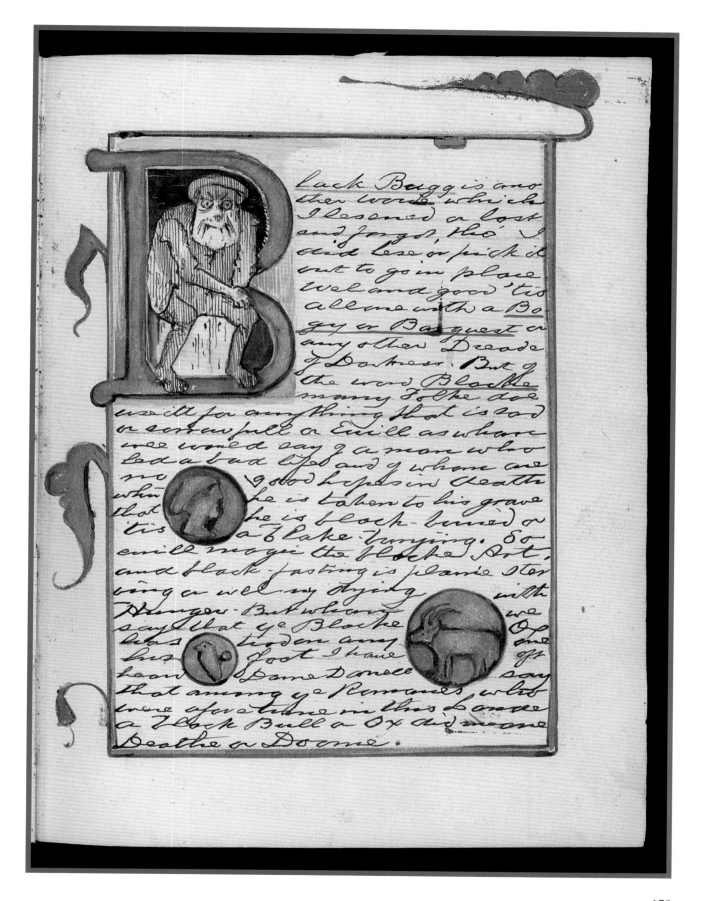

Black Bagg is ano-
ther worde which
I lesened a lost
and forgot, tho' I
did lese or pick it
out to go in place
Wel and good 'tis
all one with a Bo-
gy or Barguest or
any other Dreade
of Darkness. But of
the word Blacke
many Folke doe
use itt for any thing that is sad
or sorrowfull or Evill as where
wee would say of a man who
led a bad life and of whome are

no good hopes in Death
when he is taken to his grave
that he is black-buried or
tis a blake-burying. So
evill magic the blacke Art,
and black-fasting is plaine sterving or wel ny dying with
Hunger. But when we
say that ye Blacke Ox
has trodden any on

his foot I have oft
heard Dame Darell say
that among ye Romanes who
were afore time in this Londe
a Black Bull or Ox did meane
Deathe or Doome.

Leland
BDX 15

(1)

The Witchcraft of Dame Darrel of York

(3)

Here followeth ye Book of *ye Witchcraft of Dame Darrel of York* with account of all kinde of Fairys, *Elves*, Goblines, Bargests, *Ghostes*, Gasters, Bendys, Pixys, Pillicockes, Hobthrushes, Friar Rushes, Pictrees, Dules, Night Hagges, Giantes, Yeth-Hounds, Devilkins, Spoornes, *Robin Goodfelows* and all *theyr Kinde*.

(7)

Dame *Darrell* was called *the Wise Woman of York*. What I here write I heard her tell from time to time. *Veritas non semper valet*, he who tells great truths will pass for a Liar, but those who are wise know Truth from Lyes *and if ye can tell a Fly in a Milk-pan ye may know whether what is written here be meant for you or for your betters*. Now a *Wise Woman* is a *White Witch*, much as a Broom is a Besom, and so she was called of her best Friends

(8)

but to my Mind what she did not know of *Witchcraft* be it white or black was little worth knowing and might be put in a Flea's Eye not to speak of Anything smaller. And as I was her own Sister's Child and dwelt with her Ten Years I knew her like my pocket from the time when I came from the Ile of Jersey to dwel with her.

And when she would give a man or woman *good Luck in Love* she bade them in their Walks watch to find a red string or Ribbon or even a piece of red rag, how be it clean red wool is best. And when any one pickt it up he should say

Red is my heart's blood
Even as this string is rudd,
Therefore I pray thee
Bind her Love unto me
Until seven Doves I see,
And seven roses on a tree,
let it no longer bee.

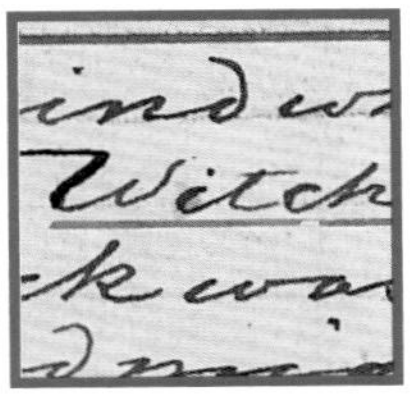

(9)

Then when he or she had pickt seven Roses from one tree and seen seven Doves he would have his will, howbeit there were other ways, and this was one – *Take the red string and if you can not finde one then beg or buy it, however it is best if found.* And then take a stone with a hole in it, but if this fails to be had take any good little peble, and cord the string all about and round it, and knot and tie it. And while you do this say:

All other maids above
[Here the name], I do love,
As this string on this stone I bind,
May my love round her heart entwine
By the power of Night
And the moon's light
While ash trees growe
And roses blowe
And rain falls in the sea
Shall her heart turn to me.

Now this must be carried in the pocket and when you

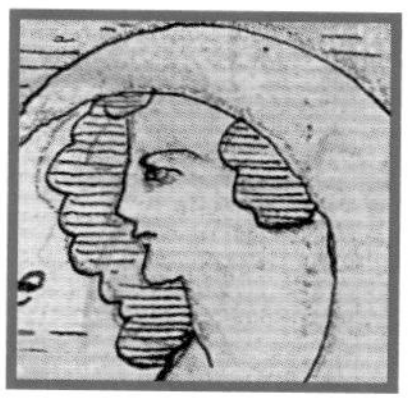

(10)

meet Maid or Man whom you want, bee bold, and you may have your will with them. Which has been full often assayed and never failed that I know of.

Another way and a rare one is this. You must paint or lim the exact Picture of the one whom you love, quite naked, and note that the better the Likeness the better will be the success. Keep this secret, let none know thereof and often look upon it. And keep about it sweet scents, musk and spices. And when the Moone is full at Midnight, or in the Season of the New Moon burne these perfumerys and Spices before it. And as you do so, sing:

Sweet is this Spicerye
But sweeter is her fair Body.
Lady Moon on high
Who seest all things from the Sky
If my love thou findest

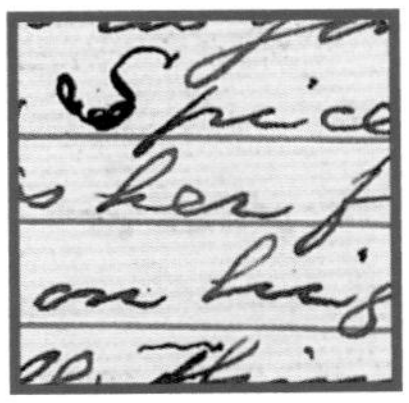

(11)

Moon as thou shinest
Turn her thought unto Me
So I will worship thee!

Fairies haunt old thorn bushes, ruins of old castles and towers, fairy rings on the downs near the Sea and open places in forrests. And if you find a large Snail shel in such a place keep it for it is a fine charm. Now this is for a Maid and she must rub it all over her Bodye by Nighte. And while so doing sing or say:

Shell if thou hast fairys seen
And has dwelt where they have been,
Mind thou my conjuration
While I make this aplication.

Then she shall put into the shell so many dried peas as it will hold. *And if a shell was so large that it coould hold fifty Peas not one more nor less the Charm was a sure one.* Then it comes to pass that in so many Days as there be Peasen she will win the love of him whom she would have. Of which Charm I can truly say *Probatum est* as Dame Darel always said when I askd her if any charme was good.

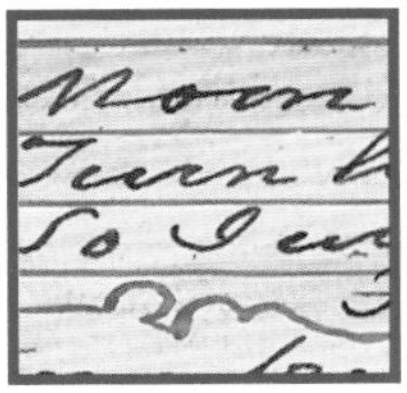

(12)

Now it comes to pass and that many a time and oft and perchance oftener that a charme fails as a Physitian be he never so wise cannot cure as Men did say in Jersey where I dweld, *Medecin est bon voisin me ne reusi pas tojours*. So there came once to my Aunt a grand lady who had tride three Spells for Love of which one had mist, one had failed, and the third had nout availed. To her *Dame Darell* said "*Yea and if thou had'st pissed thrice it would have done as much good. For thou hast a hard head and no Faith. The Devil take such a seeker who hath no will to find. Thou art blind because thou wilt not see*, thou Bitch." So my Aunt always spoke to people of *Quality* who thought the more of her for it, but to the Poorer kind she was Soft as a Kitten. Then she saide, "Now I will give thee *a spell* which would charm the Devil out of Hell."

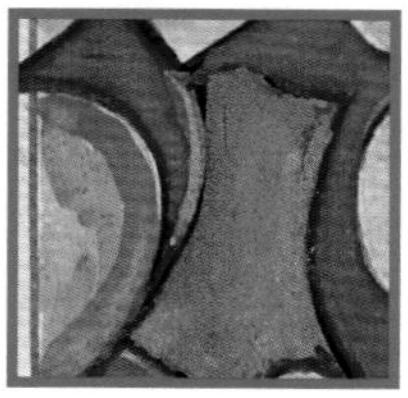

(13)

Thou must when the moon is full and bright and every star is in sight at midnight *walk stark-naked three times round about thy house* and that without an Eye sees Thee. And while thou walkest say Seven times.

"I a maiden fair forlorn,
Naked now as I was born,
As three time I pass around
This my House and Gardenes bound,
So may I thrice entwine
Round thy Heart oh Love of Mine,
Ash and Beech & Oaken Tree
Grant no eye may look on me!

And if thou findest aught while so walking be it only a Peble or a Flower, keep it for a *Charm. And if this* fail thee nothing will avail thee, *for the Fairies have no mind unto some*, and if thou beest of them, then is my Game at an end, even as FIN.IS the end of a fish. –

(14)

One day I asked Dame Darrel how one could know where Faireys *dwelt or came?* And she said "Wherever Nettles grow there are the places where they go. adowne into the Ground dwel one kind, and they are what are called *Swart Elves* and of that there is a strange History. When the Father made the world, first he created Men and then all kinds of *Fairys*, *Goblins*, *Pookas*, and ye like. Now one kind of Elfs were made first and left to drie in the Sun-lighte, but they were left too long and were mislayd, so that the first pair Brother and Sister were very dark. Then all were told to wait till Wives and Husbands were made for them. And all the other Fairies waited as they were told to do.

(15)

But the Swart Elf and his Sister being like all dark folke warm blooded would not wait and so Coupled at once. and therefore the Father condemed them to live underground. Then Swart Elf sang.

Hard is the fate
Of me and my mate,
Left in the sun
We were overdone.
Thence came the Harm
That our blood is so warm.
For that we must go
To the cold Earth below
and live out of sight
Of the sun's light.

So the Father said Thou speakst truly, therefore thou shalt not want Light or Warmness. For there is Fire within the Earth and a great light. And thou shalt have rule over Gems and Gold. So Swart Elf and his Sister rule

(16)

in the Earth. And because they abide in Heat they love all hot and prickly Things and the Nettle and Thistle and Thorns are dear to them, so that where they comes forth Nettles grow. And he who would have Luck in seeking Women, or Gold or Gems, if he know how to find them and become their friend may get all these.

Now note that if you Take a Cup and leave it by night, near a nettle, and let it be full of wine or mead or milk, and come the next day, and what was therein be gone, *this is a beginning. and note that the Cup be a new one out of which no one had ever drunk at all.* Then another time *do the same and so forth on, many* times. But if ye once begin to do this cease not so long as ye find it emptied.

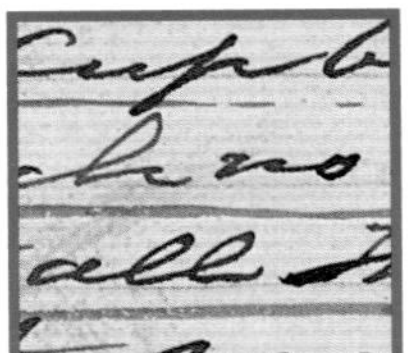

(17)

And when you want the Love of any one write on *clean Parchment* and that as well *as ye can with* all your Skill.

Elves whom no one sees
Under the Roots of Trees
Deep in the antient Hills
I pray of your good Wils
By the white bear's paw,
And the grey wolf's jaw,
The Serpent's back,
And Foxes track,
Give me the Stone
Whose power is known
Unto you alone!

Then you will find a *Stone in the cup*, be it a Peble or a Gemm. And if ye touch a Man or Woman on the Brows with it you will get their Love. *But this is not lightly come by for they give not this stone to everybody.*

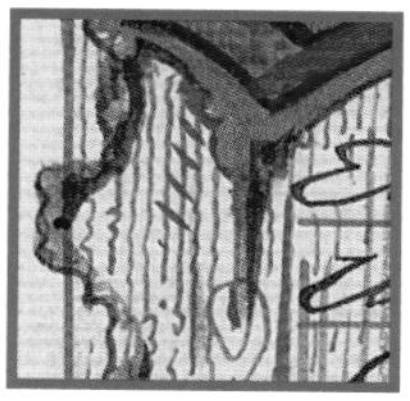

(18)

The Swart Elves be all ways thirsty because their Nature is heat. But the Elves of the Woods and Forests do incline to dainty food, because *when they were made and left to dry, as soon as ever they were done and they were right shaply and fair, but skatter and harebrained.* So insted of lying still as the Master bade them the Sister seeing an *Apple tre* full of fruit said *I hunger, let us eat yon coddes!* To which her brother Said. "*Climb my crabbat, and throw them down.*" And as she was picking and eating and throwing, came the Master who seeing the Elfe up in the tree, tho' she tried to

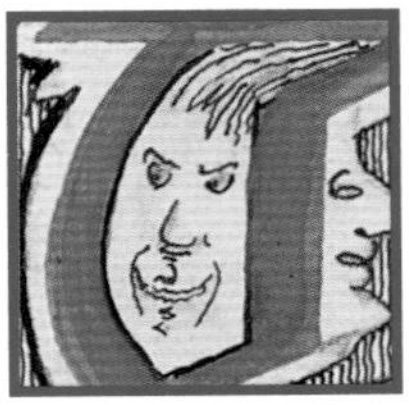

(19)

hide her Nakedness behinde the Leaves, said, Since ye are so fond of Trees ye shall ever dwell in the Woods, and for your haste to eat ye shall ever be given to eating. So it came to pass that to this day they dwell in the Forests. And he or she, *devill the difference, who will have a favour of them shall take a dish of spiced Frumenty, or a dish of figey which is made with almones figs, raisins, ginger and honey, or sugar-frutors, or a mince pye,* and let it be in a wood *best under an Oak if it may be, but where it can not be seen of Mankind.* And if it be gone the next day, do the like again. And so at last lay with your gift a Boar's tusk, and if the next day the dainty be gone and the Boar's Tusk be there, but turned over on the other side, it will be a exceeding good charm, be it for Love or any other Luck.

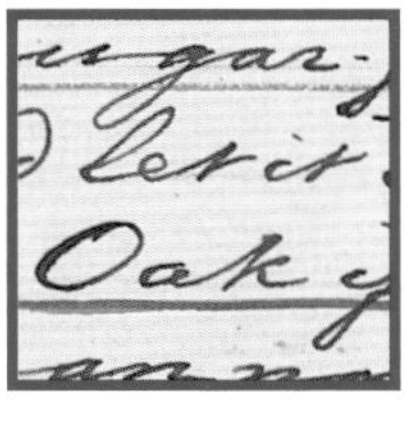

(20)

Of which Dame Darrel told me. There was once a girl named *Bessy Lacken*, she had no kith or kin and was good blood yet exceeding poor. And one day she came to my Aunt and said Dame I am as thou knowest a poor destute, but I have here an *Egg-pye* and a good one, this is all I have and I will give it to thee if ye will give me a Charm to bring me Luck." Then Dame said. Take thy Pye, child, into the Wood and leave it under an Oak, and the next time thou canst leave such things with this *Boar's Tush. And when she went one day with the tush, and it was in her poke. she sat beneath the Oak and thinking* how forlorn she was, wept. Then there came out of a Hollow in the Oak a Wood Elf, a young man he seemed, dressed all in green.

(21)

Bessy had never in all her young Life seen or dreamt of any man one hundredth part so comely as this Elfe, and her foolish little Hearte bumpt for Love. Then he said Good day, Bessy. *I have brought thee thy Fairing* and with this he gave her a *Boars tooth*, and lo it was the very same one wh'h she deemed she had in her poke. And yet again "Bessy, if thou throw that Tusk into any man's Lap, he will marry thee. Now do thou mind my words. Tomorrow the King's son and all his train will pass through York. *And when he is seated do thou draw near and he seeing thee will bid thee come to him.* Then do thou cast the *Boars Tush* into his Lap and he wil wed thee. More than that my sweet Child I can not give thee."

(22)

Bessy sat still for a little time with a beating heart and then burst into tears and said: Thou canst give me a far better Gift and that I will have. Saying this she threw the Ring into the Elf's lap. And he halsed and kissed her and said, As thou hast chosen Bessy so be it and truly it has been best for us both. And I am King of the Wood Elves in all the North, but if thou comst with me thou must leave men for evermore." Bessy answered – "Little good have men ever been to me or women either, save the Fairy-Dame Darrel." And from that day Bessy was nevermore seen by any one save my Aunt, who said that now and then she had met her of moonlit nights at the Fairy dancings in the Forest.

(23)

Now there is another kind of Fairys which live in rivers and Lakes and these are the strangest of their kinde. For many times they live as Men and Women in the World among us and pass for Humane and this came to pass in such Wise. When ye Water Elf and his Sister were made and layd in the Sunshine to dry the Father bade them *ly still till they were well baked,* but when they found it hot, and seeing a river near by in w'h a human maid and youth were swimming and wantoning, in they jumped and began to *bop and play at bawdy bo-peep, belly-bumpers and Tommy-come-tickle-me;* flirking, flisking and flipping about in the water, as merry as a thousand Griggs, for they had found stolen waters were sweet. Then came the Father and said "Since ye have found water so pleasant in water ye shall dwell. So they became Water Elves, and because they began by mingling with men

(24)

and women they are ever exceeding fond of them. *And the Water man in old times often ravisht Maides who went in to swim, while the Water witches sing sweetly to intrap young* ***[blank space long enough for "men" or "lads."]*** How be it there came a new law among them because of their exceeding Lustfulness, there being danger that all Mankind would turn to Elves or the Elves change to men. *So now they only dare to couple with human kind when they are asleep.* Then the Elf cometh and lyeth with a Damsel, and when he hath had his pleasure of her Bodie, *he layeth his hand on her Heart;* when she straight way forgets it all, nor knows anything of what has been done to her. But if a Water Elf carry this too far and spende all his Nights with Women, or if a Water-lady lye every night with Men neglecting her own kind, they are so punisht

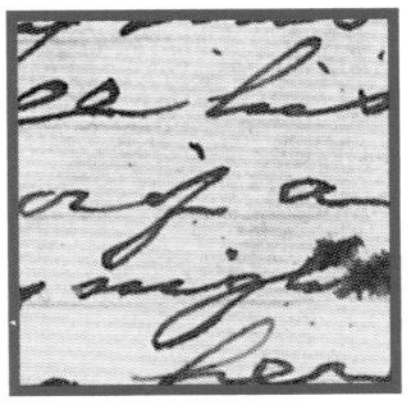

(25)

by being sent to dwell among them in humane Form, and while so they must be good and break no Laws else they must remain many Years longer away from their river or Lakes.

Now it came to pass that a very beautiful but withal wanton young lady drew the love of a Water Elf and he came and laid with her every night, nor was there one in which he did not couple with her nine times. *Then he would press his Hand on her Heart* and when she awoke she had clean forgot all that had happened. Yet she plainly perceived, not being quite an Innocent, that something had happened and that the *posnet*, as Northern folk call a little pot, had been on the fire. There with she came to Dame Darrel and askt what it might mean. Then the Dame said "Truly

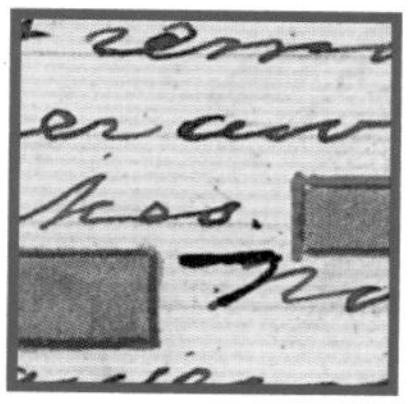

(26)

I see how it is. Thou art *Elf-ridden every night*, and that with a warrior, for when such a rider hath so faire a mare if he once gets on the saddle he spareth not *ye spur*. But if thou wilt catch and keep this Frog, go in the garden early and eate of four kinds of Leaves, Rue, Cummin, Mint and Marjoram. Then the morning or ere the Sun shines *he will lay his Hand on thy Heart* but twill nout availe, and he must obey thee like a slave. So that nighte when the Elf came she knew it and saw to her great joy that he was a very comely youth tho his Haire was green as an Emerald. *And she had her joy with him to her Heart's Content*. And when both were full fed with *amorous daintys*, he laid his hand on heart, but it was of no avail for she did but laugh and say as Dame Darrel had taught her:

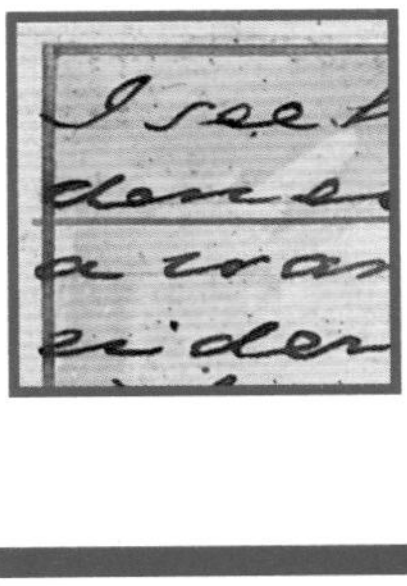

(27)

As the Rain falls on ye Hills
And to their Rivulets distils,
As the Riveret seeks the River,
Running to the Sea forever,
As the Sea doth rise to Rain,
Coming to the Hils again,
In a Ring which hath no End
And a Chain which none can rend
So I bind thee Water Elf
In my Service, to Myself.

So my Lady Marian got herself a brave Leman and as the saying is *they slept well sweetly samely in one bed for many a year.*

Those who would have aught from these Water Elves must take a new earthen Pot or tankard with a close top, and put therein some such toy as a stringe of Beads which a Girl hath worn or a Silver Ring

(28)

or chain or any such but they prize mostly a little looking glass or a pretty combe. And write on a clean paper these words and thy Name:

Elf of river sea or lake
As I come my thirst to slake
Here unto you I bring
With my love an offering
As the men of ancient days
Made their Offering allways
So whoever ye may be
I make my Offering to thee.

Then drinke of the Lake or Riveret and cast the pot in as far as ye can and sit there awhile, and so come, day by day, *till an Elf comes*. But if ye value your Virtue one straw it is a great risk, for verily one may as well entrust a Black pudding to a hungry Dog as a *Maidenhead* to such merry gentlemen or a pretty innocent boy to their Ladies.

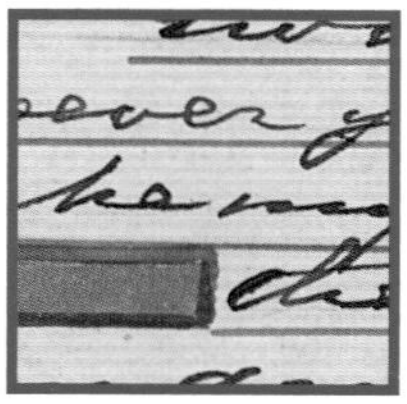

(29)

And it was said that once it became *the talk of a Town* that every Day three Sisters who were very fair Maides went to a wood a hidden place by a River, and none knew why. *So they were trackt and were seen to go the rivers Edge and took off all their Cloathes*, and when they were star-naked one cast a pebble into the river, saying some words. Then there came up a Water Elf, on whom the three Maids fastened like Bees on a Clot of Honey, and so they all *rutted and randied* and he had his will of them on the green bank, or they theirs of him. And it is told that when this fine tale was bruited aboute the three Sisters drowned themselves for shame, but others report that they did but become Water-Elfies themselves and have been seen many a time by moonlight playing about the place where they were seen with the Water-Elf.

(30)

A*dam and Eve and all Mankind came to the Fall by Curiosity*, and the Elves because they were so wild and wanton and feaky and full of *fegarys* that they could not rest when they were bid. *And when the Elves of the Air were created they were exceeding fair bonny and bright*. And as these two pretty fantekins lay in the sunshine a drying there came a Breeze and the two without more ado flew away on it merrily over hills and dales. And when the Master missed 'em and saw where they were he said *Stay where ye be*. And so from that time they have been *Aeriall Sprites*. To them go Men who are axious as to absent friends or expected events or who would fain know ther fate. *But women seek them who would have children. This comes of a very old story* that among them there are a certain Some who would

(31)

become human, and so when a woman prayed them for a child, *they went into her Belly and lay there for nine months, till borned*. And there is an old song which was sung by an Elf while he lay in his new Mothers womb.

Once over all in sunshine high
I flew on Windes thro' ye sky
Now in a Prison Cell I ly
Yet for that ne Whit care I.
Though I be in dungen dark
Star-naked eke withouten Sark
And no Sun or Moone I see
Here I live so merrily
All about is soft and warm
With no trouble or alarm
Little knows my Lady fair
Whom she doth in Belly bear.

And there is a tale told all among us *Wise Women* that in the old time a heathen Dane who had taken a Thegn in the North Umber land put him to Torture and said Ile let thee go free if thou wilt no more be a Christen man but knele to my gods. Then the Thegn laughed and said "Little doest thou kenn

(32)

thou Heathen Fool with whom thou hast to do. For my father and Mother when they grewe older and had no Heir went to a wise Woman who promist them a child. And she went to the Chief of the Sprites of the Air and asked for Aid. And because I was of Mind to be a Christen Man I went into the dark cell which we call Mother's Womb till I was borned a Babe. And for all thy Torture I care never a Whit. Thou art a Dog and all thy gods, dogs and Bitches. – And saying this he dyed. And men say that the Dane who was a Earl and all his Following became Chrisom men.

These Sprites of the Air love musick and Flowers and sweet Smels. But they fear to go near Gardens for fear of ther Enemys who guard them, or they may steal Roses. And if one can play the Lute or Pipe or anything, and has a Garden, let him go therein by night

(33)

and play as well as he may and sing.

Ye who live in Air above
Unto you I give my Love
Now this Garden shall be fre
Unto you as tis to me.
Every flower whitch is mine
From this Hour shall be thine
By the Wild Goose & the Swan
By the Eagle and the Paun
All that flies oer Land & Sea
They shall all my Witness be.

Then speak thy Wish and it may be that one will appear, but it ever comes to pass that they will haunt the Garden and grant thy Desire. These be easy Sprites to win, and they are more in number than other of the Fairey kind. When you dream that you are flying then one of them or more has come into thy Dreaming. And to draw them into thy Dreams, put a lute or the like by Any Window so that the Aire blow over its Cords and make musick and they will be atracted to come.

(34)

These are all the Chief Kinds of Elves. Some say that those of the Earth and Fire are of two Kinds but my Aunt reckoned em as one. Now there are lesser Tribes akin to them such as the House Fairys or Goblins, who come from the Wood Elves. And it is said that in the old days when the Saxones and Danes dwelt in England and much more so among the Britones before time, these House Elves lay about Houses like Cats and had no fear of Men and did much work all for a Bowl of Milk or a Jack of Ale and a Loafe. But when the Christen Faith came in they became less common though many of them were still lovesome to the gawds and glitter and gimbols of the Papists. But when the Reform drove out the Prestes, it was gone Day and Jack over the Stile with them, and they cared no more to live with Folk who looked at them all as meer Witches and Impes. However there are still some old Castles and Manors, and antient Farm Houses where a Goblin or twain still dwel secretely, and come out by Night to lye by the coles in the Chimney-place and pilfer some Scraps of Food. And of these Brownys tis said they much love Children being but a simple Folk themselves among the Fairey Kind. And they often play with them but always touch them to make them forget. And if the Master of the House be a Man of an old Family and knows the true name of the Browney, he can call him forth. And tis told of a young Lord who was in sad case from the Warrs with ner a Peny in his pung and his Land forfet, he came back to his Castel to find it bare. And as he sat all amort and alone he rememberd of a Browny that

(36)

he loved much when he was a Boy and was wont to play w'th him. So he called his Name and loe, the Goblin came forth from the Chimney-back, and with his Wife danced for Joy and hugged and embracet him. The' the Fairey led him into the Vaults *and showed him in a secret Place a very great Treasure of Coyne*, Jewels, gold-inlayd arms and Plate and said All this I give Thee. I have gathred it this nine hundred Years where Men were slain or ever an evill man or a foe came into this castle to do harm him did I despoile This I give thee and know that I was in great Fear less thou should die *for when thy race is at an end we too must perish for we began and shall end with thy Family*. So the y'g Lord was now rich and wedded well and his *Moniment* in the Church shows that he had fourteen Boys and two Maids.

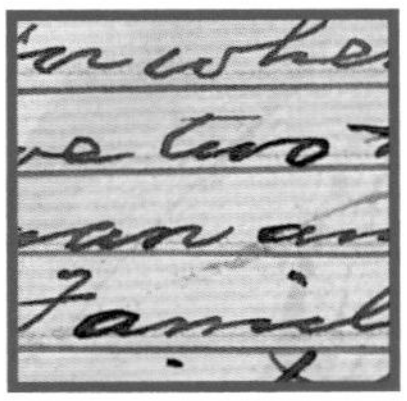

(37)

The old name for these Faireys was *Durgans* or *Derger* by which name some folk still call a very little man, or if one be very small and heavy-set they say he is *dergy*. And of some kinds it is hard to say with whom they fellowship. Now there are *Jack-Elves* who are mightyful and strong, and such as these used of yore to dwell in Swords and spears which were sure death to some one when taken in hand, *and others wond in a silken Kirtle* yet which no weapon could cut or stab. Others would live in a staff which pointed out Where gold lay hid or secret Springs and fountains ran underground. Or they had their homes in rings and coins which brought luck or in shoes in which a man could run like the wind or in Caps which made those who wore them invisible.

(38)

Of a strange kind are those whom my Aunt calld in her old Northern fashion *Logh-Elves* or the *Laughing Faerys* though they be not rightly Faireys nor Elves nor Goblins but Spirites of a sort w'h no one knows ther *Family*. They appear ever as *Men among Men* sometimes as Minstrels or Jesters and like Merry Nighters in the Sky flash and go no one doth know whither or whereuntoe. And all ther Delight is to make mischief and jape folk. Now of one of these there is a very old and strange tale. *There was an Earl in North Umber Land an evil Trole Carl the* Dame calld him, in some sort *a devil* or *Enchanter*, what he *loved* above all things was *Ridlings*, as Countryfolk call *Riddels*. There was a certain old Lord whom the Earl had so trapt in his nets that he held his life. And he sent him word

(39)

to come on a day to his Castle to be doomed but if he could make any *Riddel* which the Earl could not guess he should be *scathless*. Now ye Lord knew as little of Riddels as a old Bawd of Grace. And the Eve before the day of Tryal he sat all adrad in his home when there came a Pilgrim who craved lodging unto whom the poor Lord told his trouble. *"Little needs thou rack for that," quoth ye Pilgrim*. Do thou lend me thy Garments and Ile go and riddel him so ridlingly that thou shall be rid of him forevermore. And in the morning when he had dond the Lords cloaths he saw so like him even in the Face that no Man could tell Whitch. And when he came to the Earl, the Earl said wilt thou be doomed by my council or has thou a Riddel? "I trow, said the Pilgrim that *Doomed and damned is all one here*. Ile een abide by my Riddels. So he put one after the other till he had given ninety-eight and the Earl guessed them every one, and then said, More than an Hundred I will not answer. Quoth the Pilgrim:

"As I came to thy Castel I saw in the house *a Creature which had eight legs and four Heads yet of all this I saw but one Head*. Earl of North Umber Land guess thou my Riddel!"

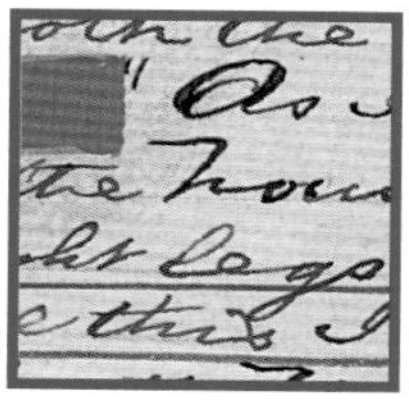

(40)

What thou didst see answered ye Earl was a woman with child but thou art uncanny and a wizard if thou speakst truly. For it is a woman with three unborn Babes in her Belly. And as he spoke there came a man who said "My Lord there is a strange thing happened For while ye sat here the wife of thy Gardener has given birth to three children." Then thee Earl Lookt Askant at the Pilgrim and said, "Give me thy hundredth Riddel thou Son of the Riding Hag, and a curse on thy riddening." Then the Pilgrime laughed and said This is my Last Riddel.

Tell me oh Earl of North Umber Land who it was lay with thy Mother the Night thou was begotten?

The Earl roared in a rage Who else byt my Father the Earl of this Land. The Pilgrim ansered: Thou lyest between thy teeth and on thy Tongue For the

(41)

Earl was but thy *Trow-father. For thy Mother was a leacherous Trull and over-troxy, and coupled with all her* Men-servants. And a Witch wife gave her Lovers the Form and Figure of ye Earl and made him sleep while these Bullys went in unto her. And the worst of them all who swiked the Earl was his own Swine-heard, and his Son art *thou as all thy Mannere shows*.

Then the Earl in a rage drew his sword and hewed at the Pilgrim. so that the blade passed clean through his Neck, but he heeded it not, and laught again like a sper or a devil, and said: *Thou dids bid me here on thy word, and said I should be safe if I could give thee a Riddel beyond thy getting. Now for thy falset thou shalt die the death of a dog and truly a dogs death it shall be.* And saying this he vanisht *out of sight before their eyes.* And as all men know that Earl was torn to death by his dogs.

(42)

In the City of York there is a Street called ye *Shambles* Therein was an Ale House. And every Chris'mas Eve therto came a Man in strange cloaths. no one knew whence he came but they cald him *Youel*, for the first word he always spake he cryed out three times Yuell Yuel Yuell! Then he would play on a lute & sing songs which no man had ever heard, and make Mirth & Game. Once there came Some one who said that a great Wolf, exceeding bold and dreadfull, because it was a very cold Winter and the Wolves were starved had come into Town and rusht into a stal and then the Door was shut on to him, and no man dared to slay him because of his great Fiercenes. The Youell laught and said If ye will see good sport come with me. And when they were at the Stall he said, Now I will slay the Wolf. And because Yuell had no Arm some one offred him a Sword but he said

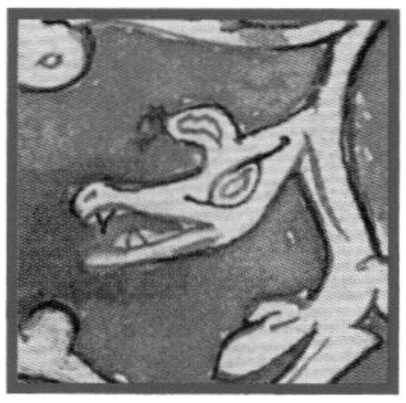

(43)

A Cat needs not a Knife to slay a Mouse, which was true of old times and yet holdeth good and I am boon as I be. Saying this he went in and closed the door, and then there was heard a great noise, but it seemed more like two men in rage *danging and illifying* one the other than a Man and a Wolf. But they spoke in a tongue w'h no man understood. And all thought it was a gabbery and japery of Yuell who was only playing at two Voices for *he was very swipper with his Tongue*. Then all was stil and Youel came forth and fastened the door and said that no man should go in till the next day and then we should have *a rare and merry Jest*. But that Night he was gone and the next Morning when men when to see the Wolf there lay a dead Man; ster-naked and it was plain that he had been strangled for his neck was *writhed arynt*. And by him lay a wolf's skin. And the dead man was one very ill

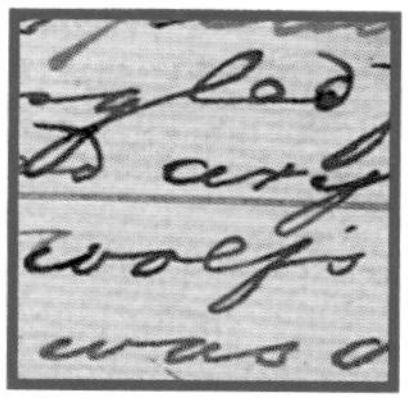

(44)

liked, cruel and evil and men were afeared of him because he was thought to be a wizard and deal with the devill. And now twas known he had been a *Were Wolf* such as we in the Ile of Jersey call in our French *Loup garou*.

Of this appearing to be as animals there are some things which I do not very well know. Once I asked Dame Darrel wherein a *Fay* was unlike a Fairy. For in ye Isle of Jersey what we call a *fé* or Fay is a spirit like a very fair Lady as large as a natural Woman who is mostly in all ye Tales as benevolent and very Friendly. And Dame Darrel said that a Fay was properly the same as a *Hamen* or *Hemen* which was a Home Spirit & a mans *Luck or Fate*. And they always appear in the Form of an Animal at first, and always *in Dreams*. And whenever ye see an *Animal* in a

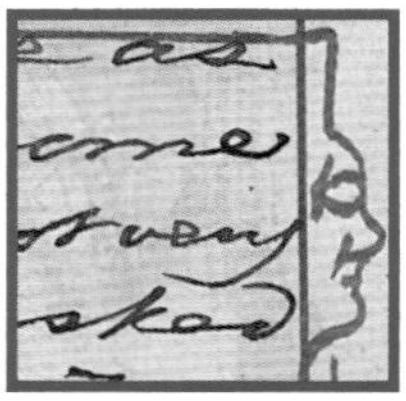

(45)

Dream it is some man's or womans Hamin. It was thought in the old Time that Everybody had one though Some said there was one to a Family, and some believed they brought good fortune. So they seem to be somewhat akin to the *House Elves* which belong'd to Families. Of this Kind is the Thrummy Cap who appears like a Dergy little old man. He liveth in the Vaults of Castles and there are many tales of him and his Kind. Yet he is not Hamin for they seem to fly in the Air. And there are Followers who are much like them, they fly after men as Birds or in other Forms. If a man see his *Follower appear to him as a Woman and lye with her she looses all her power and becomes like any other woman*. There was a Lord of great riches, he was forth from the land in a boat and saw a Hawk which flew after; one of his Men said I tro that is your Follower. That may be he answered, I will make her an Offering, and say

(46)

ing this he threw out a gold Ring. The Hawk flew scooping and scuting down and took up the Ring ere it sunk and flew away. Then arose a great Storm, the Boat was sunk all the Men drowned. The Earl swam long and saw come flying over him a very beautiful woman who taking him by the *Scruff or behind his neck held him up and so drew him ashore*. Then she took him up to a Castle among ye Rocks and made a fire and gave him meat and wine. And as he sat there *he saw on her arm the gold ring which he had thrown to the Falcon*. Then he said Art thou not my Hammen and Follower? And she said I am. The Earl answered for that I am Glad but I would thou wert as other Women because thou art so beautiful. But I will not ask it of thee to love me because then thou wouldst lose all thy fairy power.

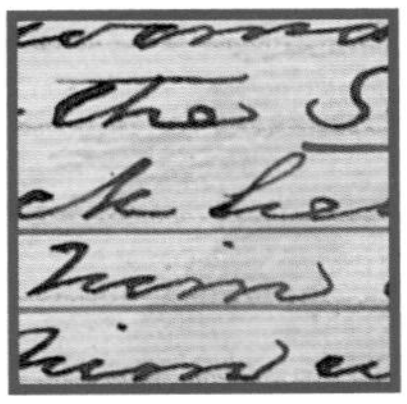

(47)

She answered I love thee so that if thou wouldst fain have me thou mays and I will be a woman and no longer a Virgin. So he lay with her and wedded her and from them came a famous family. Of them it was said that *the daughters could all fly and they kept is a great secret;* but once or twice *Something came to light. There was a randy, rascally young gentleman who meeting a young Lady of this Family one Evening* as she walkt out alone in the Moonlight by the Edge of a very high Clift *would fain have ravisht her,* and thought himself Cock-sure to succeed. But she ran and leaped over the Clift and he swore that she did not fall *but sailed out on the Wind like a Bird afar till he could see her no more. But the* next day shee was at Home and as well as ever

(48)

T*hurse is not a Faery* but *a kind of Goblin*. They be of a strange kind, uncouth and are seldom seen. Some do call them Ghosts of Witches. If you take a Sea Shell and let it lye for a time where the *Thurse* cometh first you must say over it these Words.

There was a true man yode
True Horse on true Road
Till by the true Sea
A true Shell found he
He put it to his true Ear
That he might truly hear
Thurse I truly pray thee
That thou speak as true to me.

Then coming again make thy Questions *and put the Shell to thy Ear and thou wilt hear a Sound as of the Sea and day by Day it will become like a Voice till it answers all thou* Seeks. Some use for a Shell

(49)

an old Beake or Mug or Cup such as are fisht out of the sea or are found in Stangs wherein Men cast them in old times for offerings. there is a Man in Beverly who hath twelve, all of them he found in a deep Hole in a Burn. But if ye find a Shell and there in the Markings can see the Word *Thurse* or *Thrs* it is exceeding good to answer. And Dame Darrel told of a Rock in a lone Place where was an old Ruin there dwelt a *Thurs*. In the Rock was a Hole throw which the Wind blew. Who put his Ear to that Hole on a *Thursday* could hear a Voice tell him Strange Things. And in old Drinking Horns often dwells a *Thurse*. There was a Knight who had one of these old Horns. Whenever he was in great Peril the Thurse would make it sound aloud. *One day he had gone forth to hunt and he was way laid by a certain Enemy with Twelve Men. About this time his Lady took up ye Horn* and heard it sound, and from

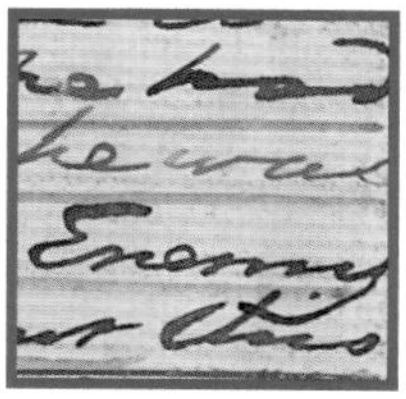

(50)

it came the Words Hurry Hurry Hurry! Then she took twenty of her Men well armed and rode forth and found her Lord in a sore strait fighting all Thirteen. Then there was a rattling and rasing fight, so that all the thirteen were slain and buryd in one hill. *Then that Lord took a Horn for his Arms with the words Free for a blast*, tho' some say it was Hurry Hurry Hurry. And when made game of him he said he cared not how *many Horns his Lady set him so that they were of that kind*. And because he had very rich Lands men said that he never wanted Corn, for so they call with us the unseen Horns which grow on the Heads of some married Men, whence the saying of a certain wife who lay with other men that she had sent her husband to Cornwall in an open Boat and that he lacked not an Oar [or a Whore] while she lived.

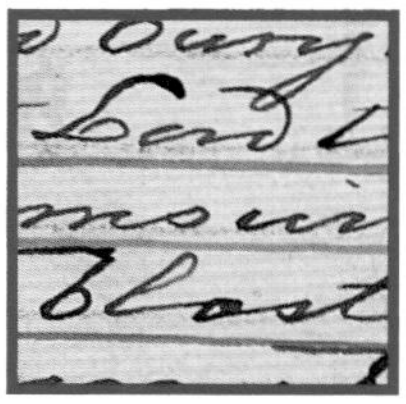

(51)

Some think that Fays be *the very little merry Faireys* of whom ther are so many pleasant Tales. Others wil have them to be *Ouphs*. Dame Darrel said that when the Elfs were made there was left but a little Piece of Clay and from this the Father made two teeny pretty little Sprights and that these alone behaved well so that they are ever happy and dance and ride on Butter Flys and sleep in Flowers. One kind of these little Ones live by the Sea. *The Land Ouphes* greatly esteem fine Limpet Shells which they wear for Helmets or use for Cups and these the *Sea Ouphes* guard with great Jealousy. Once there was a Little Girl and Boy who had been told this and when they were taken on a Time to the Sea they made good provants of such Shells

(52)

And coming home they went to a place where they deemed these Ouphes dwelt and threw there all their Shells. And who so merry and glad as these smal folk when they found this exceeding great and valuable Treasure, *truly they danced for joy.* Now the Mother of these Children was so poor that when Christmas Even came there was no bite or Sup in the House nor any *Gifts, and the Children sat a-cold and cried for Hunger and Grief. When lo* there came a great Light into the Room and a great Yule Log with Fire was in the Herth and there came in a great *Processioun of Ouphes,* every one who had got a Limpet Shell from them wearing it proudly on his head like a mighty Warrior. And their Musicians blew on Trumpets made of Straws *a Solemn March and as they Paraded around the Room and passed the Children Every Ouph* gave them a Silver Two-

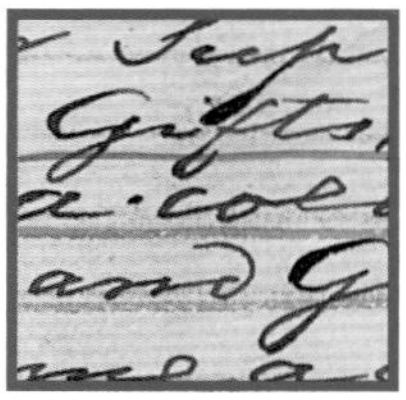

Penny Piece or a coin of the Fairy Money as men call old money. some say it is of the Romans or Saxones. Dame Darrel gave me two for a Fairing. And so they went forth leaving the Children as a-joyed as they had been sorrowfull. And their Mother grew so rich that she bought a Manor and set apart a Field and in that since it was never toucht and no one entered it. it was called the Fairys Field and they filled it with Fairy Rings and danced there every Night.

There is another Tale which is of a Youth who heard that when one eats an Egg, he should break the Shel lest Witches or Faireys make of them Boats or Cups. But he threw a whole Shell into a Bush saying *Take it ye Faireys and much good may it do you, and this he did*

(54)

whenever he ate an Egg. Not it came to pass that one day he was in a Tavern and held an Egg when a strange man in a very ancient Attire said, That Egg thou wilt never eat. Truly I will try he said, but when the Egg was opened it was full of Wool, and in the Wool was a Mark of Gold full weight. The Strange Man said Go in the Morning to the Bridge and thou wilt meet a Man with Sheep and I counsel thee to buy them whatever his Price may be. The Youth promist to do so. And in the morning he found the man who had six Sheep and his Price was a Gold Mark for all. The Youth said such a Price was never paid in all England for Sheep but for his Words sake he bought them. And as he drove them homewards at every mile he found one more Sheep in the Flock, and this was ever so every Day that whenever he drove em they encreased. Then the Youth remembered an old Tale, how that there was in a certain mountain a Drove of such Fairey

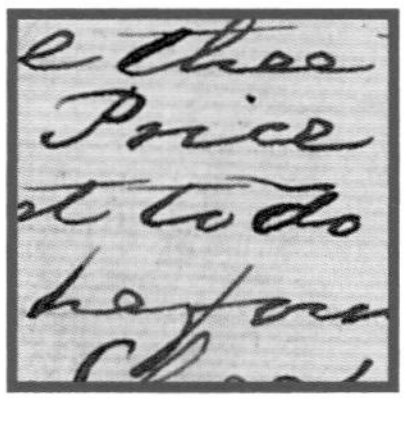

(55)

Sheep which belonged to an old king in Days of Yore. And he told his Secret to none and grew to be as rich as an Earl.

There is a round stone of many sizes from that of a nut to an Apple which Men find in Rocks or Gravell. These they call Fairey Faces or Colt Pixy or Elves Heads. Dame Darell told me that ere as Men were in the Land were only Giants and this kind of Faireys and they were a hard dour race and ill to knap with. So when the Master came he turned them all into Stone, of the Gyants were made the Rocks but of the Faireys only the Heads were steaned. Wise men do so make with these Heads, they take one on which a Face appears and make a small Body of Wood, Beech is best, and set ye Head on it. And when it is made set it in an honourable place and say:

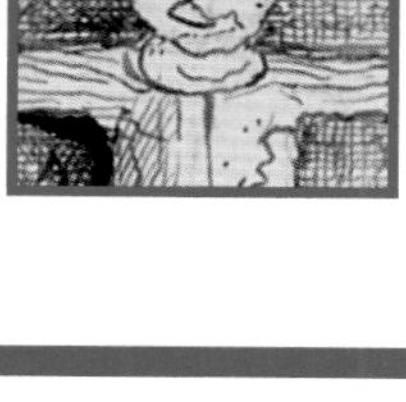

(56)

North South East West
Alto Valin ye are best
Bifer Bafer Nar and Nine
Norey, Orey, Onar, Ine,
Vindel Vandal Thraw and File
Make the Giant Kettle boil.
When the Wolves come o'er the Plain
With Vigg and Nar and Alf and Nane
Ye shall have your own again.

Yet Dame Darrel thought this but a crass work and no better than Witchcraft, nor do the Fairys of our time like it for these were their Foes of Yore. And the Strange Names in this Spell *are those who were their Chiefs in those Days*. With these Heads one can make the Dew which hangs on Rocks turn to Gold or work ill to a Foe and succeed in all Murder Rape Revenge Robbery and such pretty Trickes.

(57)

A many people theyr be yea and over many who call all this Lere of Faeries foly, and say of elves there ben none and that tis Time lost and Sense wasted to listen to such tales. Of which Dame Darrell would saye whan shee was counsayled to give no hede to Wanton Gospelers and Hereticks, "Be thou not quicke to beleve every new Doctrine yet listen well even to the verie End and heare what the teacher hathe to say." For ther was once a Tyme God wot, whan al and all y't wee now believe was called Folly and Falset and was a new Thing. Beare thou thatt in Mind.

(58)

Now there was one thinge of which D. Darrell spoke noe Worde to any other and but litel to mee ande that was she had but small faith in Blacke Witchcrafte or that Wemen solde themselves to ye Devill, for she had known ful many who was sayd to serve the Devill and devill a one was there who could conjer up half a crown or showe my Aunt anything new. But in White Witchcrafte the Dame had great beleefe, saying that Faithe in spels and charmes and great hope would cure or holpen Folke when the Devill and all his folk were afraid. Twas with their fraying tales like Rob o the Dale who when a man was scart att some Frogges, said "Bee of good cheare I trow itt is nothing but a Noyse."

(59)

N*ow I will here as well as I can, not being over Learned as ye can well see, give all the names of the* Faireys and Goblins *according to the Letters of the* Christcross and with them such Words as pertain to their kind. And first are the Alfs or Elves of whom I have written all that I know or what we call Awvish or Elvish things. With these are the Annets or Sea Guls whom some say are the Souls of Men who perisht at Sea and who for their Sins must fly about and dree their were or time of dowbt till they be set free.

Of the Letter B there is a very strange thing to be noted.

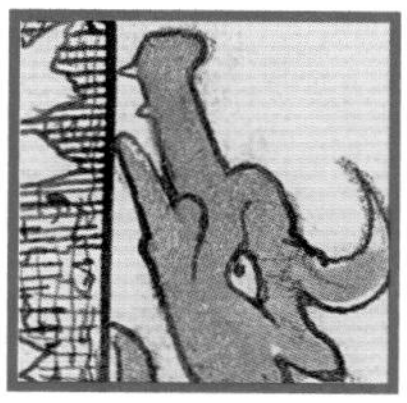

(60)

And this is that of the beings whose names begin with it are a kind of mysticall terrifying Sprights who seem more like Devills and Dunces with all than Faireys. They are all believed to be Horrific in figure, be they spinney and thin, or *dwergey* and dumpy. They seem to be all much the same, as their Names seem to be in one. These be called firstly, the *Bo*, who is a *hobb goblin*, also *the Bogg* or *Bugg* which I take to be all the same with *Boo*, *Bogy-bo*, and the *Boman* who carrys childer away or who is used to frighten them. With them and all one and the same is *Boggert*, whom some account to be a ghost, as the North Umbrians call him *Bogle*, and *Boogan* who is sometimes the Devil. And there is the *Bloody Bo* or *Bloody Bone*, but *Bone means here a Bon or Boman* and not that which is in our body. And with him goes the one calld *Boneless*, but Dame Darrell said that this

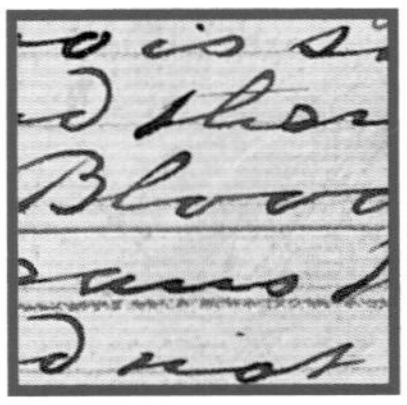

(61)

meant only a smaller Bone or his Wife. Now of this it is to be said that Ghosts and Goblins when they speak their first word is *Bow* or *Boo*. And this is to frighten Folk, and so the wild Irish in their Warrs do always rush on screaming *A-boo*, which made them so mad that as I have heard Dame Darrell say there was a Law made against the Word. Now whether the word came from Bo a goblin, or the goblins name from the cry is more than my small Wit can discern. Like unto these is the *Bargaste* or *Borguest* who is horrible over all the others to behold and who when some bad man is about to die goes howling and shrieking and skirling and skrithing a nights where men dwell and which hath been heard not long ago in York through ye Streets.

All of a kind are the *Brog the Breen* and the *Bull Beggar* which last is a *Boo-Bogey* as Dame Darrel declared.

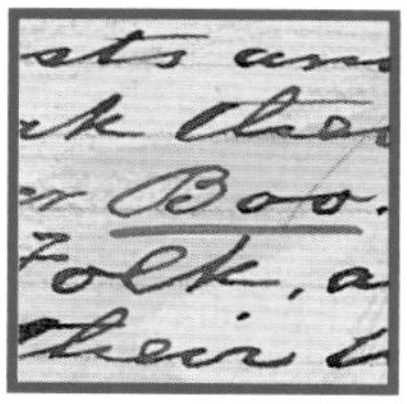

(62)

C standeth for *Church* in a picture book of the *Aphabett* which I have seen, so I will begin by the ***[long blank space]*** which are the very strange images which we see in Churches on the corbels and Everywhere and which are often plainly enough the carved pictures and portraits of *Imps*, *Goblins*, *Jack-devills*, *Bogeys* and the like. The Story runs that the Masons who built these Churches were exceeding wise and of a kind Magicions. And while they worked these *Imps* who served the *Heathen priests and Witches and Warlaws* came and vext them all they could, mislaying ther Tools, breaking their timbers and doing all the Devillments

in their power. Then the Master of the Masons turned the Imps into Stone and made them hold up arches and all kind of heavy weights for a punishment, and be trod underfoot by *Saints*. Now there is a tale that when there is a full Moon on *Saint John's* Eve then they all come down from their nooks and Horns where they sit as the Saying is, *In a Horn when the Devill is blind*, and dance and talke over the *good old Time* when everybody went to Hell and they were all so *happy*. And some say that of every Hundred, one is then set free if he will *become a Christian spirite*.

There was a Carpenter in York who being drunke one *Saint Johns* Eve went into Church and fell asleep and was not noted and so he staid there. *And it was a full moon* and when he *awoke loe* all the *Images* of the Cathedral came *crowding in*. *After that he came* no more, and then it was marked that one of the Goblins in the Church

had no more the same Face or Form or Holding that hee had afore but was all one and the same as the Carpenter – yea and his Cloathes there-to. But the Carpenter man saw never mo here below. If to the Divel he did go is more and I or any know.

C *standeth also for a Cuckoo which is a kinde of Faerie. When ye hear it for the first Time in spring when birds sing then say aloud,* Cuckoo, Cuckoo, as thou art true, Let me have that which I crave, As what I got to the Poor I gave. So give unto me, If so good it seems to be. Then make thy wish and so much as thou has geven so much wilt thou get, *but if thou asks for more thou wilt get nout. unless it be a pair of Horns. And note that all this cometh best if you see Cuckoo a sitting.* Therefore, unto, men say of ye Gowk.

If you see the Cucko sitting
And the Swalow a-flitting
And a filley Foal lying still,
You all the Year shall have your Will.

(65)

C*ats are also of their Kind, kind or unkind, uncanny Witches or Witches Darlings oft times Impes*. Best of all for Luck is a *Black cat* in a house. Therein bideth nere a Mouse. – *Therefore men say*

Kiss a black Cat
It will make you fat
Kiss a white one
It will make you lone
Kiss a black pied wi' white
A sad day and a merry Night

If you meet a black Cate in the Night and can see nout but her two eyes shining like coles, then say as she stares at you

Stir about still,
Wish me no ill.
Though it be dark,
Thine eyes I mark.

Then seek in that Place the next day and you will find two Sixpences or two pieces of gold, for all I care, *unless thou givst me one for then I hope it will be gold.* – For as the saying is If thou beest rich and givest nout thou'rt a *poor Bitch*.

(66)

A *Coricane is a Fairye who dweleth mostly in lone places, chiefly where the Rockes bee, in litel Holes where water falleth or in Caves or Springes*. He is lonely by nature and ever beareth a Horne on which he playes. It may befal *Any One to heare the Musike afar off over the Wolde*.. And on hearing it 'tis sure that great good or Evill will befal him who heares itt. Then to bring Lucke ye shall cross your Arms before you on youre Breaste and saye:

'Thou who blowst ye Horne
Who did'st play ere I was borne:
And who wilt ever playe
When I am past awaye,
Give me the Blessing which afore
Thou did'st give to men of yore!"

To hear the *Coricane* by night, Witches call to them with a Witch Whistle. –

(67)

D*werfs* or *Dergs* are *Manikins of the Elf kinde. dwel in Hills, Mountaines, Barrowes or Hillockes, and Rocks.* They mostlie wone wher Metalls be, as of Tinne Iron or Coper. Silver. *They are little, very strong and mighty in all Magic.* They doe make *Jewells and wonderful Swordes* which give Victory and slaie so many men as are apointed to their Weirde. Whan such a Sworde is once drawn it may not bee regained till itt has killed a man. *Yet there ever goeth some Evil with their Gifts.* So itt befel a King who by force made a *Derg* smithe for him a sword with golden Hilt and Gaine which shulde slay Twelve Men, but by itt were his owne sons slaine

Unto Thee, Lord,
I give the Sword
Of Great victorie,
Yet shall thy Sons
All perish anones,
And therewith be slee.

Which came to passe tho' he threw itt into a See but whan founde in after time itt still did worke its Weirde.

(68)

D*ols* are but the *Poupets* wherewith litel Maides do playe, how be it of these are a Strange Kinde and such doe Witches make of Dead Men's Bones, and these are Devills Dols, the which they give to their Children, and these Toyes walk and live. Ther was a younge maide her Name was Peronel that found one Day a Dol made of a Bone carved, drest in *red Cloth*. And Peronel not thinking said, I would I had Cherry from yon tree. Then ye Poupet answered

Thy Word to me
My Word to Thee
Ile bring the Cherry
Down from the Tre.

So the *Dol went up the Tree and came down with ye Fruite*. Till there was heard a Voice crying Bittock! Bittock! When the Dol said That is my Mistris, and flewe awaye like a Bird nor was she more seen of anyone, And this was near to Sunderland.

(69)

D*iccon* is but ye Name of a merrie Devilkin who danceth, yet is hee so well knowne that many crie out The Dickons as if he were ye Divell. He cometh ever wher Folk dance and disporte themselves. And the Dryed Leeves and the dead Leef which clingeth to ye Tree yet ever fluttreth in ye airie Wind, spinning rounde and round, and Those that flie away before the Storm as iff they were Wood are *Diccon* his Children or Litel Diccons. There was once a young maid who having has some intuse or Hurte of her Legg, could not dance. Therewith she sat ones by the wall looking on while others danset, staring like a Dassed Larke at a dasing Glasse; to her came a merrie littel unkend man with a queint Vismomie, who saide, Maiden why do not danse? To which

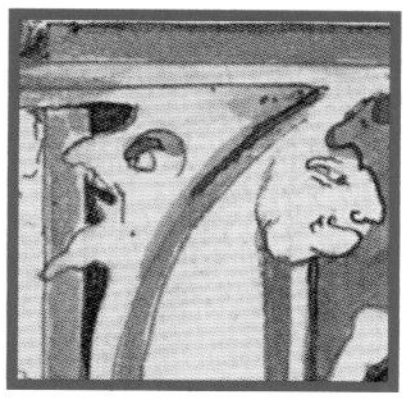

(70)

She answered Truly ’tis not of my own wil kind Sir that I *hide here on my Bace like a Brake by a Bourn* seeing the water run by whyle I lyte and can only swaie my heade to the sound. “Bellabone,” answered ye Manikin, “What aileth thee?” “What aileth is that my Leg faileth else would I fain dance forever.” Therewith the littel man betook her Legg in his hande and stript up her Juppes and Kirtel, nor could she say him *Naye!* Therewith the frene Man dyd frote her naked Leg as iff it were *Frore*, and itt became warm and was heled and saine. So she danced all night with the Stranger, as they were imbayed with Love. There with the wall did seem to open unto the *Landwide* or *Champagne* and the Two went dancing and caroling awaie behind Bush and Caprefole, and they vanisht dancing in ye Moonlighte.

(71)

D*ream Holes*. Thes be ye Sterrs, and how the Name cam was thus. Ther was of olde ere yet ye worlde begun a Gyant in whom were al Things. And hee said to himself Loe I am all alone and onlie One it wer beter gif ther were Many insted of Me. *So he gave himself to Deathe*. His bones became ye Rocks, his Flesh Earth, his Bloude the Sea, but of his Skul or Brain pan Heaven was made, and theye capt itt over ye Earth like a Lidd on a Pott. Then was the wold without Lighte – save for ye Moone. So did a great Gyant he took a greate Pine tre for a lance and prickt holes in the Skye or Skul so that ye Lighte came thro, and men had the Sterres which are onlie holes as some think to the day.

Now *Dreames* are a Kind of *Elvs that dwel in the Light and whan they saw that Holes*

(72)

had been prickt in ye Skye they crept thro' and came down to ye Earth and as was their Nature they found ther way to men and made them dreame. Some wil have itt that thes *Dreames* can not live of themselves and have no trew Life onless they can come into us, and that they ever yearn and long to thus live but can do naught without ye help of mortals. Hee or She who wolde faine have fair *Dreemes* must goe to Bed fasting and fal aslepe thinking thereof, and hee will have his Wish.

(73)

D*ule is the Devil, I doe thinke it is an Irish word*. There be men who are carneyed by the Dule or *Dule carnies*, that is, tricked or entysed by him. So is dule what is double for ye Devil is ever double-faced and lived with sinn. Dule Crooks are evill men. ther is a Flye hath the same name, all Flys are of the Devil. Dame Darrell saith Beelzebub is the devil of Flys, and ye Like, itt may wel bee. Dule is Dole or Suffering.

And itt sounds to me y't a Dule may bee as a Doll that is to say an Idoll that men worship even as Childer doe theyr dols I trow tis all one and ye Same all Idollatrie. And this minds me of a strange tale ther was a yoman who lived in ***[long blank space]*** this good man ones day in his plowing did turn upp a littl *imago* or Figure. itt was of baket Clay or Stone, had two brite Eyen like fire.

(74)

Hee knew not verily itt had been an ydoll of ye old Heathen folk that woned here afore tymes so hee gave itt to his Children to play wi' for a Dol. one Day as they played therewith came in they had set it upp for a Sainte and were playing att praying to itt. Then there came in a preest a very wise and learned Man who saide: What doe ye a praying to this accursed Dule, itt is a devill and no Seynt. Theron he tramped itt beneathe his Feete and broke itt. Out came from itt many brite and shining stones or Gemms. There yee have hee said What wil doe ye more good. As in trowth it did for the Yeman sold them for solid golde and grew riche. Truly many Men do worship in this world, many an idle or idoll Thing which were it broken would be beter for Them. For in many an old folly there is a dolly which whenn itt is broken giveth *gold token*.

(75)

D*rum is a Devilkin who sets at nought* the Saying that litle Children should be seen and never heard for he is often heard playing on a drum or Tabor in the Forest or green wood Whiche is mostly in the Autum. But few have ever sene him and some declare that Those who say theye did, *lookt at him thro' a Horne*, or that I maye not lye, thro' a Quarte Pott. which those who doe, do in faithe see wondrous Thinges, speciallie Faerys. Some say that to hear Drum is a sign of War, others that a King is to die.

Drum is like all his kin and kind, *sometimes honey and sometimes harsh* as his fancy goeth. Howbeit I have known a man of York, one Stephen Carr, who would hear no ill word spoke of Drum, and all for this that ones by Night when

(76)

he was in sore triall and hard stead, Drum helpt him out of it. And it twas this. Stephen was coming home from a Fair with a gret bag of gold, having sold and that merrily well all his Cattle, and with him were his three knaves, but he was beset by six Theeves with every strong Theef a sword or Pike, while the Knaves had but their knives and Staves. However Stephen and his men fought well "*to hard hold hard won Gold,*" as the Miller's rhyme says, yet were they about to yeeld or dye when there was heard *the rattle of a drum* close by and the sound as of many men. Whereat ye Theeves veraly believing that Soldiers were at Hand rann for their Lyves, as if the divell were lose. And so perhapps he was for devil a soldier or any other man could

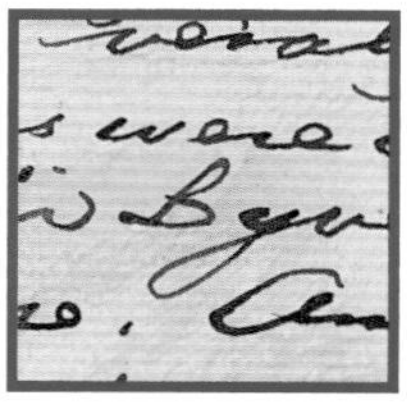

(77)

Stephen Carr see or find, far or near. Therefore all said 'twas Drum the devill who had drumd away the Theeves.

D*rudes are only Witches* among our common folk, but some say they haunt Oak Trees or use acorns in sorcery. And a man who was learned said to me They should not be called Drudes but *Dryads*, because they were a kind of *Elves*, born of the dryed Leaves which fell from Oakes, but of all this there is no word among the common folk. But the Witches called *Drudes* are known by the mark of their feet; 'tis said they can jump a mile but not fly and so it is they flee apace and afar. *Anabo!*

(78)

Now it oft haps that on trees but mostly on Oakes you may see great *Knurls or Lumps* which some cal *Boles* and from these Mazer Bowles are made which is the cause why they are cald Bowls. But some do cal them Witchs Heads for it tis said that *Drudes* or Oak Witches seek to be buryed nere Oak Trees. Than is their life, over Soule drawn into the Tree, and so their Heads grow outwards. And of yore there were fine Conjurations and Spels to make them speak. but these be nowe lost. Yet can ye drawe from Aye or No and the manner to do itt is this.

The manner to make a Bole answer.

Take Seven Oak Leefs and a powder of Thyme. And I thinke it is for Time long past. As I have found Itt in other spels for Past Time of old dayes for such Words have mostly a meaninge inside of them. And ye shall burne these mixt together to the *Bole* and saye

(79)

Drude, Drude, Drude
Tho now thow art rude
Once thow wert faire
Joly and debonair.
Let this be thy Taske
Moe I doe not ask
Unto what I pray
Answer Yea or Naye!
So shalte thow be
Ever dear to me
And may ye Woodman never fell thy Tree.

Thenn will ye hear in the Leeves of the Tree Yes or No, according to your Question. And I have heard that not far from York there was the ruine or Wals of a littel old church in which grew an Oake on which was a Drude or Bole very like a womans head, on which were all that pertains to a face, such as Eyes, Nose, Mouthe, very marvellous to behold this Heade had a neck, itt came forth oute of the Trunke as a Woman who lookt from a Window. And this Drude itt was told would talke at the Full of the Moon, unto

all who told the charme: *Erebon*.

It came to pass that the Bishop having heard this gave order that the Tree should be felld and burnt. Which was done but a workman stole the Drude and sold it to a certain witch and as I have heard it yet talks. And thus much of the Drudes, of which I have writ so much because they are so litel known though they be common in every wood.

Now will I speak of the *Eager* or *Eigir*. He is a spirit of the water, some do say he is a wild rising tide which comes in a hasty rage, others call the third wave which is mighty an *Eger* or *Eagre*. But it is a torrent or swash or great gurge ye can undirstand in which boats and men often perish. So the fisher wives do sing to him or Higre.

Eagre take the wicked man,
Let the canny folk alone.

(81)

E*lves* be Fayries without doubt or of Fairy kind, yet there are Fairys who are not Elves. Elves be light and dark, the Fairys are only light. Elves be ever small and I thinke them to be one with the Dwergs or Dwarfs. Dame Darrell thought them to have come sooner into the world. Faerys did not come out of the Light Sky World till Men grew larger and better albeit there were Gyants in those dayes and many *Drakes* ot Dragones. And of these too wil I speak anon. And *Thyme* is the bed wherein Man was bred when we tell children that Babes are found in Bedes of Thyme. Yea and all Things mortal do come thro that Portale. *Mon amy ie vous le dis*, as we did say in Jersey. In Frenche, La verite com lamour vient tojors au jour. –

The *Ellwives* I think like the *Ellmen* are Elves of the water. For there be Fishes which are called Alewives but they are Ale-wives tho in sporte Men call women who sell Ale by that name. Because they putt Water into Ale. The Ellmen are their Husbondes.

(82)

But *of this matter of Ellmen and Ellwives there is Mistery now.* and of it Dame Darrell spoke to me once on a tyme. *Least of all of these Thinges is what is known.* For as't ofte befals hee who hath store of gold and silver manifold yif he have a great Lord for a naybor who is a Stronge Theefe or such like round him, hides it away, Even so they that have greate Secretts which are their *Lyves* have litle luste to make them over to the common folk whereof to bee japed and *jibed* if no worse. Now ther bee Familys wherein *Ell Folk make their Homes*

(83)

and live in Peace, and no Mann or Woman knoweth there of, save the Master or his kin, and these feare to tell as twere come Deathe stopp Breath. Let the Secret fly thou shalt surely die. And these folk be mostly akin or sib to the Ellmen. For in the old time the Ell men often lay with the daughters of those who were wizards and witches or of the old faithe of hethene Idoles, or the Ell wemen had joye in Men, and so were born full many who had strange giftes. Tis saide they could talk wit the Deade with Drudes Heades in Okes – yea, with Streames and the Wind and old Head-Stanes and with all Images, with Spirites in ye Lakes and Hils. That was no true Ell man's sone who could not with a Witche Hasel wand or Rod find him a hidden store, nay 'tis said this Folk could see through Wals and Rockes, Ther dwelt in ***[long blank space]*** in Yorkshire, such a Family in an old House far and lone, litle did they see of other People, no one kenned

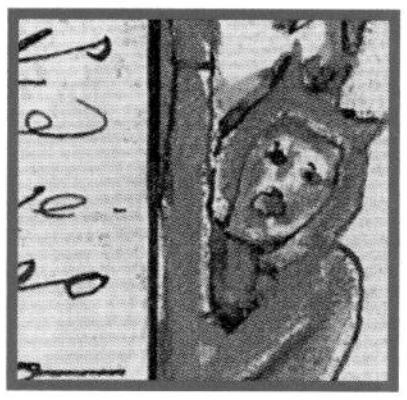

(84)

how they lived, live wel they did wanting neither meal nor malt, honey or Salte Meate or aught to eate – whence it came God knows from whome every Blessing flows, for they had no handicraft and followd no trade save that the Master had ever a good hose or Jacke to sell, or a Bulocke to swappe. But gold they all had ever in purse and went clad in brave attire. Now it befel that a certain man ever bore about him Saint John's Hearb and Rue and a charm whereby to behold hidden Things. And one day at a Fair in York he sold unto this other yeman a pair of Oxen, and he who boughte them said: to the Oxen: Go home! And in that time the seller beheld the Buyer take from his pocket a smal Impe or Goblin and sett it

(85)

on the Ox's neck. And he wened that the other saw itt not, howbeit by the Virtew of his charmes he saw all and knew that the other dealt with Ell-folk. Where *Ellwives* and *ell-men* hide, the house is aye kept clean, the cattle cared for and all the work done. In olde Familys they nurse ye Childrene that no harme befal them. There was an Elf was wont to cary a babe to the top of a very high tree, this was not far from Berwicke, there he would sit for Houres rocking up and down on a bough, singing Rock a by baby upon the Tree top. I have heard that the song came from this. I can wel believe it. the Mother took no feare, but only said –

What to my grandsire's great grandsire was done
May hapen I wene to the Elf and my son.

So there be full many Familys wherein *Ellmen* dwel and none know it, because when 'tis tolde they go awaye. As Dame Darrell said, *Plura latent quam patent*. More thinges hidden be than ere are sene by mortall Eye. –

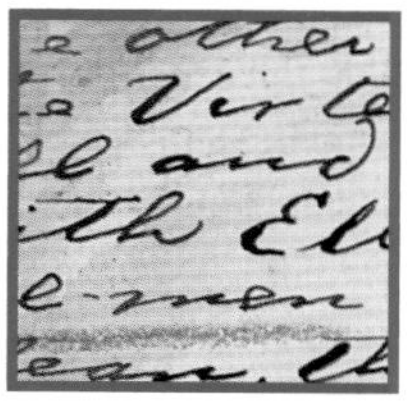

(86)

Of *Friar Rush* I telle you ther be more merry tales than true since everie Gammer in the Land hath one and the beste a Jeste. However what hee is is a Goblin that is hight Good Fellowe Robin, and his Crafte and Calling, that is to play Trickes and putt Japes on Travelers or any other men or Mayds and iff he findes none of Them, since Maydes have growne rare of late here Abouts, he mocketh any Wemen. Thus the Fyer or Lighte which is seen in Marshy Places, which some doe call Will of the Wispe which leadeth Men astray is trewlie Friar Rush with his Lanthorne, a rushing here and there in the Nighte.

(87)

Fays is noughte but the Frenshe for Fairys as I well know, since in the Isle of Jersey where I was borne theye did call them so But some Folk will so have itt that Fays are the Bubbels or Blubbers or Buls which rise and fall and dance and burst on running water. Truly they looke like little Heads which are alive. And Dame Darrell told me that whan you see a Bubbel-Fay or Bulle floating, if you bee a Mayd and counte, one two three, so many Numbres as ye can co'nt ere it burste so many Loves shall you have, or if you like itt better, so many Lemans ere you dye. I knew one who thus counted to a thousand for it was a very stiff Bulle when shee walkt away and said "Goddes mercie – that is enough for any Woman!"

(88)

F*airy Heads*. Thes be stones as of Greye Flint – the Bignes of a Wallnut. – Ye find them in Gravel and Pebles. Some doe look much like a Heade I have seen them with all the Linements of a Face. Now of these ther goeth a Tale how in the olde Time there were Fairys by the Hundred Thousand in the Land when there came an evil race of Wizzards and Witches who were kept out of the country by a Spel. And the Wizardes promist the Fayries that if they would lett them come in to the Land not a head of the Faies should be hurt and they should endure forever. But mark how they kept

(89)

their troth. For by their magic they slew all the little Faerys and turned their Heades to stones.

This is a Conjuracion of a Fairye Heade. – If ye find one which is good or like to a real Heade, Frote or rubb it with rue and Sainte John's Hearb on the night when the Moone is full, and saye

Curst be they
Who did thee slaye!
Curst for ever
Beyond deliver
In sooth and truth
By the wolfs tooth
And the bitter Thorn
And the Drak unborn
And the red Fire
And the cold Mire
By North and South
And the wolf's mouth
By East and West
But bless the Hand which gives thee rest!

Tis saide that a Heade soe enjoined will talke, and it brings Lucke. And set in the Moon-lighte, there comes to it an aeriall Body, then doth the Fairie dance merrily.

(90)

Now this is a Secret, quent and rare – that if ye tak any Peble or round Stone, but far and away the best be these Fairy-Heades, ye can hear itt say Yes or No as playne as a Pego. And this is the way as Maudlin saide to Jacke. Take a Fairy-head or Urchine, and wash it well in Springe Water nine times and say every tyme

Heade which wert
As thou art
And ere shall be
By the rook and the crow
Say to me ere I go
No or Yes – Yes or No!

(91)

This shall be done by nighte, under a full Moone, by a Wel or Poole or such Water but it must be depe and Stil. Than throw the Stone upp, so that itt fall into the Wel and as itt plumpes in ye can it say Yes or No. There was a merrie girl who had one of these fairie heds which lookt like a Damsel's face, or that of a little Virgine. and one day she threw it into a pool, and got her answer, but when she sought to finde the Stone in ye water shee could not reach itt. So she went to a House neere by and askt for a Rake. For as she saide She had loste her litle Mayden-Heade. To which a wise man made reply that he had often known a Rake to tyne a Maydenhed, or lose one, but never to finde such a Thing.

(92)

F*litter-Mice they ben Bats because they be like mice yet do theye flitt and fly like unto a Swalow. So are they most uncanny* of Fowle for the femell hath Titts and gives sucke to her Younge. And as they come out by Twilighte ever as ye Darke groweth Mirk to chason Midges and cry Cheep, Cheep like speakin wordes so are they like Humane Folk. And this cometh because they are of a Kind, Faeries. Yet would I saye Elves or Swart-Elves, of the Night yborn, runneth ye Tale, that once in a month they become like litle men and wemen Then doe they beget their kind. Whereof a Tale:

(93)

Itt fel on a Time long afore Any Bodie dremed I woulde write or that Thowe would reade these Old Wives tails that ther dewlt hard by Beverly a young Man of gentill bloud but most ungentil fortune sith he was a pore schollar. Now he dwelt in an olde House lone as any Mouse and not like a Mows in a Chese either. And not afar was a very high Hil, or steepe Rocke on topp of which was an old Tower and for as much that a great side of the Rocke had faln away no man could climbe to it. And as no body wanted to theye ene let it alone. One Even whan this Scholler was sitting by his Fyre with a Booke he found in itt

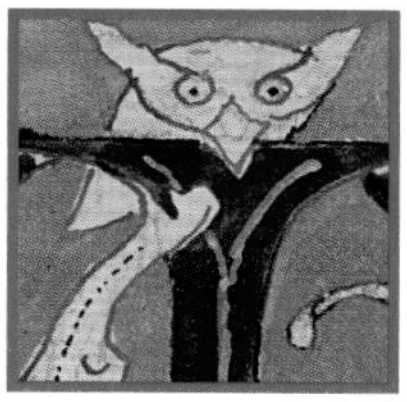

(94)

a Spel whiche all unwyting hee reade alowde and itt was a Conjuracion by which any one not a Birde or suche Beinge hearing of itt could become Humane according to itts kind male or femell. And whan he had done this he heard a crye as of Chepe, chepe, here I am as the Lamb to ye Ram So he cald *'Come in,'* and lo there entered a verie little but comely maide, all clad in soft fur. And the ende thereof she stayd by him and lay by him as Gilian did to Jocke until one nighte she sayd to him, I have Something beneath my Smocke. What is that saide he.

"And she answered sooth and faire:
Well I trowe
That thou shouldst knowe
Sith thow didst putt it there."

And this thinge was a Babe. So time past and shee was lighter for the Babe was y-born. Now the mother was ever wilde as a hawk and

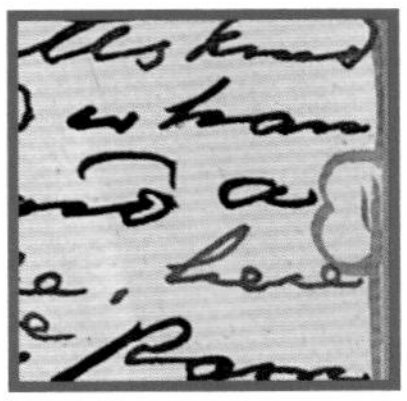

(95)

full of capricios, oft time she would Leape aboute Like mad, running after Flys, ever merry. Whan one Evening they heard from without in the Mirk a cry of "Fleta, come!" and she said That is for me. Heer can I no longer Stay, my time is ore, I cant delay. But iff thow shouldst ever bee in dire Nede, to ye childe make thy Rede. She will holpen thee in Dede.

Therewith off she ran and was no more seene. But the Childe who was now a twelmonth olde spoke to his wonder, and saide Dere Father doe not greve for my Moder has left me her Voice seens that shee hath no use for it more.

Now itt befal on a Tyme that ye Scollar was so pore hee made his mone to the Childe

(96)

And hee saide to hir. My dere Doughter today I have no Peny wherewith to buy Breade. I lacke Monney. Than the litel Maid replyed Is money those rounde shining Thinges which thow hast in thy Poke. Yea quod hee. Than she replied I know well wher to seke. And my Mother taught me ere shee went awaie how to flie Thereatt she became all at ones a Batt and flew away bot soon came back with an olde gold crown and became a Maid agen and saide There is plenty mo wher that came fro, It is pon the top of yon tower on the Rocke. So he became riche.

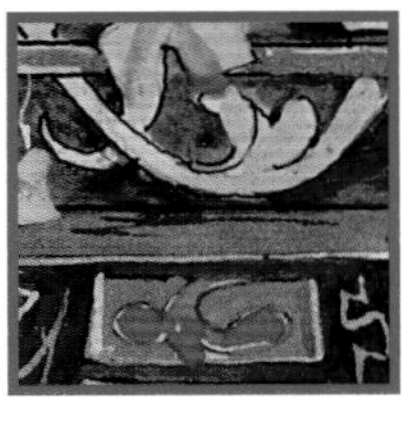

(97)

Gyants wern afore-time long agone but they ben no more in the Lande in thes Days. Some will have it that there never were any, but that is Fools Talk since we read of them in the Bible. And I have sene with my owne Eyes hanging in the market-place in ***[long blank space]*** wher itt had been for an houndred Yeres the Thy-bone of a Gyant of exceeding great Bigness

(98)

In the oldene Time and ene yet while good Kinge Arthur rayned in this Land or ere he stole three Sackes of Barley meale to make a Bag Puddinge there was a mightie Gyaunt in the Lande, who was withal as I wen a Kinde of God to the Hethen Folke, ye Divill Kens what all, however hee dieyd and was buryed and a great Stone twenty Cubits long layed over his Grave and Oke Trees grew up and hung over itt, and they are ther yett,

(99)

Nowe it byfell there was a certain Yemmen, a bold carl of quik witte, a very good fellow who going his waye one Even. And as he was carrying a carcas of a Sheep. being weary came to ye Gyants Grave and laide his sheep on it and sat down to rest. And laying itt down he said without Thout God be wi' ye! Than he saw rise oute of ye Grave a greate Giante grisly he was to see and the Gyant said Dis thou brynge this to me for an Offeryng to worshyp me Than ye Yeman who was wise aswered quikly

(100)

Itt is trew said the Yeman. I laide itt here as an Offeringe to the. Itt is a Lye replyd ye Gyant and that was layd on with a Trowell I trowe y't thous't never want for a Whet Stone. –Thereon hee lofte and they who heard itt afar off tho't it was Thounder.

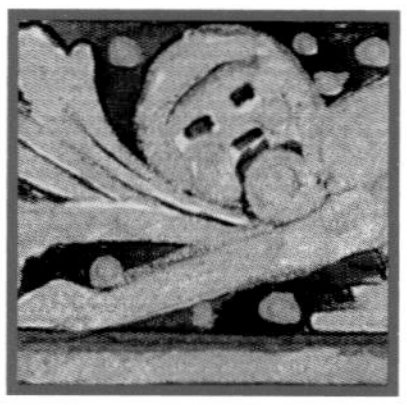

(101)

G*ally-Bird* is one whiche maketh gret feare, the Wodewale or mad bird is like it, both are witches. *Gale* or *gally* giveth drede as doth the Nightingale, tho its song be swete it singeth Woe. these be all strange thinges. So is a *Galleytrot,* a thinge like a Barghast very fearsome to beehold. some call itt Gallows bird, it beth not that, for so are things mixt. He who meets a Galley-*trot, should say:*

Ab-ba-acca-adda
Affa Agga!

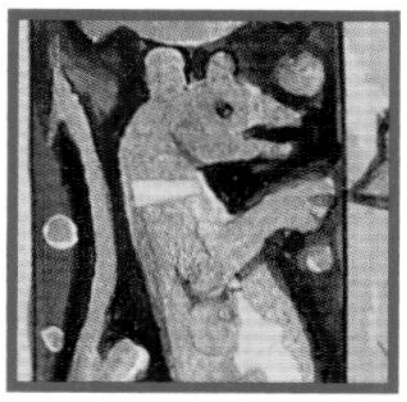

(102)

G*oose* and *the Ganse* and *Gander* is all one a gander gutted man is a leane Foole. Yet are Geese held to be wise, yea a kind of Witches for Witches doe often apere as Geese. att Michelmasstide. or keep theyr kind and Folowers in such a forme. And whan a Lord or great man dyeth than doe these noble Fowle flapp theyr Winges and skrithe and gabble like as many *Ratches in ye Skys* of an evening. And she or Hee who would conjer the *wild Geese* on the wing to flye lowe must sing.

(103)

By the white One
Which shineth as Sun
Ever in light
And in the black
Two of Night
And the Violet thre
At dawn on the Sea
And the *Blew-black Four*
Of eve, evermore.
And the *blew Six*,
Which doth entermix
Earth and Heaven
And *the Green Seven*,
And *the Yellow eight*,
And the *Orange Nine*
Which doth ever combine
With the *Red Ten*

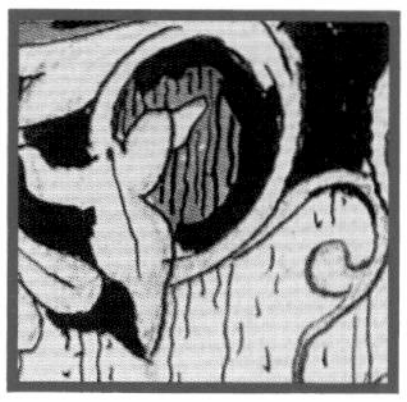

(104)

Which brings Life agen,
And the Silver *eleven*
In number uneven
And the Twelve which is seen
In the Moonrays sheen.
I conjer ye, Geese,
though high ye go,
To come down to me
and this world below.

Than will Ye Gees swoop down and this Song does as well for Duckes howbeit there are Witchs and Warlaws in the North who can bringe Fowles adown with one word or by beknyne to them with the fingeres.

(105)

[105 has a full page silver-point drawing to illustrate the rhyme on the following page.]

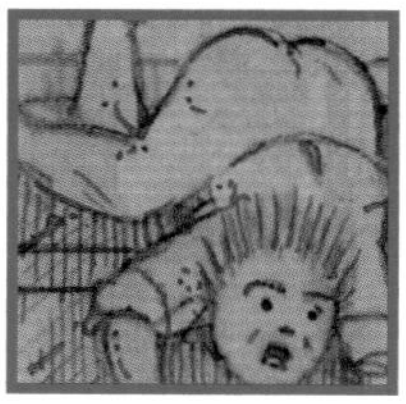

(106)

Now I have writen of the Spel to call Geese and this minds me of a folish little Song which Childern singe to a Goos but and yet Dame Darrel wold have itt and no put up, that itt was a Conjeration to plese and charm the Fowle. And itt is this.

Goosey Goosy Gandere!
Whedere dost thou wandere
Upp Steyers, down Steyers
In my Ladis Chambre:
Ther I mett a litel Boye
Who wolde not say his Preyers
I tooke him by th left Legg
And strake him doune ye Steyers.

How be it there were of yore som kinde of *Heretikes* or *Lolards* in the Land who did woship both a Goos and a Pigg, and Dame Darrell said they swore in the name of a *Bore* which they call ye Gulenborst or Borstle which is golden Bristels att New Years tide and swore what they would doe the Coming Yeere.

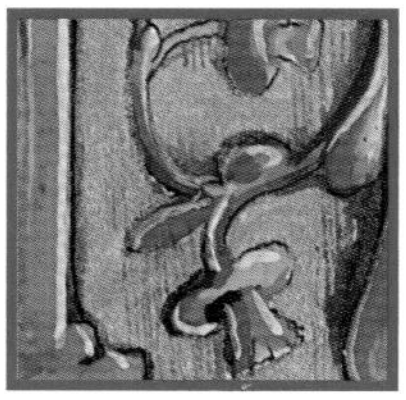

(107)

G*aster or Gaste is a spirit which causes exceeding great feare yet will I not say it is a comon Ghost,* but rather any Bugg or terible thing because as men say they are *gastered* or agast at a *Gastne* which is a specter of any kind, the Lord keep us all therefro, and all haukit Thinges!

From the nightmar and ye Gobin
Which is hight Good Falowe Robin.
And all which wandereth by night
Between the duske and morning light.

Ther was a Gentleman who lived neer **[long blank space]** in a large Manor. therein wonde a *Gaster* very horrible to behold one daye the Gentlem'n saw the *Gaster* and conjered it with a strong spel so that the spirit was agast himself and said, Now I feare thow wilt conjure me out of house and home and loe I have dwelt here this fower hundred Yeeres and done no harm. Nay re

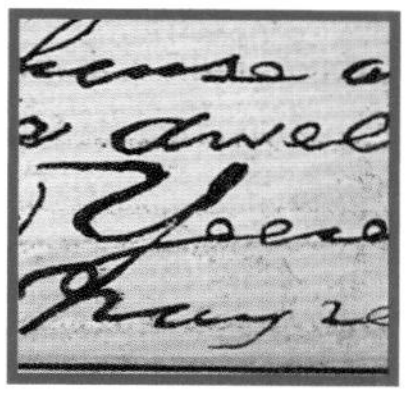

(108)

plyd the Master, I do rather conjer the to remaine an thou wilt doe somewhat for me. what wilt thou have quoth ye Gaster. Only this that whan my men servantes or Maids would steale aught from me or doe aught Amiss that thou fray them. That can I well do said the Gast till they fal down in a fullock. So he went his way and I trow from that day the Lord lost little. So the Gaster served as a horrorr and a Scar to the Crows. (Illegible) . . . . Jankin who made a *Scar for Crowes* so terrible . . . . . he was wel-nye scart to death of Itt him selfe. Truly ther be amany things which are all Funk or Gamen and Gillor as old folk say, yet which doe good, for what is a holy besant to the wise and learned may be a holy Sainte to Another. Eagles fearen naught Scarcrowes. And so a Bull-beggar is a Begger to a Bull and this ends my discorse on the Gaster.

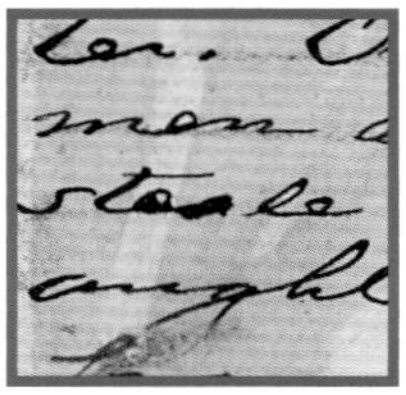

(109)

G*uest is a Ghoste* as some say and nat more but Dame Darrell would have it a Guest-gost is something more, for itt is a *Gaster* that comes straungely to a gret Feaste or Weddyngs or where many Folk be met for merryment, also to Buryalls or any kind of Croude or any manere of galliarding, as at Fairs. And these be the *Bogies* of men and wemen who while on life did ever go about to other folk and theyr Feests and Fayts and never were at Home for which they now dree their Weyrde and do Penaunce. however they doe no Harm and vanish if any one say –

Guestes Ghosts if here ye bee
I bid ye go I bid ye fle
In the name of the Trynitie
Bide no more I bid by me!
Vade in pace. Abite!

(110)

Havel is ye Slough or Skin of a snake which itt casteth off. let those who find 'Em guard 'em with care for they doe bringe good Fortune but they are beste when found by chance and nott whan sought after. Those who will never kill a snake nor make any pain or tormente to Man or Child or anie of God's creatures or in killing aughte doe gett great good Luck fro such *Havels*. Ther was a verie poore man of that ilk who hadd such Kindess that he spared all Snakes ther Lyves. So one Daye hee found a Havel and on the next there came to him a greate Estate of which he had loste al Hope and soe itt ever went wi hym, God grant us in his Grace all the Same!

(111)

Hegge is a *Hagg* or *Witch*, but chefely one who changeth the faces or favour or *Form of Children* making al that ill which was once fair. For whiche there be many Cures one is to pass the Child thro' a *cleft* Oake or other Tree, or *a Holy Stone*. Or to conjer the Witch with boiling her Clothing till shee be tormented or to hang a red Cloth or Corals on the Child but in sothe ther bee so many Savings for all this Sorowe that I have not paper enowe in my Booke to write Them all down God save Us and Ours from all Trouble!

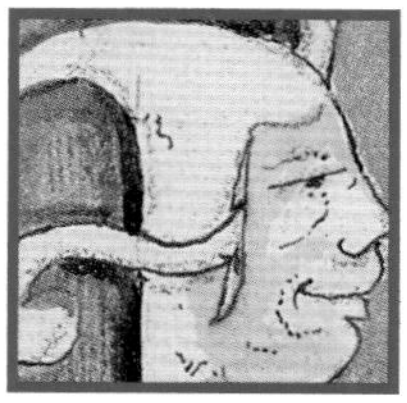

(112)

H*ella is the Nighte Mare* shee that was aforetime ye Quene or Lady in Helle of all the Witches and sent forth her Witches & Bitches to torment Christen folk in ther Dreames by Nighte howbeeit, *Mare* is not a Horse but as I thinke either *Mere*, a Mother, as we doe saye in Jersey, or as many say *Mare* for any Whore or shee-devill, or Impe or Hagg. Itt is said the Hella hath such madd delite to bee the Nightmare as Menn have to enjoy Wemen, and Wise men have Devices to intrap them and bring them to repentaunce. Yea and itt often haps that there be Nightmares among our Gossipes and Nyboures, tho no one wetes therof ne of theyre Sinns and Subtleties.

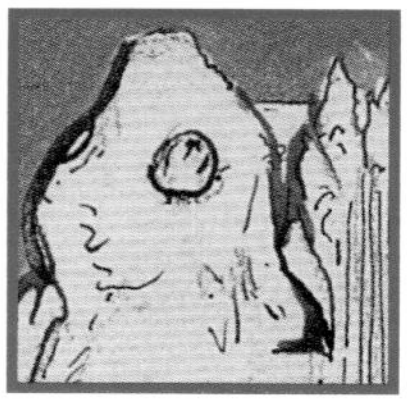

(113)

Hell wain is the greate fiery wain or wagon which is seen in the sky a nights in wh'h the witches doe ryde with theyr Quene and of which are many old Tales.

Hob goblin is soe cald from Hobb as one says Jacke O Lantern, and in sooth the same is often y-cleped Hobby Lanthorn, and itt meneth wel ny any Fende or Goblin which frayeth and friteneth.

Hob Thrush is a goblin, but not so evill. Hee is a merrie Sprite who maketh Mischief and Sporte, but seldom greate Scathe.

(114)

H*oodkin or Hodekin or Hotkin* tis al the same and means a merry Impe though a Lether bottel is also so called, Hotkin is al one with Robin Good Fellow, *but he wereth a Hoode*. It is a merry Tale that once on a time a good man who was going a long journey Left his Wife who *a loose Piece to the care of Hodekin to keep* Men from lying with her and this hee did *but had so mickle Trouble to drive her Lemans away that whan ye Husbond returned he said: "Never again Robin, for I had leefer drive a Thousand wode Swine thorough a Forest, than have the care of one Whore."*

(115)

J*emmy Burty or Berty which means one who sweats and is aheat* is al one with the Will o the Wisp and Jack o' lantern and is so cald because he maketh men to *bert* or puff and sweate who do toyle after him. There was on a tyme a man who had been by so misled by a certaine Goblinn, and so going to a Wise Woman or Warlok he gott a Magicke Lantern with which he went forth to the *marish* and whan the Burty would fain delude him he saide:

"By the Starres so brite
Which are the Dream-holes of Night!
Go thou into my Lanterne!
There shalt thou for ever burn
And for Wonder unto all,
Caste thy Image on the Wall!"

And *Dame Darrell* tolde me she had truly seen this miracle with her own Eyes how that the Impe did showe himself in Light. I trowe itt is trew.

(116)

A Kern baby is a Dol or Image made of strawe, which at Harvest tide the country folk or reapers doe make of Straw, on the fielde whan all is ingathered, of the last Sheaf. Then they bear itt before them and sing a Song untoe ye Harvest Supper. But iff ye ask mee what it al meanes I think *Kern* is *Corn*. And itt was beleved of old that this was a living *Elphe* or *Ouphe* who made ye Corne grow, and gave good luck wherefore they still worship its Image with greate Merriment. Finis. to ye Knacke

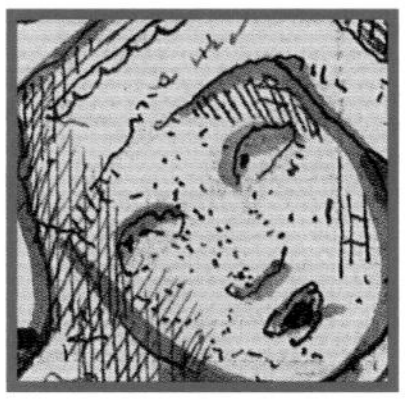

(117)

K*itty Witches* these be the Ghosts or Spectres of Wemen, or a kind of *Witchs* such as come pering and peeking out of strange places all to quappe and fray folk like a Momo. So they popp forth from betwene curtaines or fro under Bedds or in Bushes and Trees, or out Tankards, and I have heard of a drol tale how once there was a Wise Man and one Night as he took up his *Piscine* or *Chambre-pott* there rose from it the Head of a Kitty-Witch. Thenn hee clapt the Lid on, and so enchanted her that she should dwel forever in that blessed Vase, and therein shee woneth to this Day, wherever it bee. but Wher that is I know not.

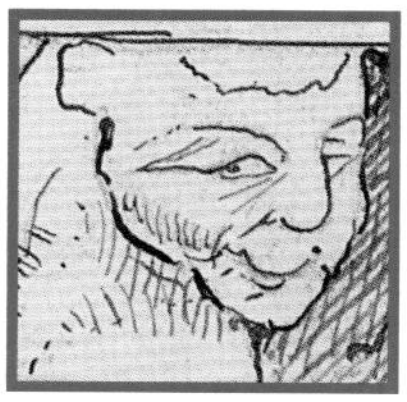

(118)

L*averock* is a Larke that is a Birde yet it is of Faery kind, and bringeth good Lucke and a merrie Heart to all who never doe itt harm but tis bad lucke to kill it. And I thinke y't ye name is from ye Frenshe word *Laricot* or Larko which is a pipe or flute which soundeth like a Larke Songe when 'tis so played And tis saide the Larke flieth in the morning upp to Heaven and asketh in its Singing Is itt time? meaning Is it time for me to come in? And a voyce answereth Not Yett. then the Larke in sorowe falleth adown to Earth. Of the Larke is a folish little ditty

Tiri liri lor peine ye Laverok song
So merrily piped ye Sparrow.
The cow brake loose and ye Pope ran home
Syr, God give you a good Morrow!

(119)

Laurence In the olde tyme ere Saintes were in the Lande ye folk had Faerys and Goblinns of a Kind and those that wer lazy and lother to work did pray to Laurence. Or as Dame Darr'l said:

Who would idle all ye Daye
Unto Laurence let him pray!
Than as ye may truly see
He'll himself a Laurence bee!

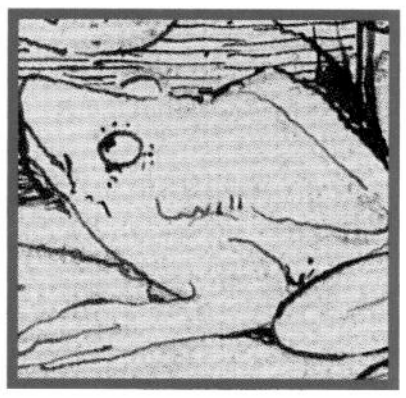

(120)

L*udlam* This I Learned from a man who came fro the South he was from Surry. There is a great Caverne called *Ludlam's Hole* in which whilome dwelt a Witch called *Dame Ludlam*, a white one who harmed none. When a man or woman had nede of aughte *They went to the Hole and walkt thre times round itt making theyer prayer. And the morowe morn what they prayed for was ever found in the Entry to ye Caverne*. Thus they did borrowe all they wanted. But one time a man borowed her *Kettle or Iron Pott*, and did nott returne Itt. And She was so angered that *from tht Day foorth Mother Ludlam wold never lend or give aught to Anybodie*.

L*oterie* is ye telling of Fortunes or Divinatione in any Way and a Lott wife or Lottellere is such a Witch, for Lots be fortunes and a *loteby is a Lemman or Lyer-bye*

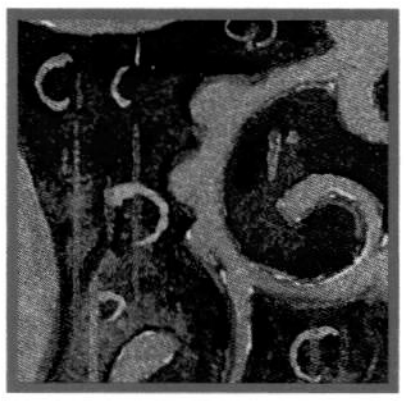

(121)

Madge was of old a nun who became a witch because shee longed for a loose Lyfe, and was at Heart a greate *Whore*. And so shee was turned into an Owle which seketh Lovers by night. Hence both Witch owls and ***[long blank space]*** are called Madge.

Of all ye Byrds I ever did se
Ye Owle is the fayrest in hir degre
For all daye long shee sitts in a tre,
And whan ye Nighte comes away flys shee
Tu whitt – too how!
Sir Knave to thou.
This song is well sung
I make you avowe.
And tis Nose! Nose! jolly red nose.
And whatt gave thee that joly red nose
Nuttmegs and cinamon spices and cloves
And they gave me this joly red nose!

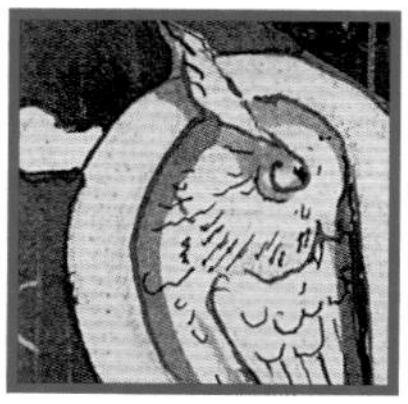

(122)

M*alise* or *Mallys* is ye Marsh mallowe or Maule, and itt is the same Word with *Malice* w'h means *witchecrafte*. and I doe think from this is *Mally* a hare. And wee in Jersey did ever ever call bad fortune *Malure* in our Frenche, whiche is like *Malire* a *Mallow* since Witchcraft bringeth woe. But both *Mallys* and *Mandragores* be used in Magick for many things. But most marvellous is the Mandrake or Man-dragon roote which hath Life or a soule and is a kinde of Devill or Elfe, whan itt groweth neathe a Gallows it springeth tis said from ye man who hangs there and screams whan itt is pulld out of the ground. Men make Images of roots which they call Mandrakes. therin is often great Deceite and Cozening for these be none true Mandrakes.

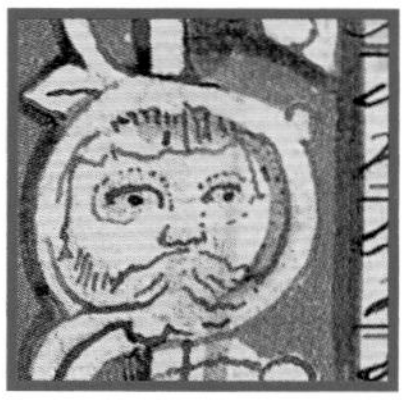

(123)

M*are meaneth many Things and all evill or mockes*. For a *Mare* is any Bugg of the Derke or Terror, also a witch or a devill or hag or Harlot or Whore. And I have herde that in some places instead of a Kerne Baby or Knacke they make in Harvest Time att the Ende the Image of Woman fro a Sheafe and call it a *Mare* and cutt the strawe which binds it like a Belt and whoop and crye: Whatt hast thow. I trow a Mare. This I wene is the true story and the *Mare* is the Mother of the Corn because Mare is mother in Frenshe.

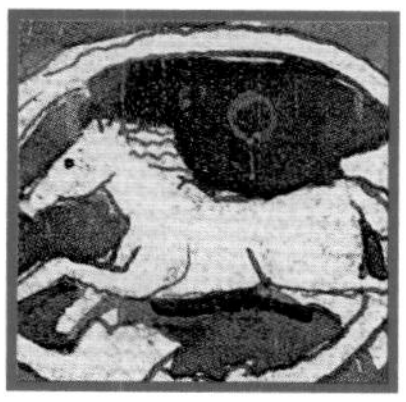

(124)

Meg *with the Wad* is all one withe Will o' the Wisp for a *Wad* means a wisp of Straw, wh'h means any idle Whiffle which is nought, like a Skendish or show on a Table which hath naught therein. But this Meg is all one I trow with the other *Madge the Howlet,* who whooreth by night, onlie that Madge is an Owle and Meg the mate of a goblin, be it *Jacke o' Lanthorn or Robyn Goodfelowe* or all of 'em first one and then another. However these be all Tales of the very old time when the Goblins were as Godds and these stories of straw and Lanthorns meant Thinges which are now unknown

(125)

Mormo is a fearsome ghost or Gaster yea a Spectre. No one I ever knew could tell much about itt, but I think itt should be called *Marmo* sith itt is a *Mar* or *Mare* which means a Bugg or *Terror*. Butt in our Frenche of Jersey we do commonly call any monkey-like figure or odd and uglie little Creature or Image a *Marmot*. so do they cal a *marmouset*, but itt did in truthe mean an odd and strange Thing ere itt did a monkey or the like. Now *Marmotter* is to murmer and mutter to oneselfe and this the *Mormo ever doth, att all Tymes*.

(126)

M*urch* meneth a *very litle Man* or a *Goblin* but more a Devilkin becaus Murchy is also Mischief. house men say *The old Murchy!* which is the old Devill. And some say Mirshty, these be Southren folk. And some call the Devill, Mischief.

Nick is a name for ye *Divell* yet it cometh not as Fooles say fro Seint Nicolas but from *Nick or Neck a Spirit of ye Water* who lives in Rivers or the Sea and was greatly feared of old time. He was also called of old Nickir. Hee dwelt in the cold sea. I doe thinke that *Nikkle*, as many doe cal *Iccles*, that is *Ice candles or Ice-shockles or Shoggles*, is all att one *with Nickel the Spirit*. He singeth often and men who have herd him say his Song is sad and sweete. He riseth up from the Water like a round *Bulle or Bubble* which is called *a Nick*, as is the round and rising Bottom of a pott or Bottel.

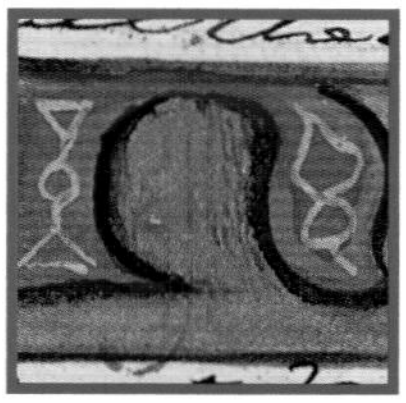

(127)

The *Night-bat or Night Mare* tis all one and the same. Itt is a woman Mare or Terror. she hath Winges of a batt. some did call itt the *Night Raven,* which hath Feadthers. Of all which there be soe many tales and rimes that I might wel fill all this Booke with them, as if it semed thatt all Bugges were Night Mares. –

(128)

And of all Spels y't ever were spelled there is nat one which is oftener said than one of the *Nightmare* to Seinte George, al be it manie do maken it Some to one Sente and some to Another. And itt is this. Firste ye shal say –

In nomine Patris et Filii et Spiritus Sanctu!
Seinte George our Ladys Knight
Hee walked by daye and eke by Nighte,
Untill ye Nightmare he found.
Her hee beate and Her he bound
Till her Troth to him Shee plite
Neer to come within his sighte
Thereas Seinte George our Lady's Knight
Named was three times thatt nighte.

And like unto this is another

"Seinte Wittold footed thrise ye Wold
Hee mett ye Nyt-mare and her 9 fold:
He bade her alighte
And her Troth plite
And arynt the, witch, arynt thee!

Arynt means May thy necke be twistyd!

(129)

N*oah's Arks* These be Cloudes which do seeme like Arkes or Boats or Shipps in the Sky. they come before *Raine* or a Storme. Itt is saide however that they are truly Shipps made by the Witches and Warlaws who lade them with *Hail Stones or Snow* and then caste itt adown and all to shente and spoyl the Corne and Graine. *There is a Tale of a certain gently man who was on a Castle* by a Magnel which shotes great stone balls. And seeing above him a Noe's Ark he with a Chalke drew on a stone ball ye Signe or a Cross and say'd *In Nomine Domini* and so shott at ye boat.

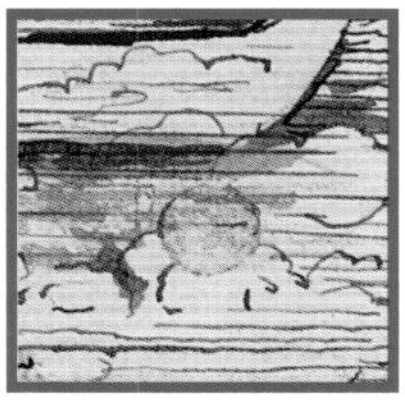

(130)

Then behold ther fell down from the Aire a Witche, a faire yonge Woman and hee knew her for a Ladye of great Renoun shee begd him *Misericorde*, being thus miscreed begged Him not to mistreat her. And he sayd Ile let the goe and say naughte iff thou leave thy Witchcraft and become a Christene. so must thou now say a *Paternoster*. so shee dyd when all at ones there came from the Boat above a Skeepe or shott of Lightening and a bolte but itt twined fro her and hurted her not as she made the sign of the Cross. So he made her his Wife and all went wel with them.

Nut-Hake or *Nutt-hack* This name is by right *Nutt Hag*. for it is of a Bird which is comonly held to bee a *Hag* or a *Witch*, for a *Jay* is a whore and a *Jay pie* or a *Nutt hacke* is a chattering bird, and eke a woman who jaweth over much. And I thinke that itt is also cald a Jay-Hawk, one who maketh mischief. And whenn one will say You Lie he cryeth *Nutt Hook*, tis all one and ye Same, for as all Roads lead to Rome all these words meane evil report. Tis all one with a *Nighte Hawkes* name.

(131)

Old *Bendy* is I wis al one with ye Devill Dame Darell sayth it is *Banedy* – for *Bane* is ever Skathe as what is *Skathy* is of mischief and so is Hee. Aso *Banned* or outlawed by the Horn of which he hath two which shows him to bee a rank Cuckold. And *bendy is also bondage* so is he evill in all as whatt bends or is bent, is crookt and evill. so is *Bendy* all twistyd even unto his talye and his Hornes which is their Meaning.

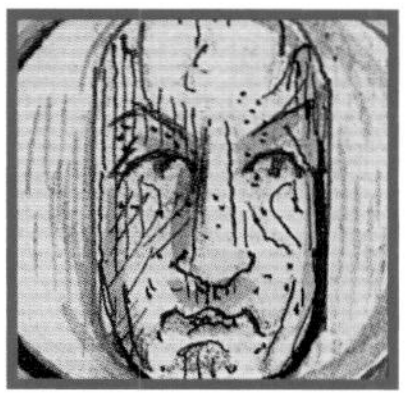

(132)

Old *Shock* is a gobblin who is is strange to se, very rough and covered with long Haire like a dog or some say a calf. so do many call a hairy dog a *Shock*. But this is no good Elfe, so do we call a man of bad fame and Name a *Shocker*, and a Good-for-Naught a *shack* who is a ragged and worthlesse felowe or Wafy. And this is one with Shag or *Shake* as when one hath to do with Wemen, and a lewde fellawe is a *Shag-ragg*.

T*here was a man of Beverley* who was ill treated by his town-folk, and all for nowt. They cald him ye *Shagg*. And it misliked him sore. One night he mett with a strange hairy kinde of Man brute who askt him: "Why so sadd?" He answered "And why not, sith all the Folk curse me and cal me *Shagg*, and God wot I have

(133)

never done Skathe to them nor theyrs And there is not a Mayde who dothe nat laffe att mee – the Divell knowes why." Then saide ye *Shock*, For this they shall dearly abye. Take thou this stoffe and whan thou dost touch Maid or Wyfe with Itt so shall she suffer and know no peace til shee hath laine by the. And so itt came to pass. For whann a Maide did gibe him or a *Giglet or gibbylot jeer him, than did* hee *jape* her and make her his *Jay,* And soe itt came to pass he had his Revenge.

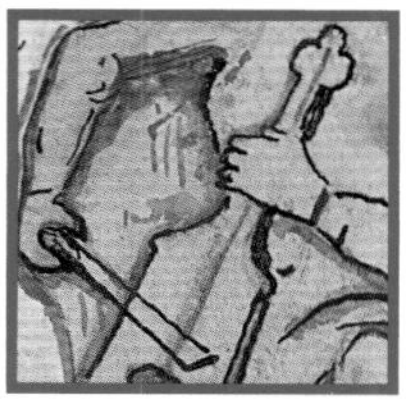

(134)

O*uphe is an Elfe, a Sprite or Faerie*, but many take it for a clumsie Goblin like the *Shack* since we doe call a rude Fellow an Oafe, as if it were the Oneliest and Chief of Fools. But these bee of the Folk to whom all that is not an Angel is un-good and all Fays devills, which is to say that God filld al the Aire and Skye and Earthe, yea and the Watres and Woodes, with Devills and Hellikins, and all to worke Evill. Whiche thing Dame Darrell woulde in no wise believe, altho' common folke in theyr Faithe have twenty Bogles and Terrors for one Good Fairy. Which did but *stablisse* as shee said y't ther was twentie times as much swill in Burrel, Bulfinche and comon *Bors* as in gentle Folke, for the beter people be, the betre do they thinke of all

(135)

P*hasmation* is all one withe a *Fantome* or anye Thinge that is fantastic or fancical or fantomy. some call em Fantasms and say they aren Ghosts of Dead. this Dame Darrel did not alow. Shee held them to bee born in many Wais even from the idle Thoughtes of Menn which escaping take on thin bodies of air or thick vapour, or fro Dreames of Love making, or are begoten by Elves on Mayds in Sleepe, or by the Elves or on one another. For al kind of Life passeth into Life anew as vapour is born of Water. –

(136)

P*ictrees are ghosts. I think of the Picts who were a folk in the lande of olden time but Dame Darrell thought it one with Pigwiggen, a very little Elf or Faery* who per hapus or happsing dwelt in Trees every one under a Leafe. A Pigling is a very small thing of smal account. And this minds me that a Pigg may come into the reckoning becaus hee who sleepeth in a Pigs crow or a Stye will have true Dreames. whereof there is an old story of a King who was betrayed by a false servant. who slept with him in a Loose. But little thinges be *piggy* as a *piggy whidden* which is the leaste in a Farowe, and *Piggins* whiche are small barels or pitchers. And a Pig Tail is the little candle to make upp a bunch. and what is small and nice is called *pickled*. Pigstyes are by som called *Pigtrees*. I had forgot itt and the least end of an anvil is a *pik iron* which is the same maybe as *Pique* a pike or a point in the *Frenshe tongue* which I spoke in Jersey. Tis also Pic or a peak Take your choice and pick out what you will fro this Pickle.

(137)

P*ixy is a Fairey* some have itt of any Kind, but they are I wene of the Elves who make Sporte and mischief with Men I thinke they are of the Pictree and Pigwiggin by the Name. Some feare to name them. They often rob orchards, or pick fruit, that is pike itt and then pyke away or pack off. They lead folk astray and wilder them. than must yee turn your cap or your coyve iff ye be a woman, or you Coate iff your a mann. So from this are men called turncotes who change their mindes for Feare as many do whan sore bested.

(138)

There is a litle folish song knoun to all yett it is a Song of a Pixy, that is –

Litel Jacke Horner
Satt in a corner
Eating a Christmass Pye
He putt in his Thumbe
and puld out a Plumme
Loe whatt a good Boye am I.

Now the Pixy hath hornes or long Eares; tis all one, and the Devill is called Old Hornie but the Pixy in a corner eating a Pye or whatever the Housewife giveth him is Jacke Horner and of thatt yee may be sure and bett on itt a sixpence iff ye have one.

(139)

P*illicock is a lewd and foul word,* but I trow that ye al know whatt itt means, al ye Same. Itt is the Cockrel without ye Cobbs, or the Pipe of a *Cornemuse* without ye Bag. Dame Darrell often said 'twas that which every Man had, and every Woman fain wold have. But *Pillicok* is indeed not *Arbor Vitae* itself, but the Elfe or Faery or Sprite which dweleth therin and inspireth it. Yee have heard a song which every grosse lass and lewde *Garson* and *Bordjor* in the Land can sing, how *Pillicock* sat upon Pillicock's hill, so that I need not geve itt. But Dame Darrel wold have it that this balade was a Conjuration or spel, tho altered.

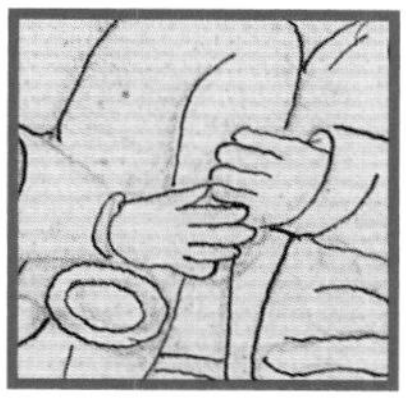

(140)

P*ucke*. Men thus call a merrie litel Elve or Faery, and Puckrels be verie smal Pucks which appeare in Glasses or Cristalls or Rings. But old *Dame Darrel would have none of this. for she said that of later times Elves and Sprights and Gobblins which were of* yore all different, are now all called one by the others' Name as som wene that all Buggs be Nighmares

(141)

Now al of this is as greate folye as to thinke that a Corn Bogle or any such Fantomy is a true ghost. For the true *Pouk* or *Porika* as he was of the olden time was a terible Spirit, whom men did feare. more as a fraying Devill than a joly merrie Elfe, and one who smelt more of brimstone then of Roses. And I have heard that *there is a fearfull Spirit who liveth in ye Sea, or in* great Watres, hee is named *Phouka,* and lieth in wayte to drowne all men. Also any ghost or spectre is called a *Puckle.* I think this is to doe with *Pucksy,* a Marish or Quakemire or muddy swampie place wher they wone, where there be *polkes* or pools. There bee many who wil aske mee What is the devill use in thus proking about among old gobs and rubbage words, and I reply, None at all to folke who have no name of any account, butt Gentil folk with faire Names or *Nomina* recken otherwise. And itt mostly befaleth that unleren and lewde men be all one with Piggs.

(142)

Q*uede or Kwade* w'h meaneth Evill is al one and ye same wi ye devill. So is a woman wi an Evil Tongue who bewrayeth and scoldeth, sour as sour, a *Qued*, for shee maketh em all quedder and shake. And some call a Prison a Qwod all because tis a bad place. I doe think that a Qued may be a Goblin who is right grum or grumpy, ever gruffling and grugging, for such ther bee among Elves as among Menn and Wemem too God wot. I would that I did not know itt to my Sorowe. Now I know that I have but littel Leerning, but whatt I have I have got *as Dickon said of his Sheep. and this I doe beleeve that man or woman who* has Lere tho itt bee never so little is beter than any Lorde who cannot reade or write, for Lewde folk who knowen naught of Leters must take all they know from Clerkes and beleeve may a Lye, as it is sayd the Blind eten many Flyes and he who cannot read is as blind as a Batt.

(143)

Quimby is I wene ye Elfe who dwelleth in every *Quim*, and a wanton and lewde Sprite itt is which doth more Michief that all others put togedere. Now this word *quim* as Dame Darrell told me is Welsh or Cwm which meaneth a clefte in a bank, or a Gulley through which mostly runns a littel Streame. Some do call it *Quem*, and others also *Quent* or *Queint*, also another word which is kin to *Quent*. Now *Quimby* is to a Woman whatt *Pillicok* is to a Man. They seeme to me to be like the Paddocks, or *Froggs which ye see in Churches*, Hee and Shee japing one another in Sinn with leacherous Eyes.

(144)

R*agamoffin is comonly enow heard of, tis a poor devill all in rags. But Dame Darel wold have itt she had* heard there was of olde a certain Devill or a Impe who was so-cald because he didd ever goe about in raggs Shee sayd to *rag* meant to beg or go a tramping and *maffin* or Moffin a simple fellowe. Thereof all, I saye naughte but truly I have heard a story which semeth to fit into this

(145)

There was an honest Jankin a good felowe. itt befel that one night late when riding home by ye Lighte of ye Mone hee was Throwne into a river and well-ny drowned. So down stream he went swimmyng but just as he deemed he should sinke hee saw on the shore a Man who putt forth his Arme till it was as long as a church steaple, it may be a hundred yards, and caught holt of hym and drew him ashore. Then he saw that ye Man who had rescowed him was all in Rags unkempt and a *Ragg Robin* indeed. Then he thankt the *Ragamoffin* and saide Wilt thou have my hose, it is al I have to yeve thee. Nay answered the ragged Man but if thow wilt change thy Coat wi' me Ile be well contented. But sweare to me that thou wilt weare my coate till thou art in thy Howse. Ay Ile do that said Jankin.

(146)

So hee set forth toe walk homeway but at every Step his Coate became so heavie that he could hardly stand. till he was in his howse and his Wife Cryed *Jesus!* who hath shente thee as Beest thow been pilled by Theeves. nay he replyed butt I met with a man who hath played a jape upon me, and made mee swere to weare this Coate home. I thinke it ways a hundred pound. As he tooke it of theye heard something jingle jingle and loe the pokets were all full of coine in good money but all very old. So hee became verye rich, and a Knight, and hee put a Ragged Robin flower into his shield. This tale hathe a fine Moral which is thatt a tattered coate may covere a good fellow.

(147)

R*alpho or Ralph.* – This is a Goblyn of whom wee know but littel hee maketh noyses in ye Housen. whan ye Children heare a tapping and rapping in the wals they saye: That is Ralph! Dame Darrell saide that of *Olde Ralph or Rolfe did mean a lustful Wolfe or one who was mad to couple with the Shee wolfe* in the tongue of the people of old. And Ralfo was I wene whatt we cald in Jersey a Loup garou or a weer wolf. sith he is called to frighten children. Itt is I do think a strange name to give to Chrisom children and call em Leacherous Wolves after a devill but many doe itt here in Yorke.

(148)

R*iding Hagg. That is a Nightmare. Some doe call it the Witch's Riding.* Yett do these troubles and deadlie Dreames not alway come fro witches. There is a merrie but unsemely Tale how a certain Gentilm'n who had a faire and very lusty Wife who was always maris appetens, did suffere from ye Nightmare every nighte and naught could rid him therefrom tho' he went to the doctor or the preest every day for possets or prayers. But one day hee came as crous and *fryke as a friskin* and cride in joy to the Frere. "*Wish me joye for I have found out whatt ailed me* and 'twas neither my Belly, Riff, nor my Brain y't were in Faulte. And whatt was it than asked the Frere in grete merveil. "Truly replied the Husband, "It was naught but my wife Jeaneton who while I slepte did helpen herself to a ride. For she was Salt. –

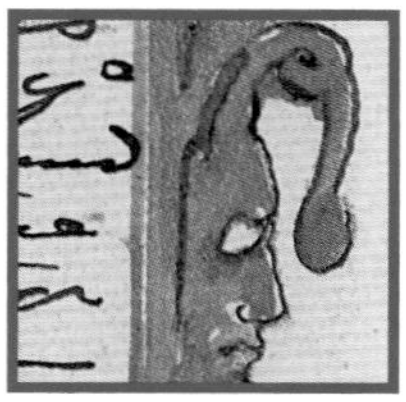

(149)

R*obyn Good fellow, his Name is soe wel-knoune that for many Folk itt is the same with every Kind of Faery and Elphe* or Goblin. – Dame Darrell did say that hee was of the newer kinde for Rob or Robin is a name for any Good felowe who loveth a Pott and a Paramoure, but shee did thinke him one with Duse or the Deuce who is a merrie litel Elfe who mockes Maides and lies wi 'em. So they say.

(150)

R*ana* is the Latin for a *Frog* or a Paddock as some doe call a Toad. But a Paddocke is trewly a Frogg and Ile tell yee why. For a *pad* or *pat* is a foot as in Frenshe it is *pied* and ther is among us a Frog Goblin called *Pad-fooit* who liveth in marishes and by water. Howbeit all Froggs are Goblins. Iff ye never hurte a Frog and will kepe one in Your House by Yow, in a Piggin or Jar of Water, all Winter, itt will be well contente and bring you Lucke above all in Love and with faire Wemen. Try itt quod Shee.

(151)

S*hagg Foal is an Elf which apereth as a little white Horse* or *Colt* I wene, every where for we had 'em in Jersaye as they are here in Yorkshire yet mostly by Rivers and the Sea. Dame Darrell sayth Hee is of verye old Time off ye Saxones. Sax is a knife so do ye comon people oft sweare by the point of ye knyfe as ye Millere did in ye Songe this *Shagg Foale*, whiche ys a *Nick or Nicker* becaus he *nicketh*, cometh by monelight and capreth like a caper cousin kindly round a man till ye man mounts him to ride. Then he runneth flene and friske into the water and jets him into it. Amen!

(152)

S*ooner* is a kind of spectre or a ghost. Itt is not a worde oftene hearde Dame D thinks it is a kind of *Visione* seen by them who are in a *Soond*, a Dreame, as the Scotch see them in Second sighte. Itt maybe for att such times as in a Dreame wee can behould strange Things such as live betwene this Life and the next or as it were in the Hall, or the *Entree Porche* betwene Out doors and In doors and of this kinde I wene is the *Sooner*.

(153)

S*pellicoat is a kind of ghost but iff ye will have my Mind o't, it is the same as the Shelly*-coat who is a Goblin of the Sea or Watres thereby, who is all overgrone wi' shels and scales and the like such as gather on ships botomes. Dame Darrel thinkes it may be Pellecoat or a coat of Sheeps pelts for there are many tales of wild folk and goblins who ever apere in such a garb and soe the two names were mixt and no wonder sith it is all among ignorante and unlered Folk that these Names are moste And the resone is that such people live more in the Wildernesses or Forestes, or by the Sea where the Fairies and all theyr kinde doe most abounde, so itt comethe to pass that they know more of such fore-beseen things than any (except a He-witch) who lives in Citys. For such Uncouthes love best lonlie and derke places afar from Townes. –

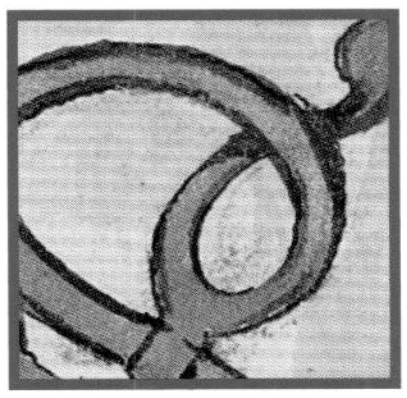

(154)

S*poorne or Sporn 'tis all one* that is a Spret or a Sprite seldom sene by any save in its tracks or spur which It leaveth in duste in Somertime but in the Snowe in Winter. And in sumere these tracks be like those of Geese tho there bee neer a Goose in the Land, but in Winter they are like ye printes of Asses hoofs and are comon enow.

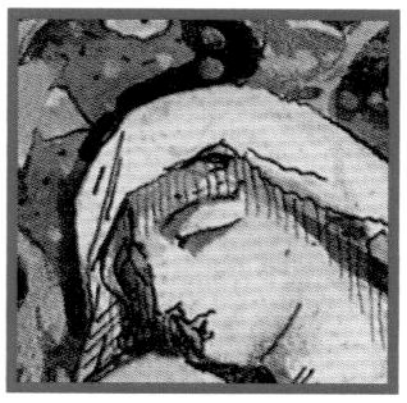

(155)

S*try is a witche just to an inche A learned man told me thatt it was a Latin word cut down* a litel for use, as on trims a collop of meate to eate and that ye Worde was *Stryga*. Itt may be butt as to *stry* is to distroy and spoile I thinke with Dame Darrel that the Folk who call 'em Strys meaned that and no more. How ever iff any one will believe that the 2 wordes together made a third even as a man and a woman make a Babe Ile nott saye that he hath not reason. And yett againe to Strye is to cure tho' itt be none so comon a word hereabouts, and manye Witches do cure the Sicke with theyr medicaments and that so well that most Folk putt more Faithe in them than in all the Phisitiouns. also doe they coste far less Expenses as ye Saw is:

Doctors be Angels whan they come to thee:
But are as Devills whan they want theyr Fee.

(156)

S*waithe is all one with a Wraith yet is the Ghost of a man who is to die Yett is not deade. Itt may be that* itt is rathe which is soone or early or before Death cometh. It is most of Nordthern folk one heares of this thing. *Whan a man sees his owne Wraith itt does not always meane his death* nor doe I beeleeve that a Wraith of Any bodie is a sure and siker sign of theyr deathe. For ther are Wizards and Warlaws who can in strange Wise go forth in many forms; such as a butterfly or mouse or a Flye or a Hare, leaving their Bodies asleep and many goe forth al in theyr owne *Likenes* yet do not dye for all thatt, nore are they ye worse for itt. However they be mostly Northumbrian or Scotch, *and it taketh a deal to kill a Scotchman God wott.* For they live on little and never die before their Tyme comes and then they liven as Ghostes.

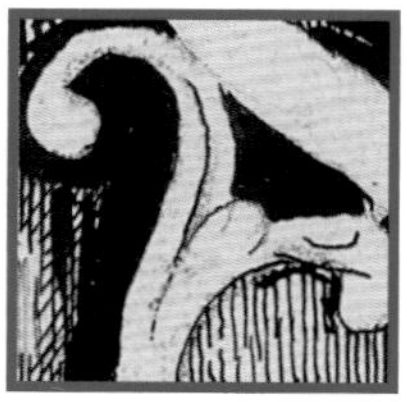

(157)

S*ea Bishoppe* is a Fish which semeth like a Preste and many Folke aren such Foles they beleve they are begoten by a Preest upo' a Sea-woman or Mere-maiden But whatt they aren in trouth is naught but a Floundre or Flundab or Skate fisshe which hath its face like a man on one syde and whan these ben drye, and painted upp and gilt they looke mervaillous like Bishops. Yett inland folk think them to be begoten by prestes. of them goe many Lies. *Some are made of Wood with a Fisshs skin and heade these be large.* And many believen that a Barnacle hatcheth into a Goose because a barnacle in its Shel hath in truthe ye very form of a litle Goosse as I have sene but I never sawe one hatcht unlesse itt was out of the brain of a Liar:

(158)

[158 has a full-page drawing of a bishop in his vestments.]

(159)

T*hrumicap or Thrummy* is a drole and wanton Impe or Gobblin or Elfe, but a Jackanapes sort all one with Faerys, but this kind doe hant old Ruines and above all old castles. Dame Darrel said twas Hodekin and that theyr ghosts of pore Children who were slain afore time of old when a Castle was builded to bring good Fortune to itt. Twas a sacrifice to their Godds. I feare itt was only too true. Thrumm seemes an old man.

(160)

T*hurse* or *Thyrs* was of old time a Gyante. Dame Darrell woulde have itt Thurse was of ye Danes. Ye scots and Irish had other Giantes of there owne. – There been a many Tales howe *that thesem Giante Folke were slayen by Jacke and Tom Hickathrift thurfout ye Lande til there was not a Scirrock of 'em left*. But if ye ken wher one lies buryed and will goe and putt some Offrandes on ye grave ye shall shourley win greate Profite. for it pleseth tham wel yat theye be still worshipt and iff a man praye them to become strong and tall he can most surely gett his desire. There be Familys wherein are great folk. Thesem are of the Giant race of olde. –

(161)

T*hirce or Thurce* is I wene all one wi' *Thursse* a giant yett many have it tis a goblin or an Elfe of a mischievous kind or kin – Or else 'tis a ghost or a *Duse* or the *Deuce himselfe*. Leet him who knows speak out, 'tis a pirn which I can not unravel. I wene twas all the same as Tib and Tom among 'em.

T*ilsterre* is a negromancer, a *sorcerer*, a magician, one who maketh his living and 'layeth his hunger by rousing the deade. Some of thesem bee wise men and as many more greate knaves and cozeneres. truly they will coze with any one like a cosin cossing and costning him but in the end the pore fonde who hoped to have ye Devills treasoury of golde findes himself with devill a Penny.

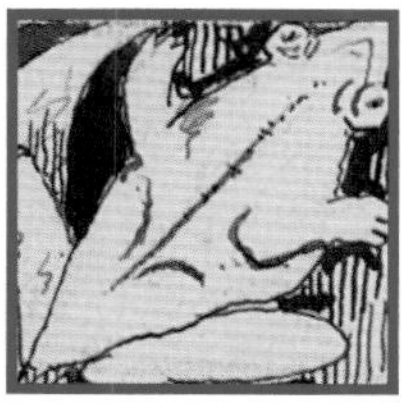

(162)

T*int is an Elfe* a Gobline. some say tis so called because it cryeth by Nighte ever *Tint! Tint!* that is *Loste!* There was a merrie Felowe tis said who once in a Wood by nighte did heare a sound as of a girl. crying out aloude *Tinte, Tint!* What has thou lost, he cride to her. "My mayden hede" she replide. "By my faithe he answered I have not seene it. Iff thou hadst given itt to mee to keepe I would have kept it a secret." Some say that *Tint* means *Teeny* or light because it is a Jack o lanthorn such as ye teen.

(163)

T*od Loury*. This is a dismall sprite or Bugg; Dame Darrell explained that itt is a death-goblin. *Tod* is a word for dead and *Larr* a sprite which fearth men and skereth them awaye. *Larren* are Ghosts of ye olden Time. they are oftenest sene in ruines of old dayes where Romanes dwelt, for Dame Darrell saide, ye name was Latine. A tod is an Ivy bushe. therein owles and Elves do comonly enhabite as doth the Ivy girle of whom I forgate to write. She is the Spirite or Faerye of the Ivy, bringeth Lucke to those who spare her Bines. Tis wel to plant them. as they growe those who have them will be protectede and favoured by their Lordes as the Ivie protecteth away the Raine and Hail. The Ivy lefe hath five points when it is stil younge but only one when olde so man loseth his 4 Senses till only one is lefte.

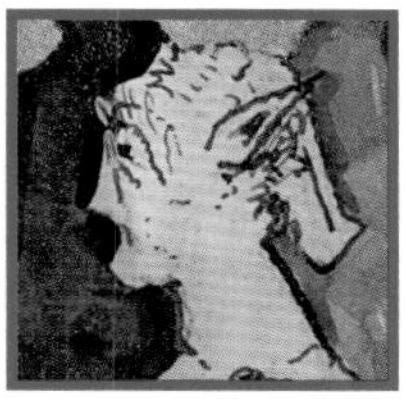

(164)

T*om Tumbler and Tom Poker are ye Names of a Goblin or Fende of whom I know Litel.* Save that the name is uset to freken Childre and that ther are Men who swere *by the Roleypoly and the Tumbling Tom.* This is as I deeme a fantom who appears tumbling Head over heels as hee goes on, or rolling over and over, like a bird which pretendeth to be wounded and goes lame to make men chase her, to get them afar from hir young ones. Or a Tumbler-Dogge.

T*oot is the Devill.* I wen hee is so-called because Hee is ever *tooting about and prying here and ther.* I did here this word fro a Soudern man wheder it bee right I wil not say. Toot is to blow a Horne and the Devill hath Hornes, so is he the Tuter of all Sinners.

(165)

T*ut is a Goblin.* I do think itt ye same with a Tod who is Death. Whenn a man is got by the *Tut* he is dying. Perchance hee is all one with the Tutivallus who gathereds upp all our sinfull idle words and beareth them to hell to await sinners. *Tilly valy!*

U*rchines bee Hedgehoggs* but there are a kind of smal Elves somewhatt like them who beare the same Name. i thinke ye Twain are mixt. Ther was a man who met an Urchine and his Wife and he said –

> "Go in peace for ye
> Have done no Harme to me."

Than ye Urch. replyed:

> "For thy gentil gof
> Thoult be well uphaft."

Ever from that tyme he had Luck.

(166)

W*aff is a sperit or ghost.* I trow tis all one with an Ouphe or Oaf. but there is ye Same word for ye Flame of a fire whan it is blown and moves like a living beeing. This brings itt to one with Hob Thrush or Jack o' Lanthorne which is like a living and moving Flame. *Waff* is also a foul earthy smel, as in a church-yard or a Vaulte. Tis I thinke an evill spirit of evil smels if not of magic-spels. *But the word cometh from waving by a wind or being Puft up as* whatever moves about is a *waft* and so these Sprites are ever on the go and swepen here and there *sans repos, voslant tojors.*

(167)

W*aith semes to be all at one with Wraith* sens it meanes the same Thinge which is the ghost of anie one not as yett deade. however tis an old worde that straying away or about losely is *wath*. even so do *waiths* stray, as men say *Wathes walken wyde*, for whan ye Soul goes owt of ye Body itt strayethe fast and farr in wyld places by lonely water fals and woody Torrents. and a *Waithe* is also any Evill and itt may bee anie Evill Spirite, or Esprit malin.

(168)

W*etche* or Weche was as I did pyne al at one wi' a Witche. but Dame Darell thinkes it is any one of lore who wets or knows or *witteth*, Sent Ninian only can tell or Tutivalls who gathers upp al our idle words. And of these are Witchens.

Warlaw is a man witch. Tis one with a War-wolf or a Gar-Wolf, gar is war, butt some say 'tis because Menne should *be ware* of them. However to be wary or ware off and waring is no far crie from War. Some cal ye word Warlockes. And truly Lacks are Sinners and itt may bee sinners God kepe us all therefro.

(169)

W*hit witch or White W'h is one who maketh hir work without ye devl or Sinne, as one that calleth* Angells and nat fendes doeth al acordyn to Christen lore. they doe make more acounte of their bookes and learning than doe ye black witches, for ye Divill loveth not Latin and the White Wizzerd ever giveth him a Bellyful of itt. Hence itt came that the whit wizards were or are for the most, broken preests *or some times whole ones*. They make great accoumpte to find treasures in old Ruines, thinges lost or Stolen. most of all to raise Spirites, and sell Reliques, Charms, Amuletts, Luck-stones, blessed medals. Some are wise and merry *other wise*, some good, but more are Whipp-Jackes and telers, Cozeners and *picaros*. For many of them with all their *Aves* are but Knaves.

(170)

Wierde is the fate or lucke or Un-luck or fortune to which a man is marked and apoynted. – So Witches and Dyviners are calld *Wierde Women* or *Wyves* because they tell a person hisn or her fortune; as Dame Darrell said what will be *werdaned.* I know not ye Word, tis like ordayned. Now as a *Wight* is a Witch because she is *wighty* or strong, and wise, so hath a *Wierde* – Wightness according as itt faleth to a man. So to *drie a wiard* is to suffer what penaunce one hath.I thinke it is as if one were a-thirst or *drien* or dry, and must *beare* with it, and truly this is to many an old Trowl the Bowl or Tos pott the worst penanc which he knows of iff hee have no Beer.

(171)

W*odwose* are wildmen. I know not if be that they are wode or mad, or becaus they wander ever in ye wods. Dame Darrell saith wose or wyse is an old worde for men, and a man is a *Wy*. but he may be a *Wy* or a *Wherefor* for al I ken, so that hee is not a *Wyfe*. This I wen is trew that of olde theyr were many such wild men who woned in the Woods who were of a kind wizards or warklokes, as all do become who live alone in such places. *Or els they weren Warwolves. theyr* ben none more in this our tyme and we can wel spare them. Little need have we I wene to see what can no more be sene.

(172)

Y*eth Hounds. of* Thes I know but litle. they ar unknown to us here. There was a Stranger of the Westland told mee that where hee woned they heared in the nighte in lone and wild places dogs howl. these Doggs had no Heads. Also tis said the Sprites of children who have mist theyr Baptism do so wayle and cry in the Woods. If they be of one kind I can not tell. Dame Darrell thinks Yeth is all the one with Sleuth Hound which is a dog that foloweth a track or slot as it dothe get or goeth. tis al one to mee.

(173)

This is al that I call to mind to this daye and Hour of Dame Darrell, *though God wote If I had wil to write all I ever heard I should nat* have moneye no credit enow to buy me ye paper and *Ink and pennes to do soe*. Now here I have to saye that I being ignorant with no skill to write have natheless sett downe what I wene are strange and unkent things and whatt are cald here *Uncoths* or News to many Scollars, tho I have done it many a time clumpish and awkert. Lett it all goe in one Stewe as the

(174)

Good wyfe saide whan she put meate and fysshe, cole and coines and apples all to stew in one pott and make a Cockagrice, whiche is a ***[long blank space]*** dish that never cometh twise alike. Now tis a strange Thing yet true that there bee many unlered Folke who are full of quainte and rare Wisdom who would be all of a dither iff made to write down what they can tell and talke, as crousely and cannily as Hearte coulde wish. and *per contra* I ever find that those who learne to write with Skil, *as Scollars, whenn they get there, have nothing left to saye or sett downe*. like Rob of the Greene who did goe from York to London to sell a wagonload of Stuffe, but whann hee got there the wagone was bare, for hee had traded away all hee hadd on the way for Bait for him and his horses. So that he had learned muche yet loste more.

(175)

Or *I may liken too too many scollers to the man who* to jumpe over a dike did firste tak a Runn ere hee lepped, but run so long that ere he gott to ye Ditch was fain to sit down and reste. And so itt is with Folke who put all theyr Witt into learning how to write well, soe that whan 'tis learnt they have no thing left to say. so there they sitt like so many Dobbeys by the brook which they don't jump over to ye other side where is the House of Fame where all are famoused who dwel therein

Wherein I tell you verily
We all of Us would like to bee.
And wherein to fess it plain
If we Could we'd ay remain.

Nowe this word *Dobby* minds me that I forgat to tell whatt a *Dobby* is, for it is a Fool and yett no Fole. At times itt is a folish doddering old Jacke or Gaffer, but mostly a Goblinn who is all one with Robin Good felow

(176)

Dobby like a Ratt or Mouse
Cometh into many a House
Castels and theyre Towers hy
Or the Graves w'h round 'em lye
Some time to a lonelie Mill,
Or a Ruine old and still:
But he loveth beste to bee
Where there is a Family,
And to serve 'em by the Night
Whence hee's a Familiar hite.
All for naught save Breade and Chese,
Hee will doe whatere they plees,
Milke ye Cows and kiss ye Maid,
Half delyted, half afrayde,
Cutt ye wood and swepe ye Floor:
Just his Duty yett no more,
For tis ever his Intent
Faithfully to work his Stent,
So that none his Faith can blame.
Fideliter Do ye the Same.

Nowe if a Made bee named *Debora* or *Debby* shee will ofte be cald Dobby and she need neer be astonned if she should meet this goblin. for there bee certaine folk with certaine

(177)

Names which Fairys and the like love. Of such names are *Gertrude* loved by Witches and *Peronell or Pernel* which is my name loved by Birds & Spirites of the Aire. *Mab* or *Mabel,* and all in *Bel,* such as *Florabel. Lucy,* for it is Light, shee is loved by ye Light Elves. *Oriana* getteth gold. *Margaret* for shee *is a Pearle. Lisbeth* shee is a *lis or* Lilye. this is Frenshe, *Fleur de Lys,* so is *Alys* or *Alice.* Of which I could write a book to shewe y't a Good name is half the Game. but lett it be a Good Name for more than that which youre Godparents gave Ye.

B*oll is another* awfull Spright who seketh People in ye Night of whom whilome I did not write. Tis all one as some say with a Balow, but Dame Darrell says Nay, for a Boll is a ghost, as of a man but a Balow is a bony and thin Bugge or Scare-crow specter. And it was ever used to frighten Babes, unto

(178)

whom theyr Nourises sang a song of Balow till they fel aslep. Itt was Balow my babe and so in time a Lulaby. Howeer it is said by some that a Balow is an angell and that to singe it to the childe is alle one as to cal it an Angell or to call em to it. So as yee may ofte hear Nowe I lay mee in my Bedd Wi' seven angels rounde my Heade Two to the lefte two to the Righte, and soe it goth onn, every childe knowes. So I think there must be two kinds of Balows. Now as balen or bally means with manye men sorowe and griefe and Mischiefe, so a Balowe is a Terror. But if yee will know whatt I think of itt it is that Balowe is deathe and itt is a Dreade and feare to all evill folk but a Joye and Messenger of Peace to the Goode.

> *Lo!* at thy finale Breath
> Have thou than no feare of Deathe
> Whan hee shall come to touch thee with his rod:
> Small cause hath hee to feare
> A sperit farr or neare
> Who hath no cause to shrinke before his God.

So may it be with all of us. Amen.

(179)

B*lack Bugg* is another worde which I lesened or lost and forgot, tho' I did lese or pick it out to go in place. Wel and good 'tis all one with a *Bogy or Barguest* or any other Dreade of Darkness. But of the word *Blacke* many Folke doe use itt for anything that is sad or sorrowfull or evill as whan wee would say of a man who led a bad life and of whom are no good hopes in death, wh'n he is taken to his grave, that he is black-buried or 'tis a black-burying. So evill magic the blacke Art, and black-fasting is plaine sterving or wel ny dying with Hunger. But whan we say that ye Black Ox has troden any one his foot, I have oft heard Dame Darrell say that among ye Romanes who were afore time in this Lande a black Bull or Ox did meane Death or Doome.

A note about the typefaces chosen for this book:

Two of them were created by Frederic W. Goudy (1865-1947), one of the most influential and prolific modern typeface designers. The typeface used for the text of *The Witchcraft of Dame Darrel* is named in his honor: Goudy, also known as Goudy Old Style, was created in 1915 for American Type Founders. Goudy is widely considered to be among the most graceful and legible of serif typefaces. The type used for the subheadings in *The Witchcraft of Dame Darrel* was also created by Frederic Goudy; known as Copperplate Gothic, this typeface was released in 1901. Cardinal font, the typeface used for the title is comparatively recent, created in 2003 by typographer Dieter Steffmann.